also by **america's test kitchen**

The Complete Summer Cookbook

Bowls

Vegetables Illustrated

The Side Dish Bible

Foolproof Fish

100 Techniques

Easy Everyday Keto

Everything Chocolate

The Perfect Pie

How to Cocktail

Spiced

The Ultimate Burger

The New Essentials Cookbook

Dinner Illustrated

Cook's Illustrated Revolutionary Recipes

Tasting Italy: A Culinary Journey

Cooking at Home with Bridget and Julia

The Complete Diabetes Cookbook

The Complete Slow Cooker

The Complete Make-Ahead Cookbook

The Complete Mediterranean Cookbook

The Complete Vegetarian Cookbook

The Complete Cooking for Two Cookbook

Just Add Sauce

How to Braise Everything

How to Roast Everything

Nutritious Delicious

What Good Cooks Know

Cook's Science

The Science of Good Cooking

The Perfect Cake

The Perfect Cookie

Bread Illustrated

Master of the Grill

Kitchen Smarts

Kitchen Hacks

100 Recipes: The Absolute Best Ways to Make the
   True Essentials

The New Family Cookbook

The America's Test Kitchen Cooking School Cookbook

The Cook's Illustrated Meat Book

The Cook's Illustrated Baking Book

The Cook's Illustrated Cookbook

The America's Test Kitchen Family Baking Book

America's Test Kitchen Twentieth Anniversary
   TV Show Cookbook

The Best of America's Test Kitchen (2007–2021 Editions)

The Complete America's Test Kitchen TV Show
   Cookbook 2001–2021

Mediterranean Instant Pot

Instant Pot Ace Blender Cookbook

Cook It in Your Dutch Oven

Sous Vide for Everybody

Air Fryer Perfection

Multicooker Perfection

Food Processor Perfection

Pressure Cooker Perfection

Vegan for Everybody

Naturally Sweet

Foolproof Preserving

Paleo Perfected

The How Can It Be Gluten-Free Cookbook: Volume 2

The How Can It Be Gluten-Free Cookbook

The Best Mexican Recipes

Slow Cooker Revolution Volume 2: The Easy-Prep Edition

Slow Cooker Revolution

The America's Test Kitchen D.I.Y. Cookbook

THE COOK'S ILLUSTRATED ALL-TIME BEST SERIES

All-Time Best Brunch

All-Time Best Dinners for Two

All-Time Best Sunday Suppers

All-Time Best Holiday Entertaining

All-Time Best Appetizers

All-Time Best Soups

COOK'S COUNTRY TITLES

Big Flavors from Italian America

One-Pan Wonders

Cook It in Cast Iron

Cook's Country Eats Local

The Complete Cook's Country TV Show Cookbook

FOR A FULL LISTING OF ALL OUR BOOKS

CooksIllustrated.com

AmericasTestKitchen.com

praise for **america's test kitchen titles**

"The book's depth, breadth, and practicality makes it a must-have for seafood lovers."

PUBLISHERS WEEKLY (STARRED REVIEW) ON *FOOLPROOF FISH*

"Another flawless entry in the America's Test Kitchen canon, *Bowls* guides readers of all culinary skill levels in composing one-bowl meals from a variety of cuisines."

BUZZFEED BOOKS ON *BOWLS*

Selected as the Cookbook Award Winner of 2019 in the Health and Special Diet Category

INTERNATIONAL ASSOCIATION OF CULINARY PROFESSIONALS (IACP) ON *THE COMPLETE DIABETES COOKBOOK*

"Diabetics and all health-conscious home cooks will find great information on almost every page."

BOOKLIST (STARRED REVIEW) ON *THE COMPLETE DIABETES COOKBOOK*

"This is a wonderful, useful guide to healthy eating."

PUBLISHERS WEEKLY ON *NUTRITIOUS DELICIOUS*

"*The Perfect Cookie*. . . is, in a word, perfect. This is an important and substantial cookbook. . . . If you love cookies, but have been a tad shy to bake on your own, all your fears will be dissipated. This is one book you can use for years with magnificently happy results."

THE HUFFINGTON POST ON *THE PERFECT COOKIE*

Selected as one of the 10 Best New Cookbooks of 2017

THE LA TIMES ON *THE PERFECT COOKIE*

"The sum total of exhaustive experimentation . . . anyone interested in gluten-free cookery simply shouldn't be without it."

NIGELLA LAWSON ON *THE HOW CAN IT BE GLUTEN-FREE COOKBOOK*

"True to its name, this smart and endlessly enlightening cookbook is about as definitive as it's possible to get in the modern vegetarian realm."

MEN'S JOURNAL ON *THE COMPLETE VEGETARIAN COOKBOOK*

"If you're a home cook who loves long introductions that tell you why a dish works followed by lots of step-by-step hand holding, then you'll love *Vegetables Illustrated*."

THE WALL STREET JOURNAL ON *VEGETABLES ILLUSTRATED*

"A one-volume kitchen seminar, addressing in one smart chapter after another the sometimes surprising whys behind a cook's best practices. . . . You get the myth, the theory, the science, and the proof, all rigorously interrogated as only America's Test Kitchen can do."

NPR ON *THE SCIENCE OF GOOD COOKING*

"The 21st-century *Fannie Farmer Cookbook* or *The Joy of Cooking*. If you had to have one cookbook and that's all you could have, this one would do it."

CBS SAN FRANCISCO ON *THE NEW FAMILY COOKBOOK*

"Some 2,500 photos walk readers through 600 painstakingly tested recipes, leaving little room for error."

ASSOCIATED PRESS ON *THE AMERICA'S TEST KITCHEN COOKING SCHOOL COOKBOOK*

"This encyclopedia of meat cookery would feel completely overwhelming if it weren't so meticulously organized and artfully designed. This is *Cook's Illustrated* at its finest."

THE KITCHN ON *COOK'S ILLUSTRATED MEAT BOOK*

"The go-to gift book for newlyweds, small families, or empty nesters."

ORLANDO SENTINEL ON *THE COMPLETE COOKING FOR TWO COOKBOOK*

"Some books impress by the sheer audacity of their ambition. Backed by the magazine's famed mission to test every recipe relentlessly until it is the best it can be, this nearly 900-page volume lands with an authoritative wallop."

CHICAGO TRIBUNE ON *THE COOK'S ILLUSTRATED COOKBOOK*

"This impressive installment from America's Test Kitchen equips readers with dozens of repertoire-worthy recipes. . . . This is a must-have for beginner cooks and more experienced ones who wish to sharpen their skills."

PUBLISHERS WEEKLY (STARRED REVIEW) ON *THE NEW ESSENTIALS COOKBOOK*

cooking for one

Scaled Recipes, No-Waste Solutions, and Time-Saving Tips

AMERICA'S TEST KITCHEN

Library of Congress Cataloging-in-Publication Data
Names: America's Test Kitchen (Firm), editor.
Title: Cooking for one : scaled recipes, no-waste solutions, and time-saving tips / America's Test Kitchen.
Description: Boston : America's Test Kitchen, 2020. | Includes index.
Identifiers: LCCN 2020023146 (print) | LCCN 2020023147 (ebook) | ISBN 9781948703284 (hardcover) | ISBN 9781948703291 (ebook)
Subjects: LCSH: Cooking for one. | LCGFT: Cookbooks.
Classification: LCC TX714 .C65432177 2020 (print) | LCC TX714 (ebook) | DDC 641.5/611--dc23
LC record available at https://lccn.loc.gov/2020023146
LC ebook record available at https://lccn.loc.gov/2020023147

AMERICA'S TEST KITCHEN
21 Drydock Avenue, Boston, MA 02210

Manufactured in the United States of America
10 9 8 7 6 5 4 3 2 1

Distributed by Penguin Random House Publisher Services
Tel: 800.733.3000

Pictured on front cover **Pomegranate-Glazed Salmon with Black-Eyed Peas and Walnuts (page 252)**

Pictured on back cover **Crispy-Skinned Chicken (page 32), Chermoula Sauce (page 68), Pan-Roasted Asparagus (page 77), Cheesy Toasted Panko (page 137), Couscous with Cumin and Pine Nuts (page 123)**

Front and back cover Food Styling **Catrine Kelty**

Photography by Steve Klise

Editorial Director, Books **Adam Kowit**

Executive Food Editor **Dan Zuccarello**

Deputy Food Editor **Stephanie Pixley**

Executive Managing Editor **Debra Hudak**

Senior Editors **Nicole Konstantinakos, Sacha Madadian, Sara Mayer, and Russell Selander**

Associate Editor **Camila Chaparro**

Test Cook **Samantha Block**

Assistant Editor **Brenna Donovan**

Editorial Assistant **Emily Rahravan**

Design Director **Lindsey Timko Chandler**

Deputy Art Director **Katie Barranger**

Photography Director **Julie Bozzo Cote**

Photography Producer **Meredith Mulcahy**

Food Styling **Catrine Kelty, Steve Klise, Chantal Lambeth, and Ashley Moore**

PHOTOSHOOT KITCHEN TEAM

Photo Team and Special Events Managers **Allison Berkey and Timothy McQuinn**

Lead Test Cook **Eric Haessler**

Assistant Test Cooks **Hannah Fenton, Jacqueline Gochenouer, Gina McCreadie, and Christa West**

Illustration **Katie Barranger**

Senior Manager, Publishing Operations **Taylor Argenzio**

Imaging Manager **Lauren Robbins**

Production and Imaging Specialists **Tricia Neumyer, Dennis Noble, and Amanda Yong**

Copy Editor **Deri Reed**

Proofreader **Pat Jalbert-Levine**

Indexer **Elizabeth Parson**

Chief Creative Officer **Jack Bishop**

Executive Editorial Directors **Julia Collin Davison and Bridget Lancaster**

contents

welcome to
america's test kitchen

This book has been tested, written, and edited by the folks at America's Test Kitchen, where curious cooks become confident cooks. Located in Boston's Seaport District in the historic Innovation and Design Building, it features 15,000 square feet of kitchen space including multiple photography and video studios. It is the home of *Cook's Illustrated* magazine and *Cook's Country* magazine and is the workday destination for more than 60 test cooks, editors, and cookware specialists. Our mission is to empower and inspire confidence, community, and creativity in the kitchen.

We start the process of testing a recipe with a complete lack of preconceptions, which means that we accept no claim, no technique, and no recipe at face value. We simply assemble as many variations as possible, test a half-dozen of the most promising, and taste the results blind. We then construct our own recipe and continue to test it, varying ingredients, techniques, and cooking times until we reach a consensus. As we like to say in the test kitchen, "We make the mistakes so you don't have to." The result, we hope, is the best version of a particular recipe, but we realize that only you can be the final judge of our success (or failure). We use the same rigorous approach when we test equipment and taste ingredients.

All of this would not be possible without a belief that good cooking, much like good music, is based on a foundation of objective technique. Some people like spicy foods and others don't, but there is a right way to sauté, there is a best way to cook a pot roast, and there are measurable scientific principles involved in producing perfectly beaten, stable egg whites. Our ultimate goal is to investigate the fundamental principles of cooking to give you the techniques, tools, and ingredients you need to become a better cook. It is as simple as that.

To see what goes on behind the scenes at America's Test Kitchen, check out our social media channels for kitchen snapshots, exclusive content, video tips, and much more. You can watch us work (in our actual test kitchen) by tuning in to *America's Test Kitchen* or *Cook's Country* on public television or on our websites. Download our award-winning podcast *Proof*, which goes beyond recipes to solve food mysteries (AmericasTestKitchen.com/proof), or listen to test kitchen experts on public radio (SplendidTable.org) to hear insights that illuminate the truth about real home cooking. Want to hone your cooking skills or finally learn how to bake—with an America's Test Kitchen test cook? Enroll in one of our online cooking classes. And you can engage the next generation of home cooks with kid-tested recipes from America's Test Kitchen Kids.

Our community of home recipe testers provides valuable feedback on recipes under development by ensuring that they are foolproof. You can help us investigate the how and why behind successful recipes from your home kitchen. (Sign up at AmericasTestKitchen.com/recipe_testing.)

However you choose to visit us, we welcome you into our kitchen, where you can stand by our side as we test our way to the best recipes in America.

facebook.com/AmericasTestKitchen
twitter.com/TestKitchen
youtube.com/AmericasTestKitchen
instagram.com/TestKitchen
pinterest.com/TestKitchen

AmericasTestKitchen.com
CooksIllustrated.com
CooksCountry.com
OnlineCookingSchool.com
AmericasTestKitchen.com/kids

introduction

as far as we're concerned, one is far from the loneliest number.

Indulging in the delight of dining alone is one of life's greatest pleasures. It's easy to reserve your special-occasion cooking for a crowd, but putting the same amount of care into your own meal preparation is just as enjoyable, if not more so—you don't have to make a mental checklist of everyone's food preferences, or worry about the overflowing sink full of dishes. The only thing you have to consider is what you want to eat. It's as simple as that.

It's not just people who live alone that find themselves solo at mealtime, though. Maybe your partner works nights, or your kids refuse to eat anything other than grilled cheese sandwiches, or you're looking for some respite from your roommates. No matter the reason, cooking for yourself should be fun, low-pressure, and delicious.

But cooking for one isn't without its challenges, from avoiding a fridge full of half-used ingredients to ending up with leftovers that become boring after the third reheat. And scaling down recipes yourself often involves awkward measurements and complicated math. Not anymore. In *Cooking for One*, we help you discover the joy of eating alone with unfussy meals that are perfectly portioned.

In order to make your cooking more flexible we made our recipes more flexible by providing leeway when having a particular ingredient—a specific nut or herb, for example—matters less than just having something crunchy or fresh to finish a dish.

"Cook what you have" is a useful mantra for the solo cook. The Kitchen Improv box with every recipe offers ideas for adding an extra layer of flavor, or altering the dish so it works for your tastes (and pantry). Ingredients themselves often lead you to another exciting meal—when you're left with extra beans or half an eggplant, we direct you to another recipe as a way to use it up. Or, check out our list of what to do with half-used ingredients on pages 22–23 for a quick reference.

In the spirit of flexibility, we organized this book with the improvisational cook in mind. Mix and match center-of-the-plate options with scrumptious side dishes in the first two chapters, or follow our guidelines for making a side the main event. In the mood for something a bit more simple? Our 5-ingredient soups are short on ingredients but not on flavor, and our clean-out-your-fridge soup recipe helps you use up the extra bits and bobs you have lying around. When you're cooking for yourself, that usually means you're on your own for cleanup. Not to worry—our One-Pan Dinners offer meals that help make that chore a little more manageable. And we didn't forget about dessert. From pantry-friendly ice cream toppings to easy microwaved cakes, we've got your sweet tooth covered (without a baking production).

This is your chance to eat whatever you want, however you want. So dig out your linen napkins or fold up a paper towel, pull up a chair or sit cross-legged on the couch, remote at the ready. Whatever your style, we're happy to have you. Let's get cooking.

makes leftovers

We don't list serving sizes with these recipes. It is *Cooking for One*, after all. Every recipe in the book makes one serving, unless there is a Makes Leftovers tag, which means it makes enough for more than one serving.

The only recipes that make leftovers are ones that make *good* leftovers—they keep well, reheat easily, and/or are easy to transform into a new meal altogether.

pantry recipe

This tag marks recipes where all of the ingredients are on the list for our well-stocked pantry (see pages 10–11). If you follow our pantry guidelines, you should have everything already on hand to make these recipes.

tip: *You can find full lists of the tagged recipes in the index.*

cook it your way

Cooking for yourself benefits from being flexible. It's challenging (and exhausting) to search high and low for recipes that fit precisely what you have on hand, or buying specialty ingredients to fit the recipes. But that doesn't mean the process should be a roll of the dice, or that the food shouldn't be absolutely delicious. Here are some general principles for cooking for yourself and tips for doing it well.

consider a smaller skillet

When cooking single proteins, a 12-inch skillet isn't necessarily your best bet. With all that empty space not occupied by chicken or fish, your pan will be dried out and smoking. Opt for a skillet that is closer in size to what you're cooking. Using a smaller skillet (see page 13) also means you should be using a smaller burner size. Reacquaint yourself with the smaller burner on your stove—it's often not in the most convenient position, but will help avoid flareups.

pay attention to visual cues

We quickly learned that single-serve proteins (such as a steak or fish fillet) cook much faster on their own than when multiple items are in the skillet. For example, our Pan-Seared Boneless Chicken Breast (page 34) cooks for just 6 minutes. Cooking two chicken breasts with the same method takes double the time. Why the difference? Heat is concentrated at the center of the pan so single proteins cook over a more focused heat source. Because of that, we lower the heat for most single-protein recipes (and reduce the cooking time). This ensures the interiors cook in the time the exteriors brown.

We also learned that an extra step is necessary so that single proteins cook evenly. When there are multiple steaks or fillets in a skillet, their proximity creates steam that gently cooks the sides as the main surface area browns. When we first tried making a single Crispy-Skinned Salmon Fillet (page 53), the sides ended up drastically underdone even when the skin was nutty brown. We found we had to turn the salmon on its sides with tongs, a step we wouldn't normally take, to make sure it was cooked all around.

dig into your pantry

Building a well-stocked pantry is critical to being a successful for-one cook (see pages 8–11). Even on nights when you don't feel like cooking something elaborate, or you didn't make it to the supermarket, you should be able to create a meal out of what seems like thin air. You can also use your pantry items to add heft to meals or tailor them to your tastes. Unlike Old Mother Hubbard, your cupboard should never be bare.

rethink your plate

When you're cooking for yourself, a meal doesn't always have to be about the protein. Side dishes, with a little bulking up, can be the star of the show. Top No-Fuss Parmesan Polenta (page 129) with Broiled Broccoli Rabe (page 85), spoon Sautéed Mushrooms with Shallots and Thyme (page 102) over toast spread with goat cheese, or build a vegetarian grain bowl. See pages 136–137 for more tips on making a side the main event.

transform leftovers

Although our recipes ensure you won't be stuck with endless leftovers, sometimes it's worth making just enough for another meal. But that doesn't mean meal-time should feel repetitive, so we provide suggestions to ensure your meal's second life is as good as the first—turn that leftover Roasted Butternut Squash (page 88) into an autumnal salad topping, or make tacos out of extra Spice-Rubbed Flank Steak with Celery Root and Lime Yogurt Sauce (page 242). See pages 284–285 for more information about leftovers.

get comfortable making swaps

You aren't always going to have exact ingredients for a recipe. But that shouldn't stop you from making the dish. In particular, two common ingredients, herbs and oil, offer more flexibility than many cooks realize. (Chives, cilantro, and basil would all taste great on many dishes; better to buy one and use it up than to buy several and let them go bad.) And here's a news flash: You can stir-fry in olive oil if that's all you have and your dish will taste fine. For this reason, we list multiple options for herbs (nuts and cheeses, too) in our recipes, and simply call for "oil," leaving it up to you to decide what works best. When substituting on your own, pay attention to potency. For example, if you're subbing cayenne for paprika, you should use less because cayenne is much spicier and will make your dish inedible (unless you have taste buds of steel). Consider the intensity of each ingredient and adjust accordingly.

herbs

We think of herbs in two categories: delicate (think: leafy fronds) and hardy (think: woody stems). Delicate herbs—like cilantro, parsley, dill, tarragon, mint, and basil—are most potent and fragrant with little to no cooking. Use them as a garnish or add them in the last moments on the heat. Hardy herbs—like rosemary, thyme, oregano, or sage—can be added at the beginning of cooking. Of course herbs have their own unique flavors, but when substituting, be sure to stick within these two categories.

oil

Thinking about oil as either one for cooking or one for finishing can help you choose the one that works best for you. Cooking oils—like canola oil, vegetable oil, avocado oil, or refined coconut oil—have high smoke points (the temperature at which the oil begins to break down), so they're great all-purpose oils for sautéing, shallow frying, and stir-frying. Finishing oils—like toasted sesame oil or chili oil—are more delicate than cooking oils. Heat causes them to become bitter, so they're better used in vinaigrettes or simple (uncooked) sauces. In our recipes, when we say "oil," we mean a cooking oil, unless specified. The exception here is extra-virgin olive oil. It's both a cooking oil and a finishing oil—use it to sauté as well as an ultraflavorful finishing drizzle.

in a pinch

Here are some ways to substitute common ingredients using what you have on hand.

ingredient	substitute with
½ cup heavy cream	½ cup evaporated milk (not suitable for whipping or baking, but fine for soups and sauces)
½ an egg	Whisk the yolk and white together and use half of the liquid
	None of our recipes call for half an egg, but keep this tip handy when doing your own recipe scaling.
½ cup buttermilk	¼ cup plus 2 tablespoons plain yogurt + 2 tablespoons whole milk
	½ cup whole milk + 1½ teaspoons lemon juice or distilled white vinegar
½ cup sour cream	½ cup plain whole-milk yogurt (other yogurts are too watery)
½ cup confectioners' sugar	½ cup granulated sugar + ½ teaspoon cornstarch, ground in a blender (not a food processor)
1 tablespoon fresh herbs	1 teaspoon dried herbs
¼ cup wine	¼ cup broth + ½ teaspoon wine vinegar or lemon juice (added just before serving)
	You can swap white vermouth for white wine if you have it.
1 teaspoon fish sauce	¼ teaspoon anchovy paste + ¾ teaspoon soy sauce

kitchen improv

Each recipe is accompanied by a Kitchen Improv box with suggestions to help you customize the recipe. They're not complete variations (and they don't have measurements)—they're there to help nudge you towards improvising to your tastes and what's in your cupboards. The dinner pictured below is the Crispy-Skinned Chicken (page 32) with Roasted Carrots (page 93). We also explain here the different suggestions we include with every recipe for riffing on the foundational recipes for a lively meal.

use what you've got

Here we offer ingredient substitutions and easy swaps to utilize what you may have on hand, ranging from varying the protein to trying different spices or vegetables.

level up

Here are ways to take your dish over the top. We give you options to drizzle, sprinkle, or garnish, adding another layer of flavor and/or texture.

get saucy

These are either ideas for sauces that would pair well with the dish, or ways to change up the sauce.

spice it up

Suggestions for spices, spice blends, and/or dried herbs that would pair well with the dish.

make it ...

We give "make it" ideas throughout the book, including Make It Heartier, Make It Vegetarian, or Make It Curried (to name a few). These are ways to tailor our recipe to your tastes.

stock up

A well-stocked pantry allows you to have more options in your cooking and to create a meal on the fly. But a pantry should be more than just canned goods and spices. We use the word "pantry" loosely—we include long-lasting ingredients like potatoes and squash, and consider the refrigerator and freezer to be an extension of the pantry. Stock your cupboards with these items (and replenish them when you're running low), and you'll never feel like "there's nothing to eat" again.

To build our pantry, we followed a few guidelines. Every item in the pantry should:

have a long shelf life

When you're cooking just for yourself, it might take you longer to get through different items. You shouldn't have to replace these items all the time.

be versatile

None of these items are single-use. You'll turn to them for a wide variety of recipes, regardless of cuisine.

be seasonless

Our pantry items don't vary from season to season. Their quality is the same year-round.

tip: *Keep a pad and paper in your kitchen and jot down a pantry item every time you run out of it. That way, when you plan your grocery trip (see page 16), you'll make sure to replace it.*

the basic pantry

oils

See page 5 for more information about using oils in the recipes in this book.

- Cooking oil (We use extra-virgin and/or vegetable oil most frequently.)

salt and pepper

Our preferred brand of kosher salt is Diamond Crystal. See page 73 for more information about adjusting measurements with other brands.

- Salt (kosher and table)
- Black peppercorns

beans and lentils

We prefer to buy canned beans for quick meals. These are the ones we use most often.

- Black beans
- Cannellini beans
- Chickpeas
- Dried lentils (brown, red, and/or green)

tomato products

- Canned tomatoes (crushed, diced, and/or whole peeled)
- Canned tomato sauce
- Tomato paste (in a tube)

dried pasta, rice, and grains

- Strand pasta (spaghetti, linguine, angel hair, and/or fettuccine)
- Short pasta (elbows, rigatoni, shells, penne, and/or farfalle)
- Orzo
- Couscous
- Rice (long-grain white or brown and Arborio)
- Coarse-ground cornmeal
- Farro
- Quinoa

dried herbs and spices

Here are the 10 we reach for the most, but your list may look a little different. Include what works best for your cooking, adding anything from allspice to za'atar.

- Cayenne pepper
- Chili powder
- Ground cinnamon
- Ground cumin
- Curry powder
- Herbes de Provence
- Oregano
- Paprika (smoked, hot, or sweet)
- Ras el hanout (see page 72 to make it yourself)
- Red pepper flakes

basic vegetables

- Alliums (onions, shallots, and garlic)
- Carrots
- Celery
- Potatoes (russet, Yukon Gold, and/or sweet potatoes)
- Butternut squash

citrus

- Lemons
- Limes

vinegars

We regularly reach for all of these vinegars, but choose a few that work best for your cooking.

- Apple cider vinegar
- Balsamic vinegar
- Red wine vinegar
- Rice wine vinegar
- White wine vinegar

bread products

- Hearty, crusty bread (see page 20 for more information about bread)
- Naan, pita, wraps, and/or tortillas (flour and/or corn)
- Panko bread crumbs

basic condiments

- Mayonnaise
- Mustard (Dijon or whole-grain)
- Hot sauce (vinegar-based and sriracha)
- Ketchup
- Honey and/or maple syrup
- Barbecue sauce
- Worcestershire sauce
- Nut butter (creamy or chunky peanut and/or almond butter)
- Soy sauce

baking items

- All-purpose flour
- Sugar (granulated, brown, and confectioners')
- Chocolate (unsweetened and your favorite type of bars or chips)
- Unsweetened cocoa powder
- Leaveners (baking soda and baking powder)
- Vanilla extract
- Unsweetened flaked coconut
- Old-fashioned rolled oats

nuts and seeds

You should have two or three types depending on your preference.

- Nuts (almonds, cashews, peanuts, pecans, pine nuts, and/or walnuts)
- Seeds (pepitas, sesame seeds, and/or sunflower seeds)

broth

- Chicken and/or vegetable

refrigerated pantry items

- Unsalted butter
- Cheeses (cheddar, Parmesan or Pecorino Romano, and/or feta or goat)
- Eggs
- Milk, heavy cream, and/or half-and-half
- Plain Greek and/or regular yogurt

the turbo-charged pantry

None of the following items are integral to having a well-stocked pantry, but these versatile ingredients are the ultimate flavor boosters. We turn to them consistently in our Kitchen Improvs, and they'll make your meals more interesting, vibrant, and flavorful.

oils

See page 5 for more information about using oils in the recipes in this book.

- Finishing oil (we use extra-virgin olive oil and toasted sesame oil most frequently)

proteins

- Canned tuna
- Tofu

flavor boosters

- White miso
- Fish sauce
- Thai curry paste (red or green)
- Mirin
- Olives
- Capers
- Canned chipotle chiles in adobo sauce
- Anchovies and/or anchovy paste
- Sun-dried tomatoes
- Dried fruit (raisins, golden raisins, dried figs, and/or apricots)

canned or jarred items

- Artichoke hearts
- Coconut milk
- Roasted red peppers

pickled vegetables

- Kimchi
- Pickles
- Pickled jalapeños
- Sauerkraut

condiments

- Asian chili-garlic sauce
- Gochujang
- Harissa
- Hoisin
- Tahini

INCLUDES THE FREEZER

frozen produce

- Frozen fruit (peaches, mango, strawberries, and/or mixed berries)
- Corn
- Edamame
- Peas
- Spinach

don't bother: *High-moisture vegetables like asparagus, bell peppers, mushrooms, snap peas, and snow peas do not freeze well, and you should avoid them both on their own and in frozen vegetable medleys.*

frozen proteins

These proteins freeze the best so they're our favorite to keep on hand. Your freezer might include more or less depending on what you like to eat and the size of your freezer.

- Bacon and/or pancetta (see page 20 for tips on freezing)
- Chicken (boneless, skinless and/or bone-in breasts and thighs, and chicken wings)
- Extra-large shrimp
- Tilapia

don't freeze out frozen seafood

Seafood's high perishability means that a lot of the seafood you eat—yes, even the "fresh" fish and shrimp you buy at the seafood counter—has been frozen. Most fish and seafood is frozen at the peak of freshness, so some argue that frozen fish is even "fresher" than fresh-caught fish that's been sitting on ice for more than a day.

We love buying bagged frozen shrimp as it's easy to thaw exactly what you need. Extra-large shrimp (21 to 25 per pound) are our go-to. This count is the most widely available in stores, and the shrimp's meaty size allows them to stay on the heat longer before turning rubbery. Because peeled shrimp tend to be drier, we prefer to buy frozen shrimp with their shells still on and peel them ourselves after defrosting. Be sure to check the label: "Shrimp" should be the only ingredient listed. In an effort to prevent darkening or water loss during thawing, some manufacturers add salt or STPP (sodium tripolyphosphate). Our tasters found an unpleasant texture in salt-treated and STPP-enhanced shrimp; the latter also had a chemical taste.

Thin fish like tilapia is our favorite frozen fish to buy as we've found its quality to be the best, likely because it freezes more rapidly than thicker fillets.

equipment for the solo chef

Cooking for yourself requires the same standard kitchen equipment you likely already own (like 10- and 12-inch skillets, a chef's knife, a cutting board, and rimmed baking sheets, to name a few). There's no need to rush out and buy tiny loaf pans or other gimmicky single-use items, but there are a few solo cooking–specific items we think are useful to have on hand.

small whisk
A miniature whisk is helpful for making single-serving salad dressings, or whisking together just a couple eggs. Our winner is the **Tovolo Mini Whisk** ($7).

digital scale
A scale comes in handy for weighing proteins and vegetables (or pasta) to ensure you've got the right portion size for the recipe. Our winner is the **OXO Good Grips 11 lb Food Scale with Pull Out Display** ($49.99) and our best buy is the **Ozeri Pronto Digital Multifunction Kitchen and Food Scale** ($11.79).

small cutting board
A full-size cutting board can be a hassle to clean. For small-scale jobs, we love the **OXO Good Grips Utility Cutting Board** ($14.95).

measuring pasta

Pasta is a tricky ingredient to measure correctly. Most of the recipes in this book call for 3 ounces, but what does that actually look like?

As a general rule, 1 cup of short pasta = 1 serving. We like to use a dry measuring cup to get this right. This might fluctuate depending on the size of the pasta—dial it back for smaller pasta like elbows or small shells, and add a little more for larger shapes like rigatoni or farfalle.

When 3 ounces of uncooked strand pasta are bunched together into a tight circle, the diameter measures about ¾ inch.

stand pasta on end to measure ▶

← 1 serving →

small saucepans

We reach for smaller saucepans (as opposed to stockpots) to make small-batch soups or whip up a better-than-the-box macaroni and cheese (see page 261). Our favorite is the **All-Clad Stainless 2qt Saucepan** ($130) and our best buy is the **Tramontina Gourmet Tri-Ply Clad 2qt Covered Sauce Pan** ($44.63).

quarter-sheet pans

When we call for a rimmed baking sheet, we mean the standard, half-sheet pans. But we also have an affinity for quarter-sheet pans—their smaller size (about the size of a sheet of letter copy paper) makes them perfect for baking just a few cookies (see page 303), or roasting a single sweet potato (see page 113). Plus, they're much easier to clean. Our winner is **Nordic Ware Naturals Quarter Sheet** ($8.99).

8-inch skillets (nonstick and stainless steel)

These diminutive skillets give new meaning to "personal pan," and are great for cooking a single protein or making the world's-best breakfast hash (see page 241). Our winning nonstick skillet is the **OXO Good Grips Hard Anodized Pro Nonstick 8-Inch Fry Pan** ($29.95), and our winning stainless-steel skillet is the **All-Clad Stainless 8" Fry Pan** ($98.49).

digital instant-read thermometer

A good thermometer takes the guesswork out of cooking. This is especially important when you may not be used to the different ways a single piece of chicken or fish cooks (see page 4). We've loved the **Thermoworks Thermapen Mk4** ($99) for years.

food storage bags

We use zipper-lock bags to keep everything from herbs to cheeses fresh (see pages 20–21). We actually mail-order **Elkay Plastics Ziplock Heavy Weight Freezer Bags** ($9.69 for 100 bags), but **Ziploc Brand Freezer Bags with Easy Open Tabs** ($5.37 for 28 bags) are a suitable supermarket option.

storage containers

Good storage containers are a must for packing up leftovers (see pages 284–285). For plastic (lighter and easier to transport), we like all of the different sizes in the **Rubbermaid Brilliance Food Storage Container** line. For glass (best for reheating) we like all of the different sizes in the **OXO Good Grips Smart Seal Container** line.

make the most of your microwave

Microwaves are for more than just reheating leftovers (see pages 284–285). We used them throughout the recipe testing process, from par-cooking potatoes to make the Fastest-Ever Baked Potato (page 105), to blooming spices to make salad dressings that pack a punch (see pages 210 and 226), to softening a shallot quickly to make Classic Tuna Salad (page 207). Here are some surprising ways to use yours.

dry fresh herbs
Place hardy herbs (see page 5) in single layer between 2 paper towels on microwave turntable. Microwave on high power for 1 to 3 minutes, until leaves turn brittle and fall easily from stems.

dehydrate citrus zest
Use a vegetable peeler to remove strips of citrus zest, avoiding the bitter pith. Place strips on paper towel–lined plate. Microwave on high power for 2 to 3 minutes, let cool, then store in airtight container. Steep in tea, pan sauces, custards, or cooking water for grains to add subtle citrus flavor.

defrost bread
Letting frozen bread thaw at room temperature actually results in dry, stale texture—the exact thing we're trying to avoid by freezing it. Instead, place slices on a plate (uncovered) and microwave them on high power for 15 to 25 seconds.

bloom spices
Cooking ground spices in fat intensifies their flavor. Microwave oil and spices in medium bowl until fragrant, about 30 seconds.

easily peel garlic
Rather than tediously peeling off the papery skin, a quick 15-second zap of the cloves in the microwave allows the skins to peel right off.

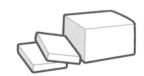

soften butter
Microwave butter at 50 percent power for 10 to 20 seconds.

quick microwave recipes

toasted nuts

Place nuts in shallow bowl or glass pie plate in thin, even layer. Microwave, stirring and checking color every minute. When nuts start to color, microwave in 30-second increments until golden brown.

fried shallots

1 Place 3 shallots, peeled and sliced thin, in medium bowl with ½ cup vegetable oil. Microwave at full power for 5 minutes. Stir, then microwave for 2 minutes. Repeat stirring and microwaving in 2-minute increments until shallots begin to brown (4 to 6 minutes), then stir and microwave in 30-second increments until shallots are deep golden (30 seconds to 2 minutes).

2 Using slotted spoon, transfer shallots to paper towel–lined plate; season with salt. Let drain and turn crisp, about 5 minutes, before serving. Sprinkle on salads and sandwiches; use cooking oil in dressings.

kale chips

For the best texture, we prefer to use flatter Lacinato or Tuscan kale. We also found that collard greens work well, but we don't recommend curly-leaf kale, Swiss chard, or curly-leaf spinach, all of which turn dusty and crumbly when crisped. Make sure to pat the kale dry thoroughly and space the pieces apart on the plate before microwaving.

1 Remove stems from 5 ounces kale (about ½ bunch). Tear leaves into 2-inch pieces; wash and thoroughly dry, then toss well with 4 teaspoons oil in large bowl.

2 Spread roughly one-third of leaves in single layer on large plate and season lightly with kosher salt.

3 Microwave for 3 minutes. If leaves are crispy, transfer to serving bowl; if not, continue to microwave leaves in 30-second increments until crispy. Repeat with remaining leaves in 2 batches. Store chips in airtight container for up to 1 week.

watt's going on?

A microwave's wattage ranges from 600 to 1,200 (the higher that number, the more powerful it is). You should have a sticker on the inside door or on the back of your microwave that tells you the wattage. We developed our recipes using 1,200-watt microwaves, but this number can vary greatly from household to household. But not to worry: For most applications a lower wattage really doesn't matter that much. Usually if your microwave is a lower wattage it means things are going to take a little longer to cook, so you'll just have to adjust times accordingly. But in some instances, lower wattage microwaves just aren't powerful enough. Our Paper Bag Popcorn (page 296), for instance, works best in a microwave with a wattage of 900 or higher.

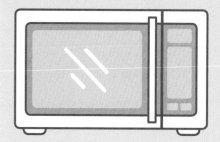

shop smarter

It's hard to navigate the supermarket as a solo cook. It seems like everywhere you look there are specials enticing you to buy far more than you need, gigantic prepackaged family-size portions, and carts that feel as big as a car. Here are some tips to help you tackle your shopping list.

at home

take stock
The grocery run really starts at home. Peek into your cupboards and refrigerator to see what you're running low on, and what's still left over from your last shopping trip. If you've already kept a running list of pantry items you've run out of (see page 8), this step will be a little easier.

make a plan
Even if you haven't specifically planned out your meals for the week (see pages 24–25), you should have a general idea about the main components of the dishes you want to make, and a list of items. This will help you cut down on impulse buys and ensure you leave with only what you need.

but first, eat
It's so much easier to overbuy when your stomach is rumbling. Have a snack before you leave, and save yourself from a detour down the chip aisle.

at the store

ditch the cart
If you're able, using a basket helps you avoid buying anything not on your list. Unless you're stocking up on pantry items, if it's too much to carry, it's probably too much to buy.

shop the perimeter
The perimeter of the supermarket is where the perishable items are—produce, dairy, eggs, and meat. Try to avoid the middle aisles as much as possible unless you're going to get something specific, or need to replenish anything in your pantry.

buy by weight
Produce is a difficult thing to buy for one—items are often sold by the bunch or in pre-portioned bags. You may have better luck in the organic section, where produce is often sold loose by the pound. (Local farmers' markets are good for this, too.)

shop the salad bar
Your supermarket's salad bar is for more than just salads—it's perfect if you need just half a cup of snap peas or a handful of spinach.

bulk up
Buying prepackaged foods like nuts, rice, and grains is almost always more expensive than buying just what you need from a bulk bin. Whether you want to buy a pound of brown rice for your pantry or a cup of quinoa for a specific recipe, you can buy as much or as little as you need. If your supermarket doesn't have a bulk section, check out a natural foods store.

counter service
Instead of buying prepackaged lunch meat and cheeses, purchase just a few slices of turkey and your favorite cheese at the deli counter. Then head to the bakery to get a single roll—making a solo hoagie has never been easier (or more cost-efficient).

take a number
If you can buy your meat at a local butcher shop or if your supermarket has a meat counter, use it. Same goes for the fish and cheese counters. You can purchase things like a single chicken breast or piece of salmon, or a smaller hunk of Parmesan. If counters aren't an option and you can only buy larger quantities, the freezer is your friend (see page 19).

things you can ask...

YOUR BUTCHER

split up that family pack
As long as it's something than can be weighed, your butcher can often split up the big packages of chicken breasts or ground meat.

tenderize it
Don't worry about pounding cuts of meat to an even size in your kitchen—your butcher can do this for you. This goes for chicken breasts (see pages 32–36), pork cutlets (see page 36), or even pork tenderloin.

YOUR CHEESEMONGER

cut down a hunk of cheese
A lot of cheese that's sold by weight is already portioned out and wrapped in plastic. Your cheesemonger can often cut a smaller portion for you and re-weigh it.

taste test
Trying something new? Maybe you want to mix up the cheeses in your Stovetop Spinach Macaroni and Cheese (page 261) or you're searching for a pre-dinner snack. Before you spring for a cheese you've never tried before, ask to sample a small piece to see if you like it.

YOUR FISHMONGER

recommend substitutions
The wide world of fish can seem pretty daunting. Check with your fishmonger about which fish are interchangeable with each other.

put it on ice
Your fishmonger can often provide you with a small bag of ice to keep your fish as fresh as possible on your way home from the store.

---

items we actually prefer buying in smaller containers

It may sound counterintuitive, but sometimes going for the smaller container can help you scale back on food waste. That way you don't have to worry about the ingredient spoiling before you can use it all up.

- Applesauce
- Juice
- Milk, half-and-half, and heavy cream

store smarter

Different types of produce have different storage requirements; some need to be placed in the coldest part of the refrigerator, some need humidity, and some don't need to be chilled at all. Storing your produce under the appropriate conditions is the key to prolonging its shelf life.

in the refrigerator

IN THE FRONT OF THE FRIDGE

These items are sensitive to chilling injury and should be placed in the front of the fridge, where the temperatures tend to be higher.

- Berries
- Citrus
- Corn on the cob
- Peas

IN THE BACK OF THE FRIDGE

These items are highly perishable and should be stored in the coldest part of the fridge.

- Cheese
- Eggs
- Milk, half-and-half, and heavy cream
- Yogurt

IN THE CRISPER

These items do best in the humid environment of the crisper.

- Asparagus
- Beets
- Broccoli
- Cabbage
- Carrots
- Cauliflower
- Celery
- Chiles and peppers
- Cucumbers
- Eggplant
- Fresh herbs
- Green beans
- Leafy greens
- Mushrooms
- Radishes
- Scallions and leeks
- Summer squash and zucchini

CHILL ANYWHERE

These items are not prone to chilling injury and can be stored anywhere in the fridge, provided the temperature doesn't freeze them.

- Apples
- Cherries
- Grapes

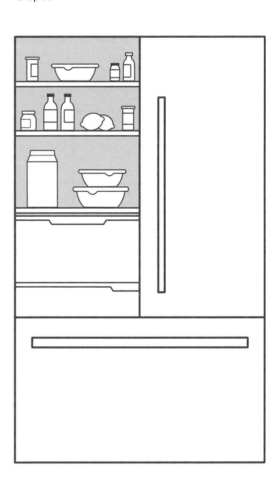

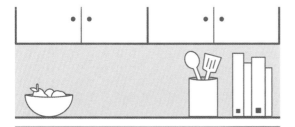

on the counter

Some produce is sensitive to chilling injury, making it subject to dehydration, internal browning, and/or internal and external pitting if stored in the refrigerator.

- Avocados*
- Bananas*
- Mangoes
- Pears
- Pineapple
- Tomatoes*
- Stone fruit (peaches, nectarines, and plums)

*Once they've reached their peak ripeness, these can be stored in the refrigerator to prevent overripening, but some discoloration may occur.

in the pantry

The following produce should be kept at cool room temperature and away from light to prevent sprouting and to prolong shelf life.

- Garlic
- Onions and shallots
- Potatoes and sweet potatoes
- Butternut squash

freezer-friendly

keep your freezer cold
The quicker foods freeze, and the fewer fluctuations in temperature once frozen, the better. Your freezer should register zero degrees Fahrenheit or colder; use a thermometer to check. Make sure your freezer is at the coldest possible setting (unlike your fridge, where the coldest setting is normally too cold).

portion liquids
Liquids can be frozen in ice cube trays and then transferred to a zipper-lock bag.

minimize headroom
In hard-sided containers, fill to ½ inch from the top and place plastic wrap on the food's surface before attaching the lid.

double wrap
For solid foods you're wrapping in zipper-lock bags, first wrap in plastic wrap and then put the food in the bag, pressing out as much air as possible before sealing.

maximize airflow
To help cold air circulate, keep food away from freezer vents.

5 ingredients you didn't know you could freeze

See pages 20–21 for how to freeze them.

1 Anchovies
2 Bread
3 Cheese
4 Leftover canned items (beans, chipotle chiles in adobo, coconut milk, and tomato paste)
5 Wine

leftover ingredient tips

It's hard to use up ingredients when you're just cooking for yourself. Here are some pesky ingredients that are common for the solo cook, and how to store them.

half an avocado

The best way to store an opened avocado is by vacuum sealing it, but that's just not practical for those of us without a vacuum sealer. Instead, store cut avocados submerged cut side down in lemon water in the refrigerator—we found that it maintains its color for up to two days, but the texture may be a bit softer and the flavor a bit tart.

anchovies and bacon

Coil up individually (to prevent sticking and to minimize surface area for freezer burn), freeze on plate, and transfer to zipper-lock bag.

berries

As soon as you bring them home, wash the berries in a bowl with 3 cups of water and 1 cup of distilled white vinegar. Drain them in a colander and rinse under running water.

Place the berries in a salad spinner lined with three layers of paper towels. Spin for 15 seconds or until the berries are completely dry. Store them in a loosely covered paper towel–lined container at the front of the fridge.

bread

We store our bread in the freezer, tightly wrapped in aluminum foil and sealed in a zipper-lock bag. We prefer buying hearty, crusty bread because it freezes much better than standard sandwich bread. Be sure to slice it before freezing. Do not store bread in the refrigerator where bread stales faster than at room temperature. See page 14 for tips on defrosting bread in the microwave.

cheese

Wrap cheese in parchment paper and then in aluminum foil and refrigerate. The paper allows the cheese to breathe, and the foil keeps out off-favors from the refrigerator and prevents the cheese from drying out. For feta cheese, if it didn't come in brine, place it in a small zipper-lock bag or airtight container and pour in just enough oil to cover. Stored this way, feta keeps for up to 4 weeks.

You also can freeze cheese (we tested extra-sharp cheddar, Brie, fresh goat cheese, and Pecorino Romano). Wrap the cheese tightly in plastic wrap, seal it in a zipper-lock bag, and freeze it for up to 2 months. Let it defrost overnight in the fridge (a 2½-hour rest on the counter also works).

canned items

beans
Drain, pat beans dry with paper towels, and transfer to zipper-lock bag. To save space, lay flat to freeze.

chipotle chiles in adobo
Freeze spoonfuls of chiles and sauce on parchment-lined baking sheet; transfer to zipper-lock bag.

coconut milk
Leftover coconut milk will last up to a week in the fridge with no depreciation in quality. For longer-term storage, transfer to an airtight container and freeze. If it separates after defrosting, blend with an immersion blender for about 30 seconds to re-emulsify, then use it as directed in recipes.

tomato paste
We prefer to buy longer-lasting tomato paste in a tube. If yours comes in a can, open ends of can, push out paste, and freeze in zipper-lock bag. Cut off only as much as needed from frozen log.

salad greens

When lettuce and other leafy greens come in bags, store them in their original packaging in the crisper drawer. Store intact heads of lettuce without packaging (or washed and dried leaves) wrapped in moist paper towels in a partially open zipper-lock bag.

fresh herbs

As soon as you bring them home, gently rinse and dry the herbs (a salad spinner works well), wrap them in a damp paper towel, and place in a partially open zipper-lock bag in the crisper drawer. The exception here is basil. Don't rinse basil before you need to use it; the added moisture will decrease its shelf life. Instead, wrap it in clean (dry) paper towels, place in a partially open zipper-lock bag, and refrigerate.

tomatoes

Contrary to popular belief, both cut and whole tomatoes actually can be stored in the refrigerator once fully ripe (for 2 days and 5 days, respectively). To keep them from picking up off-flavors, put them in an airtight container, which works better than plastic wrap at keeping out odors.

half an onion and other alliums

To store part of a chopped or sliced onion, refrigerate in a zipper-lock bag and rinse before using to remove residual odor. Store delicate scallions, chives, and leeks in a glass of water covered loosely with a zipper-lock bag.

wine

Once opened, bottles of wine are rarely usable for more than a week. But boxed wine has an airtight inner bag that prevents exposure to oxygen even after the box is opened, so the wine lasts up to 1 month. To store opened bottled wine, measure 1 tablespoon wine into each well of ice cube tray and freeze. Use a paring knife or small spatula to remove each frozen wine cube and add as desired to pan sauces.

wait to wash

With the exception of berries and most herbs, it's best to wash produce just before you use it instead of right when you get home from the grocery store. Moisture promotes the growth of mold and bacteria, which in turn causes spoilage. If you do wash produce ahead of time, make sure to dry it thoroughly before storing it.

reviving vegetables

Limp asparagus, broccoli, or celery? No problem. Trim the ends, place the vegetable upright in an inch or two of water, and loosely cover with plastic wrap before placing in the fridge.

get scrappy

save your stems Most recipes that use fresh herbs call for just the leaves. But cilantro stems are very flavorful and relatively soft and can easily be finely chopped or minced and used along with the leaves.

take stock Stash vegetable scraps in a zipper-lock bag or storage container in your freezer. Once it's full, use them to make a stock. (Same goes for that rotisserie chicken carcass.)

in a pickle Quick-pickle past-their-prime vegetables: Combine 3 parts rice vinegar, 3 parts water, and 1 part white wine vinegar with a bit of sugar in a saucepan, bring to a simmer, and pour over vegetables. Cool to room temperature before refrigerating.

feeling cheesy Save the rind of aged cheeses like Parmesan, Pecorino Romano, or Gruyère, and toss them into a soup, stock, or Sunday gravy for an umami boost.

top notch Don't toss the tops of your root vegetables. Make carrot top pesto by blending carrot greens with an equal amount of basil, sauté your beet greens, and wilt your radish tops.

tip: *Don't prep more than what you need of a vegetable. If a recipe calls for half of an eggplant or butternut squash, peeled, cut the vegetable in half first, and then peel the part you're going to use.*

use it up

To help avoid food waste, we've prepared this guide to key ingredients. So if you're making one recipe with half of a butternut squash or a few tablespoons out of a jar of sun-dried tomatoes, you can see other recipes in the book that call for them so you don't end up tossing the extras. And remember that our Kitchen Improv suggestions also include ideas for using up ingredients.

ingredient	recipe	amount	page
pantry items			
artichoke hearts	Lemon-Herb Zoodles with Artichokes, Feta, and Walnuts	½ cup	275
canned black-eyed peas	Pomegranate Glazed Salmon with Black-Eyed Peas and Walnuts	¾ cup	252
canned cannellini beans	Tuscan Tuna Salad Bowl	¼ cup	225
canned chickpeas	Moroccan Chicken Salad	½ cup	210
	Warm Spiced Couscous Salad	1 cup	228
	Vegetarian Fideos	½ cup	268
canned chipotle chiles in adobo sauce	5-Ingredient Black Bean Soup	2–3 teaspoons	150
coconut milk	Thai-Style Coconut Chicken Curry	½ cup	171
	Coconut Paletas	2 cups	320
roasted red peppers	Vegetarian Fideos	⅓ cup	268
sun-dried tomatoes	5-Ingredient Sun-Dried Tomato and White Bean Soup	3 tablespoons	153
	Tuscan Tuna Salad Bowl	1 tablespoon	225
	Italian Pasta Salad	¼ cup	226
	Garam Masala Pork Chop with Couscous and Spinach	1 tablespoon	247
	Skilled Flatbread with Goat Cheese, Sun-Dried Tomatoes, and Prosciutto	2 tablespoons	279
tomato paste	Beef and Barley Soup	1 tablespoon	160
	Clam and Cannellini Bean Stew with Sausage	1 teaspoon	178
	Simplest Ground Beef Tacos	2 teaspoons	200
	Tex-Mex Cheese Enchiladas	2 teaspoons	280
fresh produce			
avocado	Avocado Toast	½ avocado	189
	Sweet Potato–Bacon Wrap	¼ avocado	192
	Green Goodness Salad	½ avocado	213
bell pepper	Easy Cuban Black Beans	½ green pepper	130
	Sriracha-Lime Tofu Bowl	½ red bell pepper	214
broccoli	Roasted Broccoli with Garlic	1 pound	83
	Beef and Broccoli Stir-Fry	6 ounces	244

ingredient	recipe	amount	page
fresh produce *(continued)*			
broccoli rabe	Broiled Broccoli Rabe	8 ounces	85
	Sheet Pan Sausages with Sweet Potatoes, Broccoli Rabe, and Mustard-Chive Butter	4 ounces	251
butternut squash	Roasted Butternut Squash	½ squash	88
	Creamy Butternut Squash Soup	½ large squash	146
cabbage	Skillet-Roasted Cabbage with Mustard and Thyme	½ head	90
	Sriracha-Lime Tofu Bowl	½ head napa cabbage	214
	Crispy Sesame Pork Chops with Wilted Napa Cabbage Salad	¼ small head napa cabbage	248
cauliflower	Cauliflower Steak	½ head	63
	Skillet-Roasted Cauliflower with Capers and Pine Nuts	½ head	94
	Cauliflower Rice	½ head	96
	Creamy Curried Cauliflower Soup	½ head	144
eggplant	Broiled Eggplant with Honey-Lemon Vinaigrette	½ large eggplant	99
	Simple Ratatouille	½ eggplant	116
fennel	Spanish-Style Fish Stew	½ bulb	177
	Arugula and Steak Tip Salad	¼ small fennel bulb	221
dairy			
feta	Roasted Feta Potatoes	1 ounce (¼ cup)	108
	Harvest Salad	2 ounces (½ cup)	217
	Mexican Street-Corn Salad	2 ounces (½ cup)	219
	Lemon-Herb Zoodles with Artichokes, Feta, and Walnuts	1 tablespoon	275
	Asparagus and Goat Cheese Frittata	2 ounces	282
heavy cream/half-and-half	Creamiest Mashed Potato for One	2 tablespoons	106
	Creamy Curried Cauliflower Soup	¼ cup	144
	Creamy Butternut Squash Soup	2 tablespoons	146
	Whipped Cream for One	¼ cup heavy cream	289
	Dipping Hot Chocolate	¼ cup	291
	Cheesecake Parfait	1 tablespoon	306
	Banana Ice Cream	½ cup heavy cream	323
bread			
pita bread	Packable Pita Sandwich	1 (8-inch) pita bread	195
	Lamb Pita Sandwiches with Tzatziki	2 (8-inch) pita breads	196
	Cinnamon Sugar Pita Chips	1 (8-inch) pita bread	294
corn tortillas	Chipotle Shrimp Tacos	2 (6-inch) corn tortillas	203
	Tex-Mex Cheese Enchiladas	6 (6-inch) corn tortillas	280
flour tortillas	Sweet Potato–Bacon Wrap	1 (10- or 12-inch) tortilla	192
	Zucchini Quesadilla	1 (10- or 12-inch) tortilla	198
	Peanut Butter–Chocolate Quesadilla	1 (10-inch) flour tortilla	305

weekly menu & shopping list

If you maintain a well-stocked pantry (see pages 10–11), your weekly grocery list should be pretty short. Plan out your meals as much as possible, and don't forget about leftovers! (See pages 284–285 for tips on packing lunch.) Here is an example of a shopping list and meal plan to help you get to an empty fridge by the end of the week.

shopping list

- 1 (10- to 12-ounce) bone-in split chicken breast
- 6 ounces sirloin steak tips
- Fresh herbs (cilantro and basil)
- Arugula
- 1 avocado
- 1 eggplant
- 12 ounces cherry or grape tomatoes
- Hummus

sweet tooth

Make a double batch of Edible Cookie Dough (page 300) and stash it in your freezer for dessert-at-the-ready throughout the week.

monday

LUNCH

Sweet Potato–Bacon Wrap (page 192)

DINNER

Broiled Charred Kebab (page 42)

Simple Ratatouille (page 116)

tuesday

LUNCH

Leftover ratatouille with hummus and pita and a simple arugula salad

DINNER

Crispy-Skinned Chicken (page 32) with Mint Sauce (page 68) using basil instead of mint and parsley

Roasted Sweet Potato Wedges (page 113) using the extra sweet potato from Monday's lunch

thursday

LUNCH

Packable Pita Sandwich
(page 195) using the
leftover broiled eggplant
instead of eggs and sliced
cherry or grape tomatoes
instead of regular tomato

DINNER

Tex-Mex Cheese
Enchiladas (page 280)
sprinkled with cilantro,
chopped cherry or grape
tomatoes, and chopped
leftover avocado

friday

LUNCH

Leftover enchiladas,
using the same garnishes

DINNER

Pan-Seared Shrimp
(page 61)

Creamy Orzo with
Parmesan (page 127)
with thawed frozen peas
stirred in, topped with
any extra chopped cherry
or grape tomatoes

wednesday

LUNCH

Tuscan Tuna Salad Bowl
(page 225) using arugula
instead of bibb lettuce

DINNER

Use other half of eggplant
from Monday's dinner
to make Broiled Eggplant
with Honey-Lemon
Vinaigrette (page 99)

Couscous (see page 123)
+ dollop of yogurt and
Toasted Nuts (page 15)

working for the weekend

The weekends look different for everyone. You may be hosting
or attending dinner parties, traveling, or going out to eat with
friends. For that reason, we outlined a meal plan just for weekday
lunches and dinners, but that may shift depending on your lifestyle.
Use this more as a 5-day plan, and don't feel constrained to the
Monday–Friday schedule.

party for one

When you're cooking for yourself, dinner can be whatever you want it to be. But that's no reason to skimp on the pageantry. In fact, it's a great excuse to clear out your fridge, kick back, and relax. With simple snacks and sips that (bonus!) also help you use up extra produce and/or fresh herbs you may have on hand, here are some suggestions for enjoying your solo happy hour.

snack time

pull together a tapas-style meal using leftovers from the week
Use up your leftover Garlicky Braised Chickpeas (page 133), Sautéed Mushrooms with Shallots and Thyme (page 102), and/or Sautéed Radishes with Crispy Bacon (page 84), to name a few.

make a savory version of paper bag popcorn (page 296)
Try black pepper and Parmesan, barbecue, or any spice blend.

toss toasted nuts (page 15) with spices
Try cashews with curry powder, peanuts with cumin, or almonds with ras el hanout.

make kale chips (page 15) with leftover kale

make a simple frico
Sprinkle about ½ cup of grated aged cheese (like Parmesan or Asiago) into the center of a nonstick skillet over medium-high heat. Use a heatproof rubber spatula to tidy the outer edges of the cheese. Cook until the edges are lacy and toasted, about 4 minutes. Remove the pan from the heat and allow the cheese to set for about 30 seconds. Using a fork and a heatproof spatula, carefully flip the cheese wafer and return the pan to medium heat. Cook until the second side is golden brown, about 2 minutes. Slide the cheese wafer out of the pan and transfer to a plate.

use up extra feta cheese to make spicy whipped feta dip
Process ½ cup crumbled feta cheese, 1 tablespoon extra-virgin olive oil, 1 tablespoon water, 1 teaspoon lemon juice, ½ teaspoon paprika, and ⅛ teaspoon cayenne pepper together in food processor until smooth, about 20 seconds. Transfer mixture to bowl and drizzle with more olive oil.

drink time

grapefruit-rosemary spritzer

Fresh or unsweetened store-bought juice both work here. Garnish with a rosemary sprig in addition to the grapefruit twist, if you like. You can make this spritzer with or without alcohol.

- 4 ounces grapefruit juice, plus strip of grapefruit peel for garnishing
- 1 ounce blanco tequila, vodka, or London dry gin (optional)
- ½ ounce Herb Syrup with rosemary
- 4 ounces seltzer, chilled

Fill chilled glass halfway with ice. Add grapefruit juice, tequila (if using), and herb syrup and stir to combine. Add seltzer, and, using spoon, gently lift grapefruit mixture from bottom of glass to top to combine. Top with additional ice. Pinch grapefruit peel over drink and rub outer edge of glass with peel, then garnish with grapefruit peel and serve.

variation
orange-thyme spritzer
Substitute orange juice for grapefruit juice and herb syrup with thyme for rosemary syrup. Substitute orange peel for grapefruit peel.

celery gimlet

If you don't have a cocktail shaker, a mason jar is a suitable substitute in a pinch.

- 1 small celery rib, chopped, plus celery leaf for garnishing
- ¾ ounce Simple Syrup
- 2 ounces London dry gin
- ¾ ounce lime juice

Add celery and simple syrup to base of cocktail shaker and muddle until celery is broken down and all juice has been expressed, about 30 seconds. Add gin and lime juice, then fill shaker with ice. Shake mixture until fully combined and well chilled, about 30 seconds. Strain cocktail into chilled cocktail glass. Garnish with celery leaf and serve.

variation
arugula gimlet
Substitute ⅓ cup baby arugula for the celery, and vodka for the gin. Garnish with an additional arugula leaf.

mint julep

For a classic presentation, make crushed ice using a food processor. Otherwise, cubes are fine.

- ⅓ cup fresh mint leaves, plus mint sprig for garnishing
- ½ ounce Simple Syrup
- 2 ounces bourbon

1 Add mint leaves and simple syrup to mixing glass and muddle until fragrant, about 30 seconds. Add bourbon, then fill glass three-quarters full with ice. Stir until mixture is just combined, about 15 seconds.
2 Strain cocktail into chilled glass half-filled with crushed ice. Top with additional crushed ice to form mound above rim of glass. Garnish with mint sprig and serve.

variations
rye-basil julep
Substitute basil for the mint, and rye for the bourbon. Garnish with a basil sprig.

whiskey-ginger smash
Substitute 1 (1-inch) piece of fresh ginger, sliced thin, for the mint, and Tennessee whiskey for the bourbon. Garnish with an additional ginger slice.

sugar, sugar

These syrups can be refrigerated for up to 1 month. Shake well before using.

simple syrup
makes about 8 ounces

- ¾ cup sugar
- 5 ounces warm tap water

Whisk sugar and warm water together in bowl until sugar has dissolved. Let cool completely, about 10 minutes, before transferring to airtight container.

herb syrup
makes about 8 ounces

- ¾ cup sugar
- 5 ounces water
- ½ cup fresh herb leaves (basil, dill, mint, or tarragon), 12 fresh thyme sprigs, or 1 fresh rosemary sprig

Heat sugar and water in small saucepan over medium heat, whisking often, until sugar has dissolved, about 5 minutes; do not boil. Stir in herb and let cool completely, about 30 minutes. Strain syrup through fine-mesh strainer into airtight container; discard solids.

the main event

These simple recipes should be in every solo cook's arsenal, ready for creating flexible meals on the fly. Enjoy each recipe as-is, or use our tips to customize it to your tastes, whether you transform it into a whole new meal or pair it with any of the side dishes in the next chapter. Want to level up from simple seasonings? Our favorite finishers include sauces for dipping or drizzling, compound butters to add a luxe richness, spice rubs to change up the flavor profile, and flavored salts to sprinkle over the finished product. And if you're here for meal-prep purposes, storage information is included for recipes that store well.

crispy-skinned chicken

total time 35 minutes

why this recipe works Perfectly roasted chicken is one of the ultimate comfort foods, but roasting a whole chicken for one is a bit of a stretch, even for the most enthusiastic poultry fans. Choosing bone-in breasts instead offers roasted chicken appeal—plentiful juicy meat and rich, crispy skin—in a compact package. Even better? We achieved all of that roasted goodness without even turning on the oven. To get ultracrispy skin on our bone-in chicken, we dried the chicken well, seasoned it, and then placed it skin side down in a cold nonstick skillet over medium-low heat; this gave the fat a chance to render as the pan heated. We used that rendered fat to cook the chicken (without moving it) over medium-low heat, covered, until the skin was a gorgeous deep golden brown; then we flipped it and cooked it, uncovered, until the meat reached 160 degrees. Serve alongside Roasted Butternut Squash (page 88) and finish with Chermoula Sauce (page 68). You will need an 8- or 10-inch nonstick skillet with a tight-fitting lid for this recipe.

1 (10- to 12-ounce) bone-in split chicken breast, trimmed

⅛ teaspoon table salt

⅛ teaspoon pepper

kitchen improv

use what you've got Substitute 2 bone-in thighs or 2 drumsticks for the breast and cook chicken to 175 degrees, increasing the cooking time as needed and flipping drumsticks (if using) during last 5 minutes of cooking.

get saucy Drizzle with an herb sauce like Chermoula Sauce or Mint Sauce (page 68).

make it lemon-herb Sprinkle chicken with fresh or dried herbs such as rosemary, thyme, oregano, or marjoram along with the salt and pepper and then finish with a squeeze of lemon juice.

1   Place chicken, skin side up, on cutting board and cover with plastic wrap. Using meat pounder, pound thick end of breast to ¾- to 1-inch thickness. Pat chicken dry with paper towels and sprinkle with salt and pepper.

2   Place chicken, skin side down, in cold 8- or 10-inch nonstick skillet. Cover skillet, place over medium-low heat, and cook, without moving, until skin is deep golden brown, 15 to 20 minutes.

3   Flip chicken and continue to cook, uncovered, until chicken registers 160 degrees, 5 to 10 minutes. Transfer chicken, skin side up, to plate and let rest for 5 minutes. Serve. (Chicken can be refrigerated for up to 3 days.)

pan-seared boneless chicken breast

total time 25 minutes

why this recipe works Say it with us: Simple doesn't need to be snooze-worthy. The satisfying (and versatile!) chicken breast should be in every for-one cook's repertoire—it can be shredded, sliced, or chopped for salads, tacos, sandwiches, or bowls. And just because something is skinless, it doesn't mean it has to be pale and wan. To encourage good browning, we patted the chicken dry before seasoning, and we resisted moving it during the first 3 minutes of cooking in the skillet. After flipping the seared chicken, we added a splash of water to the skillet, covered it, and reduced the heat to low to finish cooking it through. The result is a golden brown, tender, evenly cooked piece of chicken with a beautiful golden crust. You will need an 8- or 10-inch skillet with a tight-fitting lid for this recipe.

1 (6- to 8-ounce) boneless, skinless chicken breast, trimmed

⅛ teaspoon table salt

⅛ teaspoon pepper

1 teaspoon oil

2 tablespoons water

kitchen improv

use what you've got Substitute 2 (3- to 4-ounce) boneless, skinless thighs for the breast and cook chicken to 175 degrees, increasing the cooking time as needed.

spice it up Sprinkle the chicken with your favorite spice blend (see page 72) along with the salt and pepper. If using a store-bought spice blend that contains salt, omit the salt in the recipe.

get saucy Drizzle with Tahini Sauce, Chermoula Sauce, or any of the sauces from pages 68–69.

1   Place chicken on cutting board and cover with plastic wrap. Using meat pounder, gently pound chicken to even thickness. Pat chicken dry with paper towels and sprinkle with salt and pepper.

2   Heat oil in 8- or 10-inch skillet over medium heat until just smoking. Add chicken and cook until well browned on first side, about 3 minutes. Flip chicken, add water, and cover skillet. Reduce heat to low and continue to cook until chicken registers 160 degrees, about 3 minutes.

3   Transfer chicken to plate, tent with aluminum foil, and let rest for 5 minutes. Serve. (Chicken can be refrigerated for up to 3 days.)

crispy breaded cutlets

total time 35 minutes

why this recipe works Crispy, tender, and juicy breaded chicken cutlets are a standby that are also endlessly riffable. Drizzle them with a sauce, pair them with a side, or, if you're feeling ambitious, go all in and turn them into a sandwich. The best part? Because you're just cooking one cutlet, you don't have to worry about changing out the oil between batches of frying as you would when cooking a number of cutlets for a larger group. We removed a step from the standard three-step breading process (flour, egg, and bread crumbs), and instead whisked the flour into the egg. Panko bread crumbs—a must for the crispiest, crunchiest coating—adhered perfectly to the cutlets. A quick sizzle in a hot oiled pan and we were in business. Freezing the chicken briefly makes slicing it in half horizontally easier.

1 (6- to 8-ounce) boneless, skinless chicken breast, trimmed

⅛ teaspoon table salt

⅛ teaspoon pepper

1 large egg

1 tablespoon all-purpose flour

¾ cup panko bread crumbs

3 tablespoons oil

kitchen improv

use what you've got Skip the halving step and substitute 2 (3- to 4-ounce) boneless pork chops (cook to 140 degrees) or 2 (3- to 4-ounce) chicken cutlets for the chicken breast.

make it chicken parmesan Add dried oregano and garlic powder to the egg mixture; cut some of the panko with grated Parmesan; top fried cutlets with tomato sauce and mozzarella cheese; broil.

make it chicken katsu Serve fried cutlets over rice with sliced cucumbers, scallions, and a simple Tonkatsu Sauce (page 69).

1 Halve breast horizontally. Place cutlets on cutting board, cover with plastic wrap and, using meat pounder, gently pound each cutlet to even ½-inch thickness. Pat chicken dry with paper towels and sprinkle with salt and pepper.

2 Whisk egg and flour together in medium bowl until smooth. Spread panko in even layer in shallow dish. Working with 1 cutlet at a time, dip in egg mixture, allowing excess to drip off, then coat in panko, pressing gently to adhere; transfer to plate and repeat with remaining cutlet.

3 Heat oil in 10-inch nonstick skillet over medium heat until shimmering. Carefully place cutlets in skillet and cook until deep golden brown and crispy, about 3 minutes per side. Transfer cutlets to paper towel–lined plate to drain and let rest for 5 minutes. Serve.

why this recipe works While chicken wings are a game day favorite, the wings you find at barrooms are often lackluster—soggy, over-sauced, and served alongside a couple of sad celery sticks. But wings deserve to be treated as more than just a snack, and their small size and no-fuss prep make them perfect for a light yet satisfying meal for one. We ditched the deep fryer and turned to a smoking hot oven—baking the wings on a wire rack let the rendered fat drip away (lining the sheet with foil under the rack makes for easy cleanup). A final stint under the broiler crisped the thin sheath of rendered skin even further to produce the delectable crunch that's often lacking, and that can hold up to any number of sauces, though we love the crispy simplicity of the plain version, too. You can leave the pointy wingtips attached for quicker prep, although they get slightly burnt; if the charred appearance bothers you, snip off the tips with a pair of kitchen shears. For a more bite-size wing, you can cut through the wing joint to create drumettes and flats.

1 pound chicken wings

1 tablespoon oil

⅛ teaspoon table salt

⅛ teaspoon pepper

1 Adjust oven rack to upper-middle position and heat oven to 475 degrees. Set wire rack in aluminum foil–lined rimmed baking sheet. Pat wings dry with paper towels, then toss with oil, salt, and pepper in bowl. Arrange in single layer on prepared rack. Bake wings until golden on both sides, 25 to 30 minutes, flipping wings and rotating sheet halfway through baking.

2 Heat broiler, then broil wings until deep golden brown and crispy, 1 to 2 minutes per side. Let rest on rack for 5 minutes. Serve.

roasted chicken wings

total time 50 minutes

pantry recipe

kitchen improv

get saucy Toss the wings in a sauce immediately after broiling. Whisk together melted butter and hot sauce for classic buffalo sauce, or try honey and lemon juice, sriracha and lime juice, or even a store-bought barbecue sauce.

level up Sprinkle buffalo-style wings with crumbled blue cheese while still hot, or try crumbled goat cheese on honey-lemon wings, or cotija on the sriracha-lime version.

juiciest stovetop pork chop

total time 20 minutes

why this recipe works With the right cooking technique a pork chop can become the perfect treat-yourself meal (why should steak have all the fun?), so we set out to develop the juiciest pork chop imaginable—without turning on the oven. Our success hinged on two key points. First, the thickness of the chop—we found ¾ to 1 inch to be the sweet spot. Any thinner and it overcooks before the flavorful browning develops, any thicker and the exterior burns before the interior is cooked. The second is the cooking method—when testing single proteins in less-crowded pans, we discovered that flipping the piece occasionally helps to create better browning and more even cooking. For seasonings, we kept it simple with just salt and pepper, but it's easy to mix it up with spices, rubs, or simple sauces. If using a spice rub, be sure to avoid any that contain sugar or the pork chop will burn. Buy the pork chop from the butcher counter to avoid having to buy a larger quantity. See pages 16–17 for more shopping tips. We love this pork chop with Broiled Broccoli Rabe (page 85).

1 (8- to 10-ounce) bone-in pork rib chop, ¾ to 1 inch thick, trimmed

⅛ teaspoon table salt

⅛ teaspoon pepper

1 tablespoon oil

kitchen improv

use what you've got Substitute a center-cut chop or boneless chop for the bone-in rib chop.

level up While the pork rests, use the pan to sauté some apple and shallot with butter and herbs. Serve over the pork.

spice it up Add a (sugar-free) spice rub like Ras el Hanout (page 72) or ground fennel to the pork with the salt and pepper.

make it glazed Microwave some apricot jam and thyme and drizzle over the finished pork.

Pat chop dry with paper towels and sprinkle with salt and pepper. Heat oil in 10-inch skillet over medium heat until just smoking. Add chop and cook until well browned all over and registers 140 degrees, 8 to 10 minutes, flipping chop occasionally and reducing heat if skillet begins to smoke. Transfer chop to plate and let rest for 5 minutes. Serve. (Pork can be refrigerated for up to 3 days.)

broiled charred kebab

total time 20 minutes

why this recipe works Though kebabs are often associated with backyard barbecues for a crowd, what's more made-for-one than a perfectly portioned single skewer? To achieve a kebab with grilled flavor indoors, we went with pieces of sirloin steak tip: The cut has a big beefy flavor and enough fat to keep the meat from drying out as it chars under the broiler. The best part about kebabs, though, is that the same method works with chicken, beef, and pork. A flavorful spice rub, whether it's ras el hanout or another of your choosing (see page 72), elevates the dish and contributes to flavorful browning. The seasoning opens up a world of possibilities—you could be enjoying a Middle Eastern–style kebab with broiled eggplant (see page 99) drizzled with yogurt, or a Korean barbecue–style version served with rice and sprinkled with scallions. Steak tips, also known as flap meat, can be sold as whole steaks, cubes, or strips. To ensure evenly sized pieces, we prefer to buy whole steaks and cut them ourselves. You will need one 10- or 12-inch metal skewer for this recipe. You can use store-bought ras el hanout or make your own (see page 72).

6 ounces sirloin steak tips, trimmed and cut into 1½-inch pieces

1½ teaspoons ras el hanout

½ teaspoon oil

⅛ teaspoon table salt

⅛ teaspoon pepper

kitchen improv

use what you've got Substitute boneless, skinless chicken thighs (cook to 175 degrees); a boneless, skinless chicken breast (cook to 160 degrees); or country-style pork ribs (cook to 140 degrees) for the steak tips.

spice it up Substitute your favorite barbecue spice rub, herbes de Provence, or even curry powder for the ras el hanout.

get saucy Instead of seasoning with ras el hanout, brush the meat with barbecue sauce, teriyaki sauce, hoisin sauce, or gochujang in step 1.

1 Adjust oven rack 4 inches from broiler element and heat broiler. Pat steak tips dry with paper towels, then toss with ras el hanout, oil, salt, and pepper in bowl. Thread steak tips onto one 10- or 12-inch metal skewer and place skewer on aluminum foil–lined rimmed baking sheet.

2 Broil until steak tips are well charred and register 120 to 125 degrees (for medium-rare), 5 to 7 minutes, flipping once halfway through broiling. Transfer steak tips to plate, remove skewer, and let steak tips rest for 5 minutes. Serve. (Steak tips can be refrigerated for up to 3 days.)

why this recipe works There's something so luxurious about a solo steak dinner—it's an excuse to pour a glass of wine, dig out a linen napkin, and slow down. But steak is hard to get right on the stovetop, and nothing kills the mood quite like a botched cook job. Too often, the meat around the perimeter is overcooked by the time the center comes to temperature. The secret is to first cook it in a very low oven, *before* quickly searing it on the stovetop, gently (and evenly) cooking the interior to the desired temperature. After its time in the oven, the now-dry exterior of the steak browns in record time, producing a beautiful crust. (And since it's in the pan for just a few minutes, there isn't time for it to lose much moisture or become overcooked.) Next to Sautéed Mushrooms with Shallots and Thyme (page 102), or Creamy Orzo with Parmesan (page 127), this is a meal worth lighting candles for.

- 1 (6-ounce) boneless strip steak, 1 to 1½ inches thick, trimmed
- ⅛ teaspoon table salt
- ⅛ teaspoon pepper
- 1 tablespoon oil

1 Adjust oven rack to middle position and heat oven to 225 degrees. Pat steak dry with paper towels, sprinkle with salt and pepper, and place on wire rack set in rimmed baking sheet. Roast until steak registers 120 degrees (for rare to medium-rare), 35 to 45 minutes.

2 Heat oil in 10-inch skillet over medium heat until just smoking. Add steak and cook until well browned all over, about 4 minutes, flipping steak every minute. Return steak to wire rack and let rest for 5 minutes. Transfer steak to cutting board and slice thin against grain. Serve. (Steak can be refrigerated for up to 3 days.)

perfect seared steak

total time 1 hour

kitchen improv

use what you've got Flank steak or rib-eye steak work great here as well.

level up Top the steak with a compound butter (see pages 70–71), or sprinkle with crumbled blue cheese or flavored salt (see page 73) while it rests.

why this recipe works You might think you need to splurge on a marbled rib-eye steak or a filet to get top-shelf steakhouse flavors at home, but you can achieve the same satisfaction with easy-to-cook (and wallet-friendly) steak tips. For a cooking method that produces juicy, well-browned steak tips, we cut the tips into 2-inch pieces and seasoned with salt and pepper. After about 8 minutes of pan-cooking, we had perfect medium-rare pieces of meat that we cut against the grain so each bite was as tender as the next. Go all-in on steakhouse splendor and serve them with Creamiest Mashed Potato for One (page 106), or layer them on a sandwich, toss with a salad, or even gussy up your breakfast with steak and eggs. If using a spice rub, be sure to avoid any that contain sugar or the steak tips will burn. Steak tips, also known as flap meat, can be sold as whole steaks, cubes, or strips. To ensure evenly sized pieces, we prefer to buy whole steaks and cut them ourselves.

6 ounces sirloin steak tips, trimmed and cut into 2-inch pieces

⅛ teaspoon table salt

⅛ teaspoon pepper

1 tablespoon oil

Pat steak tips dry with paper towels and sprinkle with salt and pepper. Heat oil in 10-inch skillet over medium heat until just smoking. Add steak tips and cook until well browned all over and register 120 to 125 degrees (for medium-rare), 7 to 10 minutes, flipping steak tips every minute and reducing heat if skillet begins to smoke. Transfer steak tips to cutting board and let rest for 5 minutes. Serve. (Steak tips can be refrigerated for up to 3 days.)

sirloin steak tips

total time 20 minutes

kitchen improv

level up Sprinkle with Fresh Herb Salt or your favorite finishing salt (see page 73).

spice it up Sprinkle any (sugar-free) spice rub on the beef with the salt and pepper before searing.

glazed meatloaf for one

total time 45 minutes

why this recipe works Meatloaf brings to mind diner-style fare for a family, but we wanted down-home goodness in a smaller package (without the assistance of cutesy, single-use, mini equipment). To mix up the classic flavor profile, we used ground pork and incorporated Asian-inspired ingredients for a meatloaf that reminded us of the filling of our favorite dumplings. To avoid the sometimes dense bounciness of dumpling filling, we added some panko and an egg yolk to the ground pork, which kept our meatloaf supermoist and tender. We pressed the meat mixture into a free-form loaf, browned it in a skillet, flipped it, and finished it in the oven in the same skillet (bonus points for less cleanup!). We glazed the loaf with a mixture of fruity, umami-packed hoisin sauce and a splash of tangy rice vinegar. We love this meatloaf paired with Lemony Skillet-Charred Green Beans (page 101) or mashed potatoes (see page 106) for a classic combo, or turned into a sandwich with melted cheese and extra hoisin for dunking.

2 tablespoons hoisin sauce

1 tablespoon rice vinegar

3 tablespoons panko bread crumbs

2 scallions, sliced thin, divided

1 tablespoon soy sauce

1 large egg yolk

1½ teaspoons grated fresh ginger or ¼ teaspoon ground ginger

1 garlic clove, minced, or ⅛ teaspoon garlic powder

6 ounces ground pork

½ teaspoon oil

kitchen improv

use what you've got You can substitute meatloaf mix or ground beef for the ground pork.

make it classic Swap out all the traditional Asian seasonings to make this a classic American-style loaf. Use parsley, Worcestershire, and thyme to season the meat, and try ketchup and cider vinegar for a glaze.

1   Adjust oven rack to middle position and heat oven to 350 degrees. Whisk hoisin and vinegar together in small bowl; set aside.

2   Combine panko, half of scallions, soy sauce, egg yolk, ginger, and garlic in medium bowl. Add pork and gently knead with your hands until just combined. Shape mixture into rough 5- by 3-inch loaf of even thickness.

3   Heat oil in 8- or 10-inch ovensafe nonstick skillet over medium heat until just smoking. Gently add meatloaf and cook on first side until well browned, 2 to 3 minutes. Carefully flip meatloaf, neatening edges as needed, and transfer skillet to oven. Bake for 10 minutes.

4   Remove skillet from oven. Being careful of hot skillet handle, brush top and sides of meatloaf with hoisin mixture. Return skillet to oven and continue to bake until meatloaf registers 160 degrees, 5 to 10 minutes. Transfer meatloaf to plate and let rest for 5 minutes. Sprinkle with remaining scallions and serve.

why this recipe works It's easy to associate lamb with a rack of lamb, the showstopper of a holiday table. But there's no reason to save this flavorful entrée for a special occasion. Let the chicken breast take a break tonight and insert some elegance into your weekly routine, without adding any work. Simply searing two chops quickly on both sides over medium heat (plenty hot enough for the small amount of meat in the pan) and then gently finishing them over lower heat creates a flavorful crust and juicy interior. We like these chops served with a simple side salad or a bright, crunchy vegetable like shaved zucchini with feta, fresh mint, and a lemony vinaigrette to contrast the richness. Buy lamb chops from the butcher counter to avoid having to purchase a larger quantity. See pages 16–17 for more shopping tips.

2 (5- to 6-ounce) lamb loin or rib chops, 1½ inches thick, trimmed

⅛ teaspoon table salt

⅛ teaspoon pepper

1 tablespoon oil

Pat chops dry with paper towels and sprinkle with salt and pepper. Heat oil in 10-inch skillet over medium heat until just smoking. Add chops and cook until well browned all over and register 120 to 125 degrees (for medium-rare), 7 to 9 minutes, flipping chops occasionally and reducing heat if skillet begins to smoke. Transfer chops to plate and let rest for 5 minutes. Serve. (Lamb can be refrigerated for up to 3 days.)

weeknight lamb chops

total time 20 minutes

kitchen improv

level up Make this entrée extra elegant with a flavored salt (see page 73) to finish.

get saucy Drizzle the lamb with a quick herb sauce like Chermoula Sauce (page 68).

why this recipe works A perfectly seared piece of salmon with a moist interior, crispy skin, and golden exterior is at home in a variety of applications, whether on its own, flaked over a salad, or accompanied by any number of vegetables, grains, or pastas. It's easy to keep it light by serving it over greens with pepitas and shaved fennel, or take it in a heartier direction with Roasted Feta Potatoes (page 108). To keep things simple for this versatile fish and avoid overcooking, we started by placing the seasoned salmon skin side down in a cold, dry nonstick skillet, and then set the burner to medium heat. The skin protected the fish from drying out while cooking and rendered to a flavorful crisp sheath (though you can easily choose to peel it off and discard once the fish is cooked). The skin's rendered fat also enabled us to sear the remaining sides of the fish (a necessary step when cooking a single piece) without any additional oil. Buy fish from the seafood counter to avoid having to buy a larger quantity. See pages 16–17 for more shopping tips.

1 (6- to 8-ounce) skin-on salmon fillet, 1 inch thick

⅛ teaspoon table salt

⅛ teaspoon pepper

Lemon wedges

1   Pat salmon dry with paper towels and sprinkle with salt and pepper. Place fillet, skin side down, in cold 8- or 10-inch nonstick skillet and place over medium heat. Cook fillet, without moving it, until skin is golden brown and bottom ¼ inch of fillet turns opaque, 6 to 8 minutes.

2   Using 2 spatulas, flip fillet skin side up and continue to cook without moving it until golden brown and bottom ¼ inch of fillet turns opaque, about 3 minutes. Flip fillet onto 1 side and cook until golden, about 1 minute. Flip fillet onto final side and cook, continuing to flip as needed, until salmon registers 125 degrees (for medium-rare), about 1 minute. Serve with lemon wedges.

crispy-skinned salmon fillet

total time 20 minutes

kitchen improv

use what you've got You can substitute wild salmon or arctic char (cook to 120 degrees).

spice it up Add a spice rub (see page 72) to the salmon with the salt and pepper in step 1.

get saucy Serve the salmon with a creamy Yogurt Sauce (page 69) or Mint Sauce (page 68).

pan-roasted cod

total time 30 minutes

why this recipe works This ultrasimple, quick recipe yields an elegant result: a tender, succulent fillet of flaky white fish sporting a chestnut brown, supersavory crust—a great component of a light, fresh meal. White fish fillets (such as cod, pollock, haddock, hake, and black sea bass) are easy to overcook, so we borrowed a technique commonly used in professional kitchens to cook a single piece of fish: Sear the fillet in a hot pan, flip, and then transfer to a hot oven to finish cooking. To brown the fish quickly before it had a chance to dry out, we added a light sprinkling of sugar, which accelerated browning without adding any discernible sweetness. This versatile fish is perfect over quinoa, or starring in fish tacos with pickled red onions and sliced avocado. Buy fish from the seafood counter to avoid having to buy a larger quantity. See pages 16–17 for more shopping tips.

1 (6- to 8-ounce) skinless cod fillet, 1 inch thick

⅛ teaspoon table salt

Pinch pepper

⅛ teaspoon sugar

1 tablespoon oil

Lemon wedges

kitchen improv

use what you've got Black sea bass, haddock, hake, or pollock can be substituted for the cod.

level up Serve with Grapefruit-Basil Relish (page 69) or Garlic-Herb Compound Butter (page 70).

1 Adjust oven rack to middle position and heat oven to 425 degrees. Pat cod dry with paper towels, sprinkle with salt and pepper, and sprinkle sugar lightly over skinned side of fillet.

2 Heat oil in 8- or 10-inch ovensafe nonstick skillet over medium-high heat until just smoking. Lay fillet sugared side down in skillet and, using spatula, lightly press fillet for 20 to 30 seconds to ensure even contact with skillet. Cook until browned on first side, 1 to 2 minutes.

3 Using 2 spatulas, flip fillet, then transfer skillet to oven. Roast until fish flakes apart when gently prodded with paring knife and registers 135 degrees, 7 to 10 minutes. Serve with lemon wedges.

lemony poached fish

total time 25 minutes

why this recipe works The beauty of this recipe is that it works with a wide range of fish types, which can be paired with any number of sauces (see pages 68–69), or side dishes like Beets with Hazelnuts and Chives (page 78) or Sautéed Baby Bok Choy with Umami Garlic Sauce (page 80) to create a lively, interesting meal. When you're cooking a fillet of fish, you might immediately think of flashing it in the pan, but it's easy to achieve the delicate flavor and superlatively succulent flesh of poached fish. For a quick, simple recipe for poached fish that yielded delicately flavored, supple fish, we came up with a few shortcuts: Using a carefully measured amount of poaching liquid allowed us to cut back on the aromatics, saving preparation time; a splash of white wine vinegar added just the right amount of acidity (a pantry-friendly solution to avoid opening a bottle of wine); and resting the fish on lemon and shallot slices added additional brightness and aroma while also preventing the bottom from overcooking. Buy fish from the seafood counter to avoid having to buy a larger quantity. See pages 16–17 for more shopping tips. You will need a 10-inch skillet with a tight-fitting lid for this recipe.

3 (¼-inch-thick) lemon slices, plus lemon wedges for serving

1 shallot, sliced thin

1 tablespoon white wine vinegar

1 (6- to 8-ounce) skinless cod fillet, 1 inch thick

⅛ teaspoon table salt

Pinch pepper

kitchen improv

use what you've got Substitute wild salmon or arctic char (cook to 120 degrees); farmed salmon (cook to 125 degrees); halibut, mahi-mahi, red snapper, or swordfish (cook to 130 degrees); or black sea bass, pollock, or haddock (cook to 135 degrees) for the cod.

level up Up the dish's aroma by adding a sprig or two of fresh herbs (we like parsley, dill, chives, or tarragon) along with the shallots.

make it ginger-soy Substitute a thinly sliced scallion and a slice or two of fresh ginger for the shallot, and substitute soy sauce for the vinegar.

1   Arrange lemon slices in single row across bottom of 10-inch skillet. Sprinkle with shallot and vinegar, then add enough water to just cover lemon slices (about 1 cup). Pat fillet dry with paper towels, sprinkle with salt and pepper, and place skinned side down on lemon slices in skillet. Bring water to simmer over medium-high heat, then cover, reduce heat to low, and cook, adjusting heat as needed to maintain gentle simmer, until fish registers 135 degrees, 6 to 8 minutes.

2   Remove skillet from heat and, using spatula, carefully transfer cod and lemon slices to paper towel–lined plate to drain. (Discard poaching liquid.) Carefully lift and tilt fillet to discard lemon slices and paper towels. Serve with lemon wedges.

golden tilapia

total time 30 minutes

why this recipe works Tilapia is meaty, mild, and tender, and we love that it freezes well so we can dig into our freezer to produce a meal on the fly. While tilapia's flavor isn't that far off from thicker fillets like cod or haddock, that doesn't mean it can be cooked the same—unlike those more delicate fish, tilapia can handle the direct heat of stovetop cooking. But it requires a bit of finessing to get right: The thick half of a thin, wide fillet rests flat on the pan and browns nicely during sautéing, but the thin half tilts up, hardly making contact at all. Splitting the fillet down its natural seam into a thick and a thin portion allowed for more precise cooking and even browning. Salting the pieces of tilapia and letting them rest for 15 minutes before cooking seasoned the mild tilapia throughout and kept the fish moist as it cooked. This style of cooking is easy to achieve with a wide variety of thin fish, and can be fancied up with sauces and spices to match all kinds of sides—we love it with a lemon-caper pan sauce served alongside Roasted Broccoli with Garlic (page 83).

1 (6- to 8-ounce) skinless tilapia fillet, split lengthwise down natural seam

⅛ teaspoon table salt

1 tablespoon oil

Lemon wedges

kitchen improv

use what you've got You can use catfish, flounder, or sole in place of the tilapia in this recipe.

level up A compound butter (see pages 70–71) or finishing salt (see page 73) ups the elegance of this dish.

get saucy Make a quick pan sauce by browning butter in the pan, and adding capers and lemon juice off the heat. Spoon over the tilapia.

1 Sprinkle tilapia with salt and let sit at room temperature for 15 minutes. Pat tilapia dry with paper towels.

2 Heat oil in 10-inch nonstick skillet over high heat until just smoking. Add tilapia to skillet and cook, tilting and gently shaking skillet occasionally to distribute oil, until golden brown, 2 to 3 minutes. Using 2 spatulas, flip tilapia and cook until second sides are golden brown, 2 to 3 minutes, reducing heat if skillet begins to smoke. Serve with lemon wedges.

why this recipe works Shrimp is the perfect ingredient for the for-one cook—if buying from the seafood counter, you can get exactly the amount you need, or if using frozen bagged shrimp, it's easy to pull out and defrost just what you need for your recipe. (They defrost quickly in a colander under running water.) Bonus: They take just minutes to cook. Pan-searing over high heat is our choice for shrimp with a well-caramelized exterior and a moist, tender interior, preserving the shrimp's plumpness and trademark briny sweetness. And using the residual heat of the skillet to finish cooking the shrimp ensures they never overcook. With little more than salt and pepper, we can go from freezer to plate in record time. This all-purpose recipe is perfect for adding to garlicky pasta, topping a light salad, or serving on polenta (see page 129) with cherry or grape tomatoes, kalamata olives, and feta for a Mediterranean twist. See page 11 for more information about frozen shrimp. You will need a 10-inch skillet with a tight-fitting lid for this recipe.

- 6 ounces extra-large shrimp (21 to 25 per pound), peeled and deveined
- ⅛ teaspoon table salt
- ⅛ teaspoon pepper
- 1 tablespoon oil

  Lemon wedges

Toss shrimp, salt, and pepper together in bowl. Heat oil in 10-inch skillet over high heat until just smoking. Add shrimp in single layer and cook until spotty brown and edges begin to turn pink, about 1 minute. Off heat, flip shrimp, cover, and cook second side using residual heat of skillet until shrimp are opaque throughout, 1 to 2 minutes. Serve immediately with lemon wedges.

pan-seared shrimp

total time 10 minutes

pantry recipe

kitchen improv

spice it up Add citrus zest, chili powder, or a spice rub (see page 72) to the shrimp before cooking.

get saucy Toss shrimp with hoisin sauce or soy sauce.

why this recipe works Meat isn't the only steak in town: When you cook a thick plank of cauliflower, it develops a substantial, meaty texture and becomes nutty, sweet, and caramelized, making it worthy of center-of-the-plate status. Recipes for cauliflower steaks abound, but many of them involve fussy transitions between stovetop and oven. Not here. We use aluminum foil to employ a steam-then-roast method with all of the cooking taking place in the oven, so your stovetop is free to whip up an accompanying side dish like Curried Lentils (page 134). It's important to start with a whole head of cauliflower—the core keeps everything intact. Look for a fresh, firm, bright white head of cauliflower that feels heavy for its size and is free of blemishes or soft spots; florets are more likely to separate from older heads of cauliflower. Luckily, cauliflower keeps for a long time in the fridge. You could make Cauliflower Rice (page 96), Creamy Curried Cauliflower Soup (page 144), or another cauliflower steak with the leftover cauliflower.

1 head cauliflower (2 pounds)

1 tablespoon oil, divided

⅛ teaspoon table salt, divided

⅛ teaspoon pepper, divided

Lemon wedges

1   Adjust oven rack to lowest position and heat oven to 500 degrees. Discard outer leaves of cauliflower and trim stem flush with bottom florets. Halve cauliflower lengthwise through core. Cut one 1½-inch-thick slab lengthwise from one half of cauliflower, trimming any florets not connected to core. (Reserve remaining cauliflower for another use.)

2   Place steak on aluminum foil–lined baking sheet and drizzle with 1½ teaspoons oil. Sprinkle with pinch salt and pinch pepper and rub to distribute. Flip steak and repeat with remaining 1½ teaspoons oil, pinch salt, and pinch pepper. Cover sheet tightly with foil and roast for 5 minutes. Remove foil and continue to roast until bottom of steak is well browned, 8 to 10 minutes. Gently flip and continue to roast until tender and second side is well browned, 6 to 8 minutes. Serve with lemon wedges.

cauliflower steak

total time 35 minutes

kitchen improv

spice it up Rub cauliflower steak with a spice rub (see page 72) when adding the salt and pepper in step 2.

get saucy A bright herb sauce like Mint Sauce or Chermoula Sauce (page 68) pairs nicely with this mild-mannered steak.

Afte

By

Owayne
drawn to ath
can rememb

As a child
up trophies
school's tra
pass the tim
played crick
the streets
makeshift
from concre

But life w
games. "I w
eating," he s

His paren
was young. F
to the United
l, leaving hi
grandmother
ers. The situ
dire that his
ily barrels of
would last th

Mr. Mcleo
remarried a
York City. Wh
one of his bro
move in with
ther on the t
soon as that p
as I got into
the fridge," he

Now 21, Mi
eyes and a re

why this recipe works Unlike American-style scrambled eggs, which are the speediest of home-cooked breakfasts, French cooks employ a more leisurely approach. They cook their eggs slowly over low heat, stirring constantly until the mixture forms small, delicate curds bound in a velvety sauce. It's remarkably rich, but made without a lick of fat. This technique can take five times as long as the American version, but the reward is eggs that are so extravagantly creamy that they linger on the palate, allowing you time to thoroughly appreciate the fullness of their flavor. Breakfast never felt so indulgent. We like them served on toast or a bagel with cream cheese, smoked salmon, finely chopped red onion or shallot, and capers, or over Pan-Roasted Asparagus (page 77) and served alongside crusty bread.

2 large eggs

Pinch table salt

2 teaspoons water, divided

1   Whisk eggs and salt in bowl until eggs are blended. Heat 1½ teaspoons water in 8-inch nonstick skillet over low heat until steaming. Add eggs and immediately stir with rubber spatula. Cook, stirring slowly and constantly scraping edges and bottom of skillet, for 4 minutes. (If egg mixture is not steaming after 4 minutes, increase heat slightly.)

2   Continue to stir slowly until eggs begin to thicken and small curds begin to form, about 4 minutes longer. (If curds have not begun to form, increase heat slightly.) If any large curds form, mash with spatula. As curds start to form, stir vigorously, scraping edges and bottom of skillet, until eggs are thick enough to hold their shape when pushed to 1 side of skillet, 4 to 6 minutes. Remove skillet from heat. Add remaining ½ teaspoon water and stir vigorously until incorporated, about 30 seconds. Serve.

creamy french-style scrambled eggs

total time 20 minutes

pantry recipe

kitchen improv

level up Minced chives, basil, parsley, or tarragon make a great garnish or stir in.

easy cheddar omelet

total time 15 minutes

why this recipe works An omelet is definitely easier to make for one—no standing over the stove like a short-order cook and tending to multiple skillets, or worrying about keeping them all warm until mealtime. We started by spraying a 10-inch nonstick skillet with some vegetable oil spray—this ensured that our omelet would come out of the skillet easily—followed by a pat of butter. After cooking and stirring the eggs until large curds formed, we briefly tilted the skillet to allow any uncooked egg to run around the pan and finished by letting the omelet cook undisturbed until just set. Our last step was to add shredded cheddar cheese and let the omelet sit in the pan, covered and off heat, until the cheese was melted. A simple, fluffy cheese omelet always hits the spot, but we think an omelet is the perfect excuse to clean out your fridge—it's easy to make a heartier version with whatever you have on hand, whether it's the end of a bag of spinach, a leftover half of a bell pepper, or a few mushrooms. You will need a 10-inch nonstick skillet with a tight-fitting lid for this recipe.

> 3 large eggs
>
> ⅛ teaspoon table salt
>
> ⅛ teaspoon pepper
>
> ½ tablespoon unsalted butter
>
> 1 ounce cheddar cheese, shredded (¼ cup)

kitchen improv

use what you've got You can use any cheese in place of cheddar. Be sure to finely grate aged cheeses like Parmesan and Pecorino Romano.

level up Add sautéed mushrooms, cherry or grape tomatoes, and/or wilted garlicky greens with the cheese: Simply sauté them in the skillet and wipe the pan clean before starting the recipe. Sprinkle the finished product with minced chives or other herbs.

1 Whisk eggs, salt, and pepper in bowl until eggs are blended. Spray 10-inch nonstick skillet with vegetable oil spray.

2 Melt butter in skillet over medium-high heat, swirling to coat skillet bottom. When foaming subsides, add eggs and cook, gently stirring and scraping bottom of skillet with rubber spatula in circular motion, until large curds begin to form and bare spots are visible on bottom of skillet, about 20 seconds.

3 Tilt skillet so uncooked eggs fill bare spots. Run spatula around edge of skillet and push cooked eggs down off sides. Let cook, undisturbed, until bottom of omelet is just set but top is still slightly wet, about 30 seconds.

4 Remove skillet from heat and sprinkle cheddar over half of omelet. Cover and let sit until cheese is melted, about 1 minute. Fold unfilled half of omelet over filled half to create half-moon shape then tilt skillet to slide omelet onto plate. Serve.

leveling up

Solo dining doesn't have to be boring—these simple recipes help you jazz up your meal with minimal effort (and without a lot of extra ingredients). A squeeze of lemon goes a long way, but it's easy to take it a step further, whether you add a stir-together spice rub to your simple salt-and-pepper seasoning, dollop your finished steak with a make-ahead compound butter, or use up your past-their-prime herbs by whisking together a quick herb sauce. We prefer using extra-virgin olive oil in these recipes because it is a higher-quality finishing oil—the flavor really makes a difference.

sauces

mint sauce
makes ¼ cup

- ¼ cup chopped fresh mint
- 3 tablespoons extra-virgin olive oil
- 2 tablespoons chopped fresh parsley
- 1 tablespoon lemon juice
- 1 small garlic clove, minced

Whisk all ingredients together in bowl and season with salt and pepper to taste.

chermoula sauce
makes ¼ cup

- 6 tablespoons minced fresh cilantro
- 2 tablespoons extra-virgin olive oil
- 1 tablespoon lemon juice
- 2 garlic cloves, minced
- ¼ teaspoon ground cumin
- ¼ teaspoon paprika
- Pinch cayenne pepper

Whisk all ingredients together in bowl and season with salt and pepper to taste.

grapefruit-basil relish

makes about 1 cup

- 2 red grapefruits
- 1 small shallot, minced
- 2 tablespoons chopped fresh basil
- 2 teaspoons lemon juice
- 2 teaspoons extra-virgin olive oil

Cut away peel and pith from grapefruits. Cut grapefruits into 8 wedges, then slice crosswise into ½-inch-thick pieces. Place grapefruit in strainer set over bowl and let drain for 15 minutes; measure out and reserve 1 tablespoon drained juice. Combine reserved juice, shallot, basil, lemon juice, and oil in bowl. Stir in grapefruit and let sit for 15 minutes. Season with salt and pepper to taste. (Relish can be refrigerated for up to 2 days.)

variation

orange-avocado relish
Substitute 1 large orange for grapefruits; quarter orange before slicing crosswise. Substitute 2 tablespoons minced fresh cilantro for basil and 4 teaspoons lime juice for lemon juice. Add 1 diced avocado and 1 small minced jalapeño chile to juice mixture with orange.

yogurt sauce

makes 1 cup
Do not substitute low-fat or nonfat yogurt here.

- 1 cup plain whole-milk yogurt
- 1 teaspoon grated lemon zest plus 2 tablespoons juice
- 1 garlic clove, minced

Whisk all ingredients together in bowl and season with salt and pepper to taste. Cover and refrigerate for at least 30 minutes to allow flavors to meld. (Sauce can be refrigerated for up to 4 days.)

tahini sauce

makes about 1 cup

- ½ cup tahini
- ½ cup water
- ¼ cup lemon juice (2 lemons)
- 2 garlic cloves, minced

Whisk all ingredients together in bowl until smooth (mixture will appear broken at first). Season with salt and pepper to taste. Let sit at room temperature for at least 30 minutes to allow flavors to meld. (Sauce can be refrigerated for up to 4 days; bring to room temperature before serving.)

tonkatsu sauce

makes about ⅓ cup
You can substitute yellow mustard for the Dijon, but do not use a grainy mustard.

- ¼ cup ketchup
- 2 tablespoons Worcestershire sauce
- 2 teaspoons soy sauce
- 1 teaspoon Dijon mustard

Whisk all ingredients together in bowl.

compound butters

garlic-herb compound butter

makes 8 tablespoons; enough for 8 servings

- 8 tablespoons unsalted butter, softened
- 2 tablespoons minced fresh sage or 1½ teaspoons dried
- 1 tablespoon minced fresh parsley
- 1 tablespoon minced fresh thyme or ¾ teaspoon dried
- 2 garlic cloves, minced

Whip butter with fork until light and fluffy. Mix in sage, parsley, thyme, and garlic and season with salt and pepper to taste. Wrap in plastic wrap and let rest to blend flavors, about 10 minutes, or roll into log and refrigerate. (Compound butter can be refrigerated in airtight container for up to 4 days or frozen, wrapped tightly in plastic, for up to 2 months.)

rosemary-parmesan compound butter

makes 8 tablespoons; enough for 8 servings

- 8 tablespoons unsalted butter, softened
- 6 tablespoons grated Parmesan cheese
- 4 teaspoons minced fresh rosemary or 1 teaspoon dried
- 2 garlic cloves, minced
- ¼ teaspoon red pepper flakes

Whip butter with fork until light and fluffy. Mix in Parmesan, rosemary, garlic, and pepper flakes and season with salt and pepper to taste. Wrap in plastic wrap and let rest to blend flavors, about 10 minutes, or roll into log and refrigerate. (Compound butter can be refrigerated in airtight container for up to 4 days or frozen, wrapped tightly in plastic, for up to 2 months.)

blue cheese compound butter

makes 8 tablespoons; enough for 8 servings

- 8 tablespoons unsalted butter, softened
- 2 ounces blue cheese, crumbled (½ cup)

Whip butter with fork until light and fluffy. Mix in blue cheese and season with salt and pepper to taste. Wrap in plastic wrap and let rest to blend flavors, about 10 minutes, or roll into log and refrigerate. (Compound butter can be refrigerated in airtight container for up to 4 days or frozen, wrapped tightly in plastic, for up to 2 months.)

mustard-chive compound butter

makes 8 tablespoons; enough for 8 servings

- 8 tablespoons unsalted butter
- 3 tablespoons minced fresh chives
- 5 tablespoons whole-grain mustard

Whip butter with fork until light and fluffy. Mix in chives and mustard and season with salt and pepper to taste. Wrap in plastic wrap and let rest to blend flavors, about 10 minutes, or roll into log and refrigerate. (Compound butter can be refrigerated in airtight container for up to 4 days or frozen, wrapped tightly in plastic, for up to 2 months.)

anchovy-garlic compound butter

makes 8 tablespoons; enough for 8 servings

- 8 tablespoons unsalted butter, softened
- ¼ cup minced fresh parsley
- 2 anchovy fillets, rinsed and minced
- 1 tablespoon lemon juice
- 2 garlic cloves, minced

Whip butter with fork until light and fluffy. Mix in parsley, anchovies, lemon juice, and garlic and season with salt and pepper to taste. Wrap in plastic wrap and let rest to blend flavors, about 10 minutes, or roll into log and refrigerate. (Compound butter can be refrigerated in airtight container for up to 4 days or frozen, wrapped tightly in plastic, for up to 2 months.)

spice rubs

ras el hanout
makes ½ cup

If you can't find Aleppo pepper, you can substitute ½ teaspoon paprika plus ½ teaspoon red pepper flakes.

- 16 cardamom pods
- 4 teaspoons coriander seeds
- 4 teaspoons cumin seeds
- 2 teaspoons anise seeds
- 2 teaspoons ground dried Aleppo pepper
- ½ teaspoon allspice berries
- ¼ teaspoon black peppercorns
- 4 teaspoons ground ginger
- 2 teaspoons ground nutmeg
- 2 teaspoons ground cinnamon

Process cardamom pods, coriander seeds, cumin seeds, anise seeds, Aleppo pepper, allspice, and peppercorns in spice grinder until finely ground, about 30 seconds. Stir in ginger, nutmeg, and cinnamon. (Ras el hanout can be stored in airtight container for up to 1 month.)

barbecue rub
makes ½ cup

- 3 tablespoons chili powder
- 3 tablespoons packed brown sugar
- 2 teaspoons pepper
- ¾ teaspoon cayenne pepper

Combine all ingredients in bowl. (Barbecue rub can be stored in airtight container for up to 1 month.)

classic steak rub
makes ½ cup

- 2 tablespoons peppercorns
- 3 tablespoons coriander seeds
- 4 teaspoons dried dill
- 2 teaspoons red pepper flakes

Process peppercorns and coriander seeds in spice grinder until finely ground, about 30 seconds; transfer to small bowl. Stir in dill and pepper flakes. (Steak rub can be stored in airtight container for up to 1 month.)

salts

fresh herb salt

makes ½ cup

We love the texture that the coarse grains of kosher salt lend to a finished dish, so we prefer to use kosher salt in our flavored salts. We develop our recipes with Diamond Crystal kosher salt. Note that ½ cup Diamond Crystal kosher salt = 6 tablespoons Morton kosher salt, so if you are using Morton, you need to use ¾ of the given amount of salt.

- ½ cup kosher salt
- 1 cup minced fresh chives, dill, or tarragon

Using your hands, rub salt and chives in large bowl until well combined. Spread mixture into even layer on parchment paper–lined rimmed baking sheet. Let sit at room temperature, away from direct sunlight, until completely dry, 36 to 48 hours, stirring every 12 hours to break up any clumps. (Salt can be stored in airtight container for up to 1 month.)

cumin-sesame salt

makes 6 tablespoons

- 2 tablespoons cumin seeds
- 2 tablespoons sesame seeds
- 2 tablespoons kosher salt

Toast cumin seeds and sesame seeds in 8-inch skillet over medium heat, stirring occasionally, until fragrant and sesame seeds are golden brown, 3 to 4 minutes. Transfer to spice grinder and let cool for 10 minutes. Pulse seeds until coarsely ground, about 6 pulses. Transfer to bowl and stir in salt. (Salt can be stored in airtight container for up to 1 month.)

smoked salt

makes ½ cup

- ½ cup kosher salt
- 1 teaspoon liquid smoke

Combine salt and liquid smoke in bowl, then spread onto large plate. Microwave, stirring occasionally, until only slightly damp, about 2 minutes. Let sit until completely dry and cool, about 10 minutes. (Salt can be stored in airtight container for up to 1 month.)

sides to match or eat on their own

No need to keep your side dishes on the sidelines—the beauty of solo dining is that you get to decide what makes a meal. Serve these satisfying sides with options from chapter 1, mix and match them with each other for a vibrant (and often vegetarian) dinner, or use our tips to bulk up side dishes to give them center-of-the-plate status. Many sides have a robust afterlife, too, from sandwich or omelet fillings to grain bowl add-ins and pizza toppings.

why this recipe works Finding fresh, crisp asparagus at the market is like hitting the springtime produce jackpot (luckily, it's a lot easier than winning the lottery). Pan roasting produces deeply flavored asparagus for a side that will make any meal feel fancy. With a few simple additions these spears could also serve as your main dish. Arranging half of the asparagus with their tips pointed in the opposite direction of the other half allows them to fit more evenly in one layer for better browning; sprinkling them with a teaspoon of water and covering the pan for the first few minutes is just enough to steam them a bit so they become perfectly crisp-tender. Leftovers can be sliced and added to a salad, or folded into scrambled eggs or an omelet. This recipe works best with asparagus that is at least ½ inch thick near the base. Do not use pencil-thin spears as they will overcook. Trim the bottom 1 inch from each asparagus spear. You will need a 12-inch skillet with a tight-fitting lid for this recipe.

1 teaspoon oil

12 ounces thick asparagus, trimmed

1 teaspoon water

¼ teaspoon table salt

Pinch pepper

1 teaspoon lemon juice

1   Heat oil in 12-inch skillet over medium heat until shimmering. Add half of asparagus to skillet with tips pointed in one direction and add remaining asparagus with tips pointed in opposite direction. Using tongs, distribute spears in even layer. Sprinkle with water, salt, and pepper, cover, and cook until asparagus is bright green and still crisp, 3 to 4 minutes.

2   Uncover, increase heat to medium-high, and cook until asparagus is tender and well browned on all sides, 4 to 6 minutes, rearranging spears as needed. Off heat, sprinkle with lemon juice and season with salt and pepper to taste. Serve. (Asparagus can be refrigerated for up to 2 days.)

pan-roasted asparagus

total time 20 minutes

makes leftovers

kitchen improv

level up Sprinkle with toasted panko (see page 137) or grated Parmesan, or make a quick gremolata from minced garlic, fresh parsley, and grated lemon zest.

make it a meal Serve with a poached or fried egg (see page 139).

SIDES TO MATCH OR EAT ON THEIR OWN

77

beets

with hazelnuts and chives

total time 40 minutes

makes leftovers

why this recipe works When it comes to storage vegetables, beets are hard to beat: The jewel-toned root vegetables, which pack a punch of earthy sweetness, will last for weeks in your fridge, perfect for the weeks you didn't make it to the grocery store. But we didn't want it to feel like they take too long to cook. Rather than wrapping and roasting—typical beet protocol—we halved whole unpeeled beets and gently simmered them in a small amount of liquid in a covered saucepan. This method gave us tender beets with concentrated flavor in less than half an hour, just enough time to whisk together a quick vinaigrette for the still-warm beets to drink up and chop some nuts and fresh herbs. The skins slip right off when the beets are tender and slightly cooled. Serve alongside a white flaky fish (see pages 54–56) for an unexpected yet delicious meal. Beets are classic with hard-cooked eggs, so we like to turn leftovers into a salad for lunch the next day by tossing with greens, hard-cooked eggs (see page 139), and canned chickpeas. Use beets that are 2 to 3 inches in diameter for this recipe.

3 beets (10 ounces), trimmed and halved	Pinch pepper
¼ teaspoon table salt, divided	1 tablespoon chopped skinned toasted hazelnuts, pistachios, or walnuts
1 tablespoon balsamic vinegar	1 tablespoon chopped fresh chives, mint, or parsley
1 tablespoon oil	

kitchen improv

level up Sprinkle with crumbled cheese (goat, feta, or blue), dollop with yogurt, and/or add orange or grapefruit segments.

make it a meal Serve over baby spinach, arugula, or seasoned grains.

1   Place beets, cut side down, in single layer in medium saucepan. Add 1 cup water and ⅛ teaspoon salt, then bring to simmer over medium-high heat. Reduce heat to low, cover, and simmer until beets are tender and tip of paring knife inserted into beets meets no resistance, 18 to 26 minutes.

2   Drain beets, then transfer to cutting board. When beets are cool enough to handle, rub off skins with paper towel or dish towel, then cut into ½-inch wedges. (Beets can be refrigerated for up to 1 week.)

3   Whisk vinegar, oil, remaining ⅛ teaspoon salt, and pepper together in medium bowl. Add beets and toss to coat, then season with salt and pepper to taste and sprinkle with nuts and herbs. Serve.

sautéed baby bok choy

with umami garlic sauce

total time 15 minutes

why this recipe works Crisp, slightly sweet, and, well, adorable, baby bok choy is tailor-made for a solo side dish. Unlike mature bok choy, which is often chopped into small pieces for cooking, baby bok choy's allure lies in showcasing its diminutive (and perfect single-serving) size—and yes, you only need one. In this recipe, we cut the bok choy in half lengthwise to create more surface area for attractive browning you'll be proud to plate up. An initial stint of steaming gave the stem halves the head start they needed to soften just a bit before sautéing. Our sauce, an assertively complex mixture of fish sauce, brown sugar, and pepper flakes, is a pungent and spicy complement to the delicate bok choy. You can use two smaller heads of baby bok choy, but if using, cut the steam time down to 1 minute. They will not develop as much browning, but they are still a suitable option. You will need an 8- or 10-inch nonstick skillet with a tight-fitting lid for this recipe.

1½ tablespoons water, divided

¾ teaspoon fish sauce

½ teaspoon brown sugar

⅛ teaspoon cornstarch

Pinch red pepper flakes

2 teaspoons oil, divided

1 head baby bok choy (4 ounces), halved, washed thoroughly, and dried

1 small garlic clove, minced

kitchen improv

use what you've got If you don't have fish sauce, you can use a combination of soy sauce and anchovy paste (see page 5 for more information).

get saucy Switch up the sauce by omitting the ingredients in step 1, and instead whisking together oyster sauce, grated fresh ginger, and sesame oil for a salty, savory finish, or try honey and orange zest for a bright-yet-sweet alternative.

make it a meal Serve with tofu over rice and sprinkle with crumbled nori sheets and nuts.

1 Whisk 1 tablespoon water, fish sauce, sugar, cornstarch, and pepper flakes together in small bowl; set aside.

2 Heat 1½ teaspoons oil in 8- or 10-inch nonstick skillet over medium heat until shimmering. Add bok choy, cut side down, and remaining 1½ teaspoons water and immediately cover skillet. Cook, covered, until leaves begin to wilt, 1 to 2 minutes. Remove lid, add garlic and remaining ½ teaspoon oil, and reduce heat to medium low. Continue to cook, stirring occasionally, until all water has evaporated and bok choy is deep golden brown, 1 to 2 minutes longer. Add fish sauce mixture and cook, stirring constantly, until sauce is thickened and coats bok choy, about 15 seconds. Season with salt and pepper to taste. Serve.

why this recipe works Roasting broccoli turns the fibrous, chalky raw florets that are synonymous with salad bar disappointment into a deeply flavorful Jack-of-all-trades vegetable that is equally at home next to chicken or beef as it is as the star of a grain bowl or pasta dish. For even browning, we made sure to maximize contact with the baking sheet by slicing the crowns in half and cutting each half into uniform wedges, and also cutting the peeled stalks into rectangular pieces slightly smaller than the more delicate wedges. Sugar sped up browning and added a hint of sweetness, and preheating the baking sheet ensured the broccoli started sizzling the second it hit the sheet. Toss leftovers with pasta and crumbled hot Italian sausage, or make an elevated grilled cheese by sandwiching chopped pieces between bread with jarred roasted red peppers and provolone cheese. Make sure to trim away the outer peel from the broccoli stalks as directed; otherwise, it will turn tough when roasted.

roasted broccoli
with garlic

total time 35 minutes

makes leftovers

1 pound broccoli

1 tablespoon oil

1 garlic clove, minced

¼ teaspoon sugar

¼ teaspoon table salt

Pinch pepper

Lemon wedges

1 Adjust oven rack to lowest position, place aluminum foil–lined rimmed baking sheet on rack, and heat oven to 500 degrees. Cut broccoli horizontally at juncture of crowns and stalks. Cut crowns into 4 wedges if 3 to 4 inches in diameter or 6 wedges if 4 to 5 inches in diameter. Trim tough outer peel from stalks, then cut into ½-inch-thick planks, 2 to 3 inches long.

2 Combine oil, garlic, sugar, salt, and pepper in medium bowl. Add broccoli and toss to coat. Working quickly, lay broccoli in single layer, flat sides down, on preheated sheet. Roast until stalks are well browned and tender and florets are lightly browned, 9 to 11 minutes. Season with salt and pepper to taste. Serve with lemon wedges. (Broccoli can be refrigerated for up to 2 days.)

kitchen improv

level up Substitute shallot for the garlic, add fennel seeds, and finish with grated Parmesan.

make it a meal Toss broccoli with quinoa, chopped toasted nuts, chopped scallions, and lots of fresh herbs, then drizzle with Tahini Sauce or Yogurt Sauce (page 69).

make it italian Toss roasted broccoli with olives, sun-dried tomatoes, chopped anchovies, or pesto before serving.

SIDES TO MATCH OR EAT ON THEIR OWN

why this recipe works There's no reason to be bitter about broccoli rabe when you cook the notoriously sharp-tasting vegetable with our superfast method. Most of broccoli rabe's bitterness comes from an enzymatic reaction triggered when the florets are cut or chewed, so we kept the leafy parts of the vegetable whole—they charred beautifully in the oven, adding crunch and savory depth. Because the heat from broiling deactivated the enzyme, much of the bitterness was tamed. Tossing the pieces with garlicky oil gave an extra layer of spiciness that contrasted nicely with the assertive broccoli rabe, making a robust accompaniment to mains like the Juiciest Stovetop Pork Chop (page 40). Or enjoy it on its own as the central component to a vegetarian meal so you can eat this special vegetable any night of the week. If you have raw broccoli rabe to spare, use it in Sheet Pan Sausages with Sweet Potatoes, Broccoli Rabe, and Mustard-Chive Butter (page 251).

broiled broccoli rabe

total time 20 minutes

makes leftovers

8 ounces broccoli rabe, trimmed

1 tablespoon oil

1 garlic clove, minced

¼ teaspoon table salt

Pinch red pepper flakes

Lemon wedges

1 Adjust oven rack 4 inches from broiler element and heat broiler. Cut tops (leaves and florets) of broccoli rabe from stalks, keeping tops whole, then cut stalks into 1-inch pieces. Transfer to aluminum foil–lined rimmed baking sheet.

2 Combine oil, garlic, salt, and pepper flakes in bowl then pour over broccoli rabe and toss to coat. Broil until exposed leaves are well browned, 2 to 2½ minutes. Using tongs, toss to expose unbrowned leaves. Return sheet to oven and continue to broil until most leaves are lightly charred and stalks are crisp-tender, 2 to 2½ minutes. Season with salt and pepper to taste. Serve with lemon wedges. (Broccoli rabe can be refrigerated for up to 2 days.)

kitchen improv

make it a meal Serve broccoli rabe on top of polenta (see page 129); stir it into cooked pasta and top it off with a fried egg (see page 139) and a sprinkle of toasted panko (see page 137); or use it as an omelet filler along with sun-dried tomatoes and an assertive cheese.

skillet-roasted brussels sprouts

with lemon and pecorino

total time 15 minutes

why this recipe works Fifteen minutes is all you need to make this absolute star of a side dish: sprouts that boast brilliant green rounded sides and crisp-tender interiors contrasted with nutty-sweet, crusty facades. Starting in a cold pan allows the sprouts to heat slowly and release their moisture, so they steam without additional flavor-dampening liquid. The best part of this single-serving size? With fewer sprouts involved, you can be sure they all make direct contact with the skillet. Over intense, direct heat, the tiny cabbages develop a deeply caramelized crust that is delightfully thick and dark, contributing a rich, nutty sweetness. Lemon juice and tangy Pecorino Romano cheese brighten everything up. Look for small brussels sprouts that are 1 to 1½ inches in diameter. You will need an 8- or 10-inch nonstick skillet with a tight-fitting lid for this recipe.

4 ounces brussels sprouts, trimmed and halved

1 tablespoon oil

⅛ teaspoon table salt

Pinch pepper

¾ teaspoon lemon juice

1 tablespoon grated Pecorino Romano or Parmesan cheese

kitchen improv

level up Add some chopped toasted nuts.

spice it up Add a pinch of red pepper flakes and a small minced garlic clove to the skillet in step 2.

make it a meal After cooking, add some gochujang and substitute sesame seeds for the Pecorino. Serve over rice with a fried egg (see page 139) and kimchi.

1 Arrange brussels sprouts in single layer, cut side down, in 8- or 10-inch nonstick skillet, then drizzle with oil and sprinkle with salt and pepper. Cover skillet, place over medium-high heat, and cook until sprouts are bright green and cut sides have started to brown, about 4 minutes.

2 Uncover and continue to cook until cut sides of sprouts are deeply and evenly browned and paring knife slides in with little to no resistance, 1 to 2 minutes longer, adjusting heat and moving sprouts as necessary to prevent them from overbrowning.

3 Off heat, sprinkle with lemon juice and season with salt and pepper to taste. Sprinkle with Pecorino and serve.

roasted butternut squash

total time 40 minutes

makes leftovers

pantry recipe

why this recipe works If you're cooking for one you might be reluctant to put a butternut squash in your cart. We get it—it's large and unwieldy, and seems like a lot of food. But we think that's part of its beauty. A single squash can yield two different sides, each with the potential to be served twice, making it a meal-prepper's dream. Plus, butternut squash is downright delicious. The plank-like pieces provide ample surface area for even browning, and are easily personalized with spices or herbs, either before or after roasting. Best of all, butternut squash's natural sweetness, moist flesh, and long storage time make it a particularly good go-to for a pantry-friendly meal: a perfect companion to proteins like Crispy-Skinned Chicken (page 32), or when served alongside lentils (see page 134) for a vegetarian meal. This is a hefty portion for one, but leftovers are perfect reheated as is, tossed into salads or cooked grains, or stirred into pasta with brown butter, sage, and grated Parmesan. You can make Creamy Butternut Squash Soup (page 146) with the other half of the squash.

½ butternut squash (1 pound), peeled, seeded, halved lengthwise, and sliced crosswise ½-inch thick

2 teaspoons oil

¼ teaspoon table salt

⅛ teaspoon pepper

kitchen improv

level up Sprinkle with chopped toasted nuts or seeds, za'atar, crumbled cheese (goat or feta), pomegranate seeds, chopped fresh herbs (cilantro, parsley, or mint), and/or pickled red onion.

spice it up Toss squash with spices like cinnamon, curry powder, chipotle pepper, smoked paprika, dried thyme, or dried rosemary before roasting.

get saucy Drizzle with a garlicky Yogurt or Tahini Sauce (page 69).

Adjust oven rack to lowest position and heat oven to 450 degrees. Toss squash with oil, salt, and pepper and spread in even layer on aluminum foil–lined rimmed baking sheet. Roast until well browned and tender, 20 to 30 minutes, flipping slices once halfway through cooking. Season with salt and pepper to taste. Serve. (Butternut squash can be refrigerated for up to 1 week.)

skillet-roasted cabbage

with mustard and thyme

total time 35 minutes

makes leftovers

why this recipe works Vegetables that store well, like cabbage, are great for when life gets in the way of our best grocery shopping intentions. But if you think cabbage is only good for shredding into coleslaw or sauerkraut, think again. When cut into thick wedges and seared in a skillet, cabbage transforms into a sweet, silky vegetable whose caramelized layers create the perfect nooks and crannies for soaking up a quick, flavorful sauce of butter, fresh thyme, and mustard. Leftovers reheat well or can be chopped up and mixed in with Creamiest Mashed Potato for One (page 106) for a quick version of Irish colcannon. When halving the cabbage, turn it core side up to help ensure that you slice evenly through it; each wedge needs a piece of intact core so the wedges don't fall apart when flipped. You will need a 12-inch nonstick skillet with a tight-fitting lid for this recipe. You can make Crispy Sesame Pork Chops with Wilted Napa Cabbage Salad (page 248) with the other half of the cabbage.

6 tablespoons water, divided

3 tablespoons unsalted butter, divided

½ head (1 pound) green, napa, or savoy cabbage, cut into 4 (2-inch) wedges

¼ teaspoon table salt

½ teaspoon minced fresh thyme or ¼ teaspoon dried

⅛ teaspoon pepper

1½ teaspoons Dijon mustard

kitchen improv

level up Sprinkle with chopped herbs, chopped toasted nuts (see page 15), and/or crumbled goat cheese.

make it a (curried) meal Omit mustard and substitute curry powder for thyme. Add halved cherry or grape tomatoes and chickpeas with the curry powder and pepper in step 3. Sprinkle with chopped cilantro before serving.

make it miso Omit thyme and substitute white miso for mustard. Sprinkle with minced fresh chives before serving.

make it Italian Omit thyme and mustard. Add sliced garlic and red pepper flakes with the thyme in step 3. Sprinkle with shaved Parmesan cheese before serving.

1 Combine ¼ cup water and 1 tablespoon butter in 12-inch nonstick skillet. Arrange cabbage wedges in single layer in skillet, cut side down. Sprinkle wedges with salt and cook over medium heat, uncovered, until water has evaporated and wedges are well browned, 15 to 18 minutes.

2 Flip wedges to second cut side, add remaining 2 tablespoons water to skillet, and cook, covered, until wedges are tender and second side is well browned, 2 to 4 minutes longer.

3 Transfer wedges to plate. Reduce heat under skillet to medium-low, then add remaining 2 tablespoons butter and cook until butter is melted and bubbling, 30 seconds to 1 minute. Stir in thyme and pepper and cook until fragrant, about 30 seconds. Off heat, stir in mustard. Return cabbage wedges to skillet and gently turn to coat in butter mixture and season with salt and pepper to taste. Serve. (Cabbage can be refrigerated for up to 2 days.)

why this recipe works You don't need 20/20 vision to see that carrots are one of the most popular vegetables around. And for good reason—their satisfying crunchiness makes them a great healthful snack on their own. But roasting them intensifies their sweetness and flavor, making them something even more special. (They also last a long time in your fridge, making them a perfect pantry-friendly addition to your meal.) When cooking carrots, texture is paramount. Undercooked carrots are better suited for rabbits; overcooked carrots are dry and leathery. These roasted carrots are just right—tender, sweet, and well-browned. Serve with Crispy-Skinned Chicken (page 32) for a classic combination. Leftovers reheat well, and are also great cold on a salad or chopped and tossed into a stir-fry.

6 carrots (1 pound), peeled and halved lengthwise

1 tablespoon oil

¼ teaspoon table salt

¼ teaspoon pepper

Adjust oven rack to lowest position and heat oven to 450 degrees. Toss carrots with oil, salt, and pepper and spread in even layer cut sides down on aluminum foil–lined rimmed baking sheet. Roast until tender and cut sides are well browned, 20 to 30 minutes. Season with salt and pepper to taste. Serve. (Carrots can be refrigerated for up to 2 days.)

roasted carrots

total time 35 minutes

makes leftovers

pantry recipe

kitchen improv

get saucy A bright herb mixture like Chermoula Sauce (page 68) contrasts with the carrot's sweetness nicely.

make it a meal Add roasted carrots to any salad (grain or vegetable based); use them for the base of a veggie sandwich; or serve over Greek yogurt and top with chopped nuts and herbs.

skillet-roasted cauliflower

with capers and pine nuts

total time 35 minutes

makes leftovers

why this recipe works We love cauliflower as the main event (see page 63), but it's also the perfect simple side to accompany a wide variety of dishes—and it's easy to switch up the flavor profile with different add-ins. Oven-roasting the florets transforms them into caramelized nuggets, but it can be time-consuming. Starting the cauliflower in a cold pan and allowing the florets to steam in their own moisture before removing the lid and letting them brown delivers roasted results in less than half the time. It is important not to lift the lid from the skillet during the first 5 minutes of cooking. Add leftovers to a curry (see page 171), or finely chop and mix with an egg, flour, and spices to make cauliflower cakes. You will need a 12-inch nonstick skillet with a tight-fitting lid. You can make Cauliflower Rice (page 96) with the other half of the cauliflower.

½ head cauliflower (1 pound), cored and cut into 1½-inch florets

2 tablespoons oil, divided

¼ teaspoon table salt

¼ teaspoon pepper

1 tablespoon capers, rinsed and minced

½ teaspoon grated lemon zest, plus lemon wedges for serving

2 tablespoons pine nuts or chopped walnuts, toasted

1 tablespoon minced fresh chives, parsley, or basil

kitchen improv

use what you've got Substitute green or kalamata olives for the capers for a similarly briny punch.

level up Add anchovy paste with the capers for an umami-packed flavor boost.

make it simple You can omit the capers, nuts, and/or herbs for an even simpler preparation.

1 Combine cauliflower, 1 tablespoon oil, salt, and pepper in 12-inch nonstick skillet. Cover and cook over medium-high heat until cauliflower starts to brown and edges just start to become translucent, about 5 minutes.

2 Uncover and continue to cook, stirring every 2 minutes, until florets turn golden brown in many spots, about 12 minutes. Push cauliflower to edges of skillet. Add remaining 1 tablespoon oil, capers, and lemon zest to center and cook, stirring with rubber spatula, until fragrant, about 30 seconds. Stir cauliflower into caper mixture and continue to cook, stirring occasionally, until cauliflower is tender but still firm, about 3 minutes.

3 Off heat, season with salt and pepper to taste and sprinkle with pine nuts and chives. Serve with lemon wedges. (Cauliflower can be refrigerated for up to 2 days.)

cauliflower rice

total time 30 minutes

makes leftovers

kitchen improv

make it a meal Wilt leafy greens in the rice and top with a fried egg (see page 139).

make it curried Add curry powder just before stirring in the cauliflower in step 2 and substitute cilantro for the parsley.

make it Thai-inspired Add Thai curry paste, substitute canned coconut milk for the broth, and substitute scallion for the parsley.

why this recipe works Rice is nice, but sometimes it's nicer still to make it with one of the most healthful vegetables you can find. We think that riced fresh cauliflower tastes far superior to the prepackaged stuff, and the best part is that it reheats well so it's worth the extra effort. The key is to not skimp on the salt, as it's necessary to draw out the moisture of the cauliflower, allowing it to break down and cook faster. Broth, opposed to water, brings its own flavor boosts, but think of cauliflower rice as a blank slate. Turn leftovers into "fried rice" by sautéing with extra veggies, scrambled egg, and soy sauce and topping with sriracha. In addition to a small saucepan, the recipe works with a 10-inch nonstick skillet. If using a skillet, cook the rice covered for 8 to 10 minutes and uncovered for 1 to 2 minutes. You can make Skillet-Roasted Cauliflower with Capers and Pine Nuts (page 94) with the other half of the cauliflower.

½ head cauliflower (1 pound), cored and cut into 1-inch florets

1 teaspoon oil

1 small shallot, minced

¼ cup chicken or vegetable broth

¼ teaspoon table salt

1 tablespoon minced fresh parsley, chives, or basil

1 Pulse cauliflower in food processor until finely ground into ¼- to ⅛-inch pieces, 6 to 8 pulses, scraping down sides of bowl as needed.

2 Heat oil in small saucepan over medium-low heat until shimmering. Add shallot and cook until softened, about 3 minutes. Stir in processed cauliflower, broth, and salt. Cover and cook, stirring occasionally, until cauliflower is tender, 10 to 13 minutes.

3 Uncover and continue to cook, stirring occasionally, until cauliflower rice is almost completely dry, about 3 minutes. Off heat, season with salt and pepper to taste and stir in parsley. Serve. (Cauliflower rice can be refrigerated for up to 2 days.)

why this recipe works There's more to sliced eggplant than eggplant Parm, and this quick, easy side is a more vibrant (but just as satisfying) application—and its meatiness makes eggplant more than just a side dish. Salting the eggplant draws out moisture and collapses some of the eggplant's cells so it isn't a sponge for oil; just a tablespoon brushed on the slices is enough to keep them from drying out in the oven. While eggplant peel is completely fine to eat, when broiled it becomes tough and stringy; because this cooking method is mostly hands-off, peeled eggplant holds together here. To dress up our side, we drizzled the creamy, lightly charred rounds with a bright and sweet vinaigrette of honey and lemon, then sprinkled them with refreshing mint and briny capers. The warm eggplant absorbed the vinaigrette, completely transforming the slices. Store the eggplant and vinaigrette separately. Slice up leftover rounds and add to a green or pasta salad, or layer with melted mozzarella cheese between crusty bread for a vegetarian sandwich. We prefer to use globe eggplant because it's easy to find, but using a whole Italian or Japanese eggplant would also work (and help you avoid extra raw eggplant). If you do have raw eggplant to spare, use it in Simple Ratatouille (page 116).

broiled eggplant

with honey-lemon vinaigrette

total time 35 minutes

makes leftovers

½ large eggplant (12 ounces), peeled and sliced into ¼-inch-thick rounds

¼ teaspoon plus ⅛ teaspoon table salt, divided

2 tablespoons oil, divided

2 teaspoons honey

2 teaspoons lemon juice

⅛ teaspoon pepper

1 tablespoon chopped fresh mint, basil, or parsley

2 teaspoons capers, rinsed and minced

1 Spread eggplant on paper towel–lined plate, sprinkle all over with ¼ teaspoon salt, and let sit for 15 minutes. Meanwhile, whisk 1 tablespoon oil, honey, lemon juice, pepper, and remaining ⅛ teaspoon salt together in bowl; set vinaigrette aside until ready to serve.

2 Adjust oven rack 4 inches from broiler element and heat broiler. Thoroughly pat eggplant dry with paper towels. Line rimmed baking sheet with aluminum foil and spray with vegetable oil spray. Arrange eggplant in single layer on prepared sheet, and brush with remaining 1 tablespoon oil. Broil eggplant until mahogany brown and lightly charred, 3 to 4 minutes per side. (Eggplant can be refrigerated for up to 2 days.)

3 Transfer eggplant to clean plate and season with salt and pepper to taste. Drizzle with vinaigrette and sprinkle with mint and capers. Serve.

kitchen improv

level up Add pantry-friendly vegetables (jarred roasted red pepper slices or halved artichoke hearts).

get saucy Substitute pomegranate molasses for the honey and lemon juice, or substitute Tahini Sauce (page 69) for the oil and honey.

make it a meal Serve over couscous, sprinkle with chopped toasted nuts, and dollop with yogurt.

SIDES TO MATCH OR EAT ON THEIR OWN

why this recipe works Green beans are perfect for the for-one cook—they're often sold by weight, so it's easy to buy the precise amount you need. Burning your beans is an unexpected yet utterly delicious way to cook them—they're blistered, with a soft chew and concentrated flavor. Many skillet-charred green bean recipes require precooking the green beans before charring them in the skillet. We found multiple steps unnecessary, and came up with a hybrid method (adding water and oil at the outset) that first steams then chars the beans. The water provided a steaming agent, which allowed the green beans to cook through, covered, until crisp tender. After uncovering, the oil charred the outside of the beans, giving them a deep, almost smoky flavor. Once the beans finished cooking, we tossed them in both lemon zest and juice for a bright hit of citrus. These beans would go great with our Glazed Meatloaf for One (page 48) or Crispy-Skinned Chicken (page 32), and are especially delicious cold in a salad the next day. You will need a 10-inch nonstick skillet with a tight-fitting lid for this recipe.

lemony skillet-charred green beans

total time 15 minutes

makes leftovers

8 ounces green beans, trimmed

2 tablespoons water

1 tablespoon oil

⅛ teaspoon table salt

⅛ teaspoon pepper

½ teaspoon grated lemon zest plus 1 teaspoon juice

Combine green beans, water, oil, salt, and pepper in 10-inch nonstick skillet. Cover and cook over medium-high heat, shaking pan occasionally, until water has evaporated, 6 to 8 minutes. Uncover and continue to cook until green beans are blistered and browned, about 2 minutes. Off heat, stir in lemon zest and juice and season with salt and pepper to taste. Serve. (Green beans can be refrigerated for up to 2 days.)

kitchen improv

level up Add toasted panko (see page 137) and/or toasted sesame seeds.

make it spicy Omit the lemon, add red pepper flakes when you take the cover off, and finish with chili-garlic sauce.

sautéed mushrooms

with shallots and thyme

total time 35 minutes

makes leftovers

why this recipe works Yes, Julia Child taught us that for optimum browning you should "never crowd your mushrooms." But we found a way to cram them all in the skillet and achieve both even cooking and gorgeous golden browning (sorry, Julia). By overloading the skillet and extending the cooking time past when the mushrooms released their liquid, they gave up just enough liquid to eventually fit in a single layer without shrinking to nothing. We then turned up the heat until the liquid was completely evaporated, ensuring even browning. A quick coating of butter at the end added luxurious depth. Finally, to balance the richness, just a splash of vinegar brought some well-balanced acidity to the mushrooms. Meaty and savory without the effort of cooking a steak, mushrooms are the perfect addition to round out a fast and satisfying meal. Leftovers reheat easily in the microwave and are delicious when tossed with pasta; they're even a great way to elevate your takeout pizza.

1 teaspoon oil

12 ounces white or cremini mushrooms, trimmed and halved if small or quartered if large

¼ teaspoon table salt

1 tablespoon unsalted butter

1 small shallot, minced

1 teaspoon minced fresh thyme, rosemary, tarragon, or oregano

2 teaspoons sherry or balsamic vinegar

kitchen improv

use what you've got You could use any variety of mushroom with this method.

make it a meal Serve on toast with a swipe of goat cheese, or spoon over polenta (see page 129) or our Creamy Orzo with Parmesan (page 127).

1 Heat oil in 10-inch skillet over medium-high heat until shimmering. Add mushrooms and salt and cook, stirring occasionally, until mushrooms release liquid, about 5 minutes. Increase heat to medium-high and cook, stirring occasionally, until liquid has completely evaporated, about 8 minutes longer. Add butter, reduce heat to medium, and continue to cook, stirring occasionally, until mushrooms are well browned, about 8 minutes longer.

2 Add shallot and thyme and cook until shallot is softened, about 3 minutes. Add vinegar and cook until liquid has evaporated, about 30 seconds. Season with salt and pepper to taste. Serve. (Mushrooms can be refrigerated for up to 2 days.)

why this recipe works A baked potato is the best way to conjure a dinner from a seemingly empty pantry. Of course you could serve it as a side dish, seasoned simply with butter and salt and pepper. But if you add enough toppings it becomes a meal that stands on its own—its simple flavor means it is ready to be topped with any combination of garnishes. We started by microwaving a russet potato—our choice for its high starch content (read: fluffiness)—to drastically cut down on cooking time. Finishing it in the oven for a mere 20 minutes was enough to yield a piping hot, tender interior that we topped with all the traditional fixings.

1 russet potato (8 ounces),
   unpeeled

Adjust oven rack to middle position and heat oven to 450 degrees. Meanwhile, poke potato several times with fork. Microwave potato, uncovered, until slightly soft to touch, 6 to 12 minutes, flipping over halfway through cooking. Place microwaved potato directly on oven rack and bake until skewer glides easily through flesh, about 20 minutes. Pierce center of potato with fork several times to create dotted X. Press in at ends of potato to push flesh up and out. Serve.

fastest-ever baked potato

total time 35 minutes

pantry recipe

kitchen improv

use what you've got Substitute sweet potato for russet: Place a piece of aluminum foil underneath the potato in the oven to catch any drips and start checking for doneness 5 minutes early.

make it traditional Top with sour cream, scallions or chives, and crumbled bacon.

make it cheesy Top with shredded cheddar, Gruyère, or fontina, or crumbled goat or feta cheese.

make it a meal Go for higher-protein toppings like chopped hard-cooked eggs, smoked fish, or chickpeas.

creamiest mashed potato for one

total time 25 minutes

pantry recipe

why this recipe works Often associated with Thanksgiving, mashed potatoes are a crowd favorite, but they feel like a hassle to make for just one person. (And who wants gloppy reheated mashed potatoes?) We wanted to eat mashed potatoes year-round (and not have to share), so we found a way to make the creamiest version of the stuff in less than 30 minutes. A Yukon Gold was our choice for its creamy butteriness, perfect for a no-fuss single serving of mashed potato. Butter for flavor and heavy cream for richness gave us a decadent result for one of those treat-yourself nights.

1 Yukon Gold potato (8 ounces), peeled, halved, and sliced ½ inch thick

2 teaspoons table salt

2 tablespoons heavy cream or half-and-half, room temperature

2 tablespoons unsalted butter, melted

kitchen improv

use what you've got Instead of heavy cream or half-and-half you could use any type of milk, yogurt, or sour cream (adjusting consistency with liquid as needed).

level up Stir in roasted garlic and grated Parmesan, fresh herbs, jarred horseradish, wasabi paste, scallions, and/or shredded cheddar cheese.

1 Place potato slices and salt in medium saucepan and add cold water to cover by 1 inch. Bring to boil over medium-high heat, then reduce heat to medium-low and simmer, stirring once or twice, until potatoes are tender, 8 to 11 minutes.

2 Drain and return potatoes to saucepan. Using potato masher, mash potatoes until mostly smooth, then stir in cream and butter. Season with salt and pepper to taste and serve immediately.

roasted feta potatoes

total time 40 minutes

makes leftovers

kitchen improv

use what you've got Use sweet potato or peeled celery root in place of the Yukon Golds.

make it a meal Load it up with shredded chicken or pork for a poutine-like indulgence (minus the gravy).

why this recipe works While the crisp exteriors and creamy interiors of go-to roasted potatoes are too delicious to be boring, sometimes you might want to shake up your spud routine. Here, briny feta brightens up creamy Yukon Gold potatoes for a side dish that is just as elegant as it is simple. After roasting the potatoes on their own until spotty brown, we sprinkled them with crumbled feta and sliced scallions and popped them back in the oven until the scallions softened and the feta melted into creamy pockets of salty richness. They're delightful alongside Sirloin Steak Tips (page 47) for a solo date night, or eaten directly from the baking sheet while standing over your counter. (They're that good.) Leftovers make a fabulous hash—top with a runny fried egg to take it to the next level.

2 small Yukon Gold potatoes (12 ounces), unpeeled, sliced into ¼-inch-thick rounds

1 tablespoon oil

¼ teaspoon table salt

⅛ teaspoon pepper

1 ounce feta or goat cheese, crumbled (¼ cup)

2 scallions or chives, sliced thin

Adjust oven rack to middle position and heat oven to 475 degrees. Toss potatoes with oil, salt, and pepper and arrange in single layer on aluminum foil–lined rimmed baking sheet. Roast potatoes until spotty brown and tender, 15 to 20 minutes. Sprinkle potatoes with crumbled feta and scallions and continue to roast until cheese is just softened, about 5 minutes. Season with salt and pepper to taste. Serve. (Potatoes can be refrigerated for up to 2 days.)

sugar snap peas

with pine nuts and tarragon

total time 15 minutes

why this recipe works We all know you can steam, stir-fry, or slice raw snap peas and throw them into a salad, but you rarely see them as the star of your dish. This recipe takes bright snap peas out of the supporting role and into the spotlight. Sautéing them with garlic and red pepper flakes contributes an assertiveness to the delicate flavors. Rich, buttery toasted pine nuts contrast the fresh snap peas, and the subtle licorice flavor of the tarragon is an unexpected (yet still classic) addition that ties the whole dish together and infuses a bit of style without added work. Once you pair this simple side dish with Golden Tilapia (page 58) or feature it as a fresh component in a grain bowl, you'll never think of snap peas as a mere garnish again. You will need an 8- or 10-inch skillet with a tight-fitting lid for this recipe.

1 teaspoon oil	Pinch red pepper flakes
4 ounces sugar snap peas, strings removed and halved crosswise	1 tablespoon chopped fresh tarragon, mint, or basil
1½ teaspoons water	1 tablespoon pine nuts, or chopped almonds or walnuts, toasted
1 small garlic clove, minced	
¼ teaspoon table salt	

kitchen improv

use what you've got Minced shallot can be used in place of the garlic.

make it a meal Serve on top of any cooked grain (see pages 124–125) and sprinkle with crumbled cheese, or serve over toast spread with ricotta.

Heat oil in 8- or 10-inch skillet over medium heat until shimmering. Add snap peas and water, immediately cover, and cook for 2 minutes. Uncover, add garlic, salt, and pepper flakes, and continue to cook, stirring frequently, until moisture has evaporated and snap peas are crisp-tender, 1 to 2 minutes. Off heat, stir in tarragon and season with salt and pepper to taste. Sprinkle with pine nuts and serve.

why this recipe works We love roasting wedges: They require minimal prep (no peeling, no fussing over cutting even cubes), and their generous size gives them eat-with-your-hands appeal. But while potato wedges feel like a steakhouse side, roasted sweet potato wedges have a more distinctive—yet still complementary—flavor that also makes them an unexpected match for a wide variety of dishes, or as a savory snack dipped in an herby ranch dressing. And they're oh-so-simple to prepare. With nothing more than olive oil, salt, and pepper and a quick visit to a hot 450-degree oven (you don't even need to flip them!), the wedges become caramelized and sweet on the outside and soft and creamy on the inside. Be sure to scrub and dry the whole potato thoroughly before cutting it into wedges.

roasted sweet potato wedges

total time 35 minutes

1 sweet potato (12 ounces), unpeeled, cut lengthwise into 1½-inch-wide wedges

1 tablespoon oil

¼ teaspoon table salt

⅛ teaspoon pepper

1   Adjust oven rack to middle position and heat oven to 450 degrees. Line rimmed baking sheet with aluminum foil and spray with vegetable oil spray. Toss all ingredients together in bowl.

2   Arrange potato wedges, cut sides down, in single layer on prepared sheet. Roast until sides in contact with sheet are dark golden brown and wedges are tender, 20 to 25 minutes. Season with salt and pepper to taste. Serve.

kitchen improv

level up Sprinkle with minced fresh cilantro, parsley, or chives or try any of the sauces, butters, rubs, or salts from pages 68–73.

spice it up Before roasting, toss wedges with your favorite spice blend (barbecue, Latin, curry powder, Cajun, or Old Bay), or give them smoky heat (try smoked paprika or chipotle chile powder), or a warming spice (cinnamon, cumin, or cardamom).

SIDES TO MATCH OR EAT ON THEIR OWN

sautéed radishes

with crispy bacon

total time 30 minutes

makes leftovers

why this recipe works Radishes generally serve one of two purposes: tossed raw on top of a salad for crunch, or pickled and added to a taco for piquant bite. This sells this vegetable short, however; the real magic happens when you cook and caramelize radishes. To give cooked radishes another flavor element beyond sweet-spicy, we started with one of our favorite foods, bacon. This provided our crispy garnish, and the rendered fat gave us a smoky base for cooking. A finishing touch of red wine vinegar woke everything up, and with a little fresh herbs we were satisfied with our not-so-ordinary take on the peppery radish. Oh, and try not to snack on the crispy bacon before you're ready to serve. Maybe cook two pieces just in case. Enjoy leftovers the next morning with your eggs (after all, there is bacon), or later in the day on a salad.

1 slice bacon, chopped fine

8 ounces radishes, trimmed and halved if small or quartered if large

¼ teaspoon table salt

Pinch pepper

1 garlic clove, minced

1 teaspoon red wine vinegar

1 teaspoon minced fresh chives, parsley, or scallions

kitchen improv

level up A sprinkle of Fresh Herb Salt (page 73) would make a nice finish to this dish.

make it a meal If your radishes come with greens, wash them and cook them in the skillet with the radishes briefly before serving. Serve with a smear of hummus and pita for a casual dinner.

make it vegetarian Omit the bacon and add oil to the skillet in place of the bacon fat.

Cook bacon in 8- or 10-inch nonstick skillet over medium heat until crispy, 5 to 7 minutes. Using slotted spoon, transfer bacon to paper towel–lined plate. Pour off all but 1 teaspoon fat from skillet. (If necessary, add oil to equal 1 teaspoon.) Add radishes, salt, and pepper, reduce heat to medium-low, and cook, stirring occasionally, until radishes are lightly browned and crisp-tender, 12 to 16 minutes. Stir in garlic and vinegar and cook until fragrant, about 30 seconds. Off heat, stir in chives, season with salt and pepper to taste, and sprinkle with bacon. Serve. (Radishes can be refrigerated for up to 2 days.)

simple ratatouille

total time 25 minutes

makes leftovers

why this recipe works This classic Provençal meal celebrating late summer's bounty of vegetables is usually a time-consuming dish that feeds a crowd, but we streamlined it by omitting some of the traditional watery vegetables (bell peppers and zucchini) that required time to eradicate their excess moisture. Instead, we focused on three essential components: eggplant, garlic, and tomatoes. Browning cubes of eggplant and then adding halved cherry or grape tomatoes gave us flavorful caramelization and softened the vegetables without making them mushy. Adding a touch of anchovy paste with the garlic and a few spoonfuls of briny capers at the end added the complexity and depth of flavor we wanted in our quick-cooking dish. Even eggplant haters were asking for seconds. We like the look and texture (and minimal prep!) of this dish with unpeeled eggplant, but if you prefer you can peel the eggplant. Extra-virgin olive oil is a perfect match for the Provençal flavors here; we recommend a drizzle of good quality oil as a finishing touch. If you have raw eggplant to spare, use it in Broiled Eggplant with Honey-Lemon Vinaigrette (page 99). We prefer to use globe eggplant because it is easy to find, but using a whole Italian or Japanese eggplant would also work (and help you avoid extra raw eggplant).

2 tablespoons plus 2 teaspoons oil, divided	6 ounces cherry or grape tomatoes, halved (1 cup)
½ eggplant (8 ounces), cut into ¾-inch pieces	½ cup chicken or vegetable broth
⅛ teaspoon table salt	2 teaspoons capers, rinsed and minced
Pinch pepper	1 tablespoon chopped fresh basil, mint, or parsley
2 garlic cloves, minced	
⅛ teaspoon anchovy paste	

kitchen improv

level up Top ratatouille with cheese (Parmesan, fresh mozzarella, feta, or goat), chopped toasted nuts (see page 15), chopped olives, or chopped sun-dried tomatoes.

make it a meal Add jarred roasted red peppers or artichoke hearts, cannellini beans, or an egg (see page 139). Serve over toast, pasta, or grains (see pages 124–125).

1 Heat 2 tablespoons oil in 12-inch nonstick skillet over medium-high heat until shimmering. Add eggplant, salt, and pepper and cook until eggplant is browned and tender, 6 to 8 minutes.

2 Reduce heat to medium-low then stir in remaining 2 teaspoons oil, garlic, and anchovy paste and cook until fragrant, about 30 seconds. Stir in tomatoes and broth and simmer until liquid has evaporated and tomatoes have broken down slightly, 5 to 7 minutes. Stir in capers, season with salt and pepper to taste, and sprinkle with basil. Serve. (Ratatouille can be refrigerated for up to 2 days.)

why this recipe works While we love meal planning (see pages 24–25), there's something nice about a perfectly portioned serving of rice—fluffy rice is best when it's freshly made. When we jumped into this idea, we thought we had this recipe in the bag. After all, rice seems like an easy enough dish to make, but scaling it for one turned out to be challenging. The ratio of liquid to rice had to be just right, and maintaining that ratio was key—bringing the broth to a simmer with the lid on helped limit evaporation and avoid crunchy, uneven rice. For really great long-grain white rice with distinct, separate grains that didn't clump together, we rinsed the grains first to get rid of any excess starch. To avoid the pitfall of often "sogged out" rice, we placed a dish towel between the lid and pot after cooking to absorb excess moisture and ensure dry, fluffy grains. You can use water in place of the broth in this recipe, though the flavor of the rice will be much simpler.

⅔ cup chicken or vegetable broth

⅓ cup long-grain white rice, rinsed

Pinch table salt

Pinch pepper

1   Bring broth to simmer in covered small saucepan over medium heat. Stir in rice, salt, and pepper and return to simmer. Cover, reduce heat to low, and simmer gently until rice is tender and all liquid is absorbed, 12 to 15 minutes. (If rice is tender but liquid remains in saucepan, continue to cook over low heat, uncovered, until remaining liquid has evaporated, 1 to 2 minutes.)

2   Off heat, lay clean dish towel underneath lid and let sit, covered, for 5 minutes. Gently fluff rice with fork and season with salt and pepper to taste. Serve.

easiest-ever white rice

total time 30 minutes

pantry recipe

kitchen improv

use what you've got You can use just about any type of long-grain white rice in this recipe (basmati, jasmine, Texmati, or others).

level up Stir in dried apricots and cardamom, and serve with a dollop of yogurt and a drizzle of oil.

make it a meal Serve with stir-fried veggies, or add canned beans, sliced andouille sausage, and a fried egg (page 139), then top it off with hot sauce.

easiest-ever quinoa

total time 30 minutes

why this recipe works All you need are a few tablespoons—yes, you read that correctly—of protein-packed quinoa to bulk up a vegetarian meal, or serve as a stick-to-your-ribs side. For the most flavorful quinoa with a perfect tender-crunchy texture, we had to get incredibly precise with our measurements of both the quinoa and broth in order to concentrate flavor in every last bite. We used the same foolproof method as our single-serving rice (see page 119)—starting the grain in already-simmering broth, then cooking covered over low heat before removing the lid for the last few minutes of cooking to allow for any additional liquid to evaporate. We like the convenience of prewashed quinoa; rinsing removes quinoa's bitter protective coating (called saponin). If you buy unwashed quinoa, rinse it and pat it dry. You can use water in place of the broth in this recipe, though the flavor of the quinoa will be much simpler.

½ cup chicken or vegetable broth

3 tablespoons prewashed white quinoa

Pinch table salt

Pinch pepper

kitchen improv

make it a meal Add baby spinach or arugula, sprinkle with chopped nuts, and drizzle with plain yogurt.

1   Bring broth to simmer in covered small saucepan over medium heat. Stir in quinoa, salt, and pepper and return to simmer. Cover, reduce heat to low, and simmer gently until quinoa is tender and all liquid is absorbed, about 15 minutes. (If quinoa is tender but liquid remains in saucepan, continue to cook over low heat, uncovered, until remaining liquid has evaporated, 1 to 2 minutes.)

2   Off heat, lay clean dish towel underneath lid and let sit, covered, for 5 minutes. Gently fluff quinoa with fork and season with salt and pepper to taste. Serve.

why this recipe works Couscous comes together in record time when you want a meal at the ready without dirtying a lot of dishes or using a whole lot of brain power. Bonus: Its neutral flavor profile makes it perfect for endless adaptations. We wanted to really pack this pasta with punch by layering the recipe with complex flavors that included an endless list of variations. Spice came first. We opted for warm cumin, and by cooking it in oil we bloomed it to awaken its flavor. We then quickly toasted the couscous, which highlighted its nuttiness, before adding our flavorful broth to hydrate the grain. Within 5 minutes the magic happened, and we were rewarded with this incredibly easy and flavorful side dish that we enlivened with pine nuts and fresh herbs. We love this couscous paired with Weeknight Lamb Chops (page 51) for an easy yet elegant dinner.

couscous
with cumin and pine nuts

total time 20 minutes

1 teaspoon oil	Pinch pepper
⅛ teaspoon ground cumin	1 tablespoon pine nuts, or chopped walnuts or pecans, toasted
⅓ cup couscous	
½ cup chicken or vegetable broth	1 tablespoon minced fresh cilantro, parsley, or chives
Pinch table salt	

Heat oil in small saucepan over medium heat until shimmering. Add cumin and cook until fragrant, about 30 seconds. Stir in couscous and cook until grains are just beginning to brown, about 3 minutes. Stir in broth, salt, and pepper, cover, and remove pan from heat. Let sit until couscous is tender, about 5 minutes. Fluff grains with fork, stir in pine nuts and cilantro, and season with salt and pepper to taste. Serve.

kitchen improv

level up Stir in chopped dried fruit like apricots, figs, or golden raisins before serving.

get saucy Any of the sauces on pages 68–69 would be a nice finishing touch for the couscous.

make it a meal Stir in shredded chicken and top with crumbled feta or goat cheese.

make-ahead grains

We love making more than one serving of grains for the week and storing them in the fridge to bulk up a salad, use as the base of a vegetarian bowl, or whip up a quick stir-fry on the fly.

master recipe for grains

To cook the grains (opposite), bring water to boil in large pot. Stir in grain and table salt and cook until tender, following timing indicated. Drain well. All of these grains can be cooked, cooled, and then refrigerated in an airtight container for up to 3 days. Season with salt and pepper to taste before serving.

reheating grains

To reheat grains, microwave in covered bowl until hot throughout, fluffing with fork halfway through (timing will vary depending on the quantity and type of grains used).

buckwheat

dry amount ¾ cup
water 2 quarts
salt ½ teaspoon
cooking time 10 to 12 minutes
cooked yield 2 cups

bulgur

dry amount ¾ cup
water 2 quarts
salt ½ teaspoon
cooking time 5 minutes
cooked yield 2 cups
note You can use medium-
or coarse-grind bulgur.

pearl barley

dry amount ¾ cup
water 2 quarts
salt ½ teaspoon
cooking time 20 to 40 minutes
cooked yield 2 cups

farro

dry amount ¾ cup
water 2 quarts
salt ½ teaspoon
cooking time 15 to 30 minutes
cooked yield 2 cups

freekeh

dry amount ¾ cup
water 2 quarts
salt ½ teaspoon
cooking time 30 to 45 minutes
cooked yield 2 cups

black rice

dry amount ¾ cup
water 2 quarts
salt ½ teaspoon
cooking time 20 to 25 minutes
cooked yield 2 cups

brown rice

dry amount ¾ cup
water 2 quarts
salt ½ teaspoon
cooking time 25 to 30 minutes
cooked yield 2 cups
note Use long-grain rice.

white rice

dry amount ¾ cup
water 2 quarts
salt ½ teaspoon
cooking time 10 to 15 minutes
cooked yield 2 cups
note Use long-grain rice.

wild rice

dry amount ¾ cup
water 2 quarts
salt ½ teaspoon
cooking time 35 to 40 minutes
cooked yield 2 cups

oat berries

dry amount ¾ cup
water 2 quarts
salt ½ teaspoon
cooking time 30 to 40 minutes
cooked yield 1½ cups

wheat berries

dry amount ¾ cup
water 4 quarts
salt ½ teaspoon
cooking time 60 to 70 minutes
cooked yield 1½ cups

why this recipe works After a long day, when you're looking for comfort in a bowl, cozy up to this creamy, cheesy pasta. While we love traditional risotto (see page 258), we wanted an easy alternative that would be ready in a fraction of the time. Orzo pasta was the answer: It helped us create a quick and satisfying dish with the same rich body of risotto, but without the need to add measured amounts of liquid in stages. We cooked the orzo in a small amount of broth to create tender, flavorful grains; stirring the pasta frequently released its starches, creating a creamy, risotto-like texture. Finishing it with a generous handful of Parmesan cheese intensified its richness and flavor. While we'd happily eat this all on its own, it pairs perfectly with any number of proteins, or with hearty roasted vegetables. If the finished orzo is too thick, stir in hot water, a few tablespoons at a time, to adjust the consistency.

creamy orzo
with parmesan

total time 30 minutes

pantry recipe

1 tablespoon unsalted butter

1 small garlic clove, minced

¼ cup orzo

1 cup chicken or vegetable broth

Pinch table salt

¼ cup grated Parmesan cheese

Melt butter in small saucepan over medium heat. Add garlic and cook until fragrant, about 30 seconds. Stir in orzo and cook for 1 minute. Stir in broth and salt, bring to simmer, then reduce heat to medium-low. Simmer gently, stirring often, until orzo is tender and creamy, 13 to 15 minutes. Off heat, vigorously stir in Parmesan until creamy and season with salt and pepper to taste. Serve.

kitchen improv

level up Sprinkle with fresh chopped herbs or add some crunch with crisped bacon, pancetta, or prosciutto.

get saucy Dollop with pesto or drizzle with chili oil.

make it a meal Add quick-cooking or no-cook vegetables (thawed frozen peas, blanched asparagus or green beans, chopped sun-dried tomatoes, halved cherry or grape tomatoes, or halved baby artichoke hearts); top with chicken, shrimp, steak, or roasted vegetables.

SIDES TO MATCH OR EAT ON THEIR OWN

why this recipe works Polenta is a make-it-a-meal mainstay—it's a hearty, creamy base that pairs nicely with just about any topping. But when you're looking for little more than a resting place for other elements of your meal, the last thing you want is to be tied to the stove. Our trick? Adding a pinch of baking soda—it cut cooking time in half and eliminated the need for stirring, giving us the best quick polenta recipe. While you might not expect it, polenta reheats well—cover and warm in the microwave, adjusting consistency with hot water as needed.

2½ cups water

¼ teaspoon table salt

Pinch baking soda

½ cup coarse-ground cornmeal

1 ounce Parmesan cheese, grated (½ cup)

1 tablespoon unsalted butter

1 Bring water to boil in small saucepan over medium-high heat. Stir in salt and baking soda. Slowly add cornmeal in steady stream, stirring constantly. Bring mixture to boil, stirring constantly, about 30 seconds. Reduce heat to lowest possible setting and cover.

2 After 5 minutes, whisk cornmeal to smooth out any lumps, making sure to scrape down sides and bottom of saucepan. Cover and continue to cook, without stirring, until cornmeal is tender but slightly al dente, 8 to 10 minutes longer. (Polenta should be loose and barely hold its shape; it will continue to thicken as it cools.)

3 Off heat, stir in Parmesan and butter and season with salt and pepper to taste. Cover and let sit for 5 minutes. (Polenta can be refrigerated for up to 2 days.)

no-fuss parmesan polenta

total time 30 minutes

makes leftovers

pantry recipe

kitchen improv

use what you've got You can use just about any hard cheese in place of the Parmesan, like Pecorino Romano, aged Manchego, or aged gouda.

level up Drizzle with extra-virgin olive oil and sprinkle with chopped fresh herbs.

make it a meal Top polenta with Sautéed Mushrooms with Shallots and Thyme (page 102), Roasted Carrots (page 93), Broiled Broccoli Rabe (page 85), or any of the eggs on page 139.

SIDES TO MATCH OR EAT ON THEIR OWN

easy cuban black beans

total time 20 minutes

makes leftovers

kitchen improv

use what you've got Although green bell pepper is traditional, any type of bell pepper could work.

level up Sprinkle with chopped cilantro, thinly sliced scallions, shredded cheese, chopped tomatoes, and/or pickled jalapeños.

make it a meal Serve with rice, quinoa, or other grains, or with plantain chips, sliced avocado, a dollop of sour cream, and hot sauce.

why this recipe works We love shortcuts in the kitchen, as long as they don't sacrifice quality, and when it comes to beans, the canned variety is frequently the best way to go: They are quick and easy, but also give us the added bonus of using their body-building bean liquid, also known in plant-based circles as aquafaba. But we wanted to do a little more than simply open a can, so we drew inspiration from Cuba, where spiced black beans are a staple of the cuisine. We found that a quick sofrito of shallots, garlic, and bell pepper combined with cumin and oregano added plenty of earthy, fragrant flavor to our simple canned black beans. Mashing part of the beans gave them a creamy texture, but leaving a portion whole kept the dish from becoming soup. These beans are even better the next day—leftovers make an excellent breakfast when tucked into a soft taco with a fried egg and salsa. Serve with lime wedges, if desired. See Quinoa Salad with Red Bell Pepper and Cilantro on page 231 for an idea for using up any extra bell pepper.

1 tablespoon oil

1 large shallot, minced

½ green bell pepper, chopped fine

2 garlic cloves, minced

¼ teaspoon dried oregano

¼ teaspoon ground cumin

⅛ teaspoon pepper

1 (15-ounce) can black beans, drained with liquid reserved

1 Heat oil in medium saucepan over medium heat until shimmering. Add shallot and bell pepper and cook until softened and beginning to brown, 4 to 6 minutes. Stir in garlic, oregano, cumin, and pepper and cook until fragrant, about 30 seconds.

2 Off heat, add ½ cup beans and all reserved bean liquid and mash with potato masher until mostly smooth. Stir in remaining beans. Cook over medium heat until warmed through, 2 to 3 minutes. Season with salt and pepper to taste. Serve. (Black beans can be refrigerated for up to 2 days.)

why this recipe works Chickpeas are a pantry staple—they're perfect for adding some oomph (and heft!) to grain bowls, salads, and vegetarian side dishes. But here, we let them shine: The dish is little more than chickpeas and sticky-sweet toasted garlic; it has the flavor of hummus with the hearty savor of whole beans. As in our Easy Cuban Black Beans (page 130), we relied on the bean liquid for a ton of pantry-friendly flavor, as well as its role as a thickener for a rich sauce that practically glazed the chickpeas. This dish tastes like it took hours, when it can actually be on your table in less than 20 minutes. Leftovers are delicious cold over a salad the next day, or reheated and eaten with a piece of toasted bread. You will need an 8- or 10-inch skillet with a tight-fitting lid for this recipe.

garlicky braised chickpeas

total time 15 minutes

makes leftovers

2 tablespoons oil

2 garlic cloves, sliced thin

1 large shallot, minced

1 (15-ounce) can chickpeas

1 tablespoon minced fresh parsley, cilantro, or chives

1 teaspoon lemon juice, plus lemon wedges for serving

1 Cook oil and garlic in 8 or 10-inch skillet over medium-low heat, stirring occasionally, until garlic turns pale gold, about 2 minutes. Stir in shallot and cook until softened and lightly browned, about 2 minutes. Stir in chickpeas and their liquid, cover, and cook until chickpeas have warmed through, about 2 minutes.

2 Uncover, increase heat to medium, and simmer until liquid has reduced slightly, about 3 minutes. Off heat, stir in parsley and lemon juice and season with salt and pepper to taste. Serve with lemon wedges. (Chickpeas can be refrigerated for up to 2 days.)

kitchen improv

spice it up Sauté a dried spice (like cumin, curry powder, or coriander) with the shallot in step 1.

make it a meal Add cooked pasta and/or wilted greens, or serve over a swoosh of lemony yogurt with a side of pita.

SIDES TO MATCH OR EAT ON THEIR OWN

133

curried
lentils

total time 55 minutes

makes leftovers

pantry recipe

why this recipe works Creamy and tender, aromatic and nurturing—this curried lentil side is easy to pull together on a weeknight; makes a meal with a simple side of rice, quinoa, or roasted vegetables (like squash or sweet potatoes); and reheats beautifully for lunch the next day. Unlike other legumes, hearty, earthy lentils don't take hours to cook, so they're great to keep in your pantry. We paired them with low-prep staples you'll likely already have—curry powder, garlic, and shallot—and cooked them in just enough savory broth so that we didn't need to drain them, concentrating all the flavors into every last bite.

1 tablespoon oil

1 shallot, minced

2 garlic cloves, minced

2 teaspoons curry powder

2 cups chicken or vegetable broth

½ cup dried brown or green lentils, picked over and rinsed

kitchen improv

level up Sprinkle with cilantro, parsley, chives, thinly sliced scallions, chopped tomatoes, crumbled goat or feta cheese, and/or drizzle with yogurt.

make it a meal Stir in cubed tofu and serve with rice or naan.

1 Heat oil in small saucepan over medium-low heat until shimmering. Add shallot and cook until softened and lightly browned, 3 to 5 minutes. Stir in garlic and curry powder and cook until fragrant, about 30 seconds. Stir in broth and lentils and bring to simmer. Reduce heat to low, cover, and cook until lentils are tender, 30 to 35 minutes.

2 Uncover, increase heat to medium, and simmer, stirring often, until liquid has reduced slightly, 3 to 5 minutes. Season with salt and pepper to taste. Serve. (Lentils can be refrigerated for up to 2 days.)

making a side the main event

Whether you're looking for inspiration for transforming your leftovers or want to bulk up your side dish to make it a meal, we've got you covered. These strategies are useful beyond this book to help you create quick, filling, and easy meals using what you have on hand. Mix and match ideas from each category, double (or triple!) up on toppings, pair multiple side dishes together to compose an entrée, or all of the above. Customize your meal to be just the way you like it.

start with a base
Give your vegetable side dish some support by serving it over:

- Rice or grains (see pages 124–125)
- Cauliflower Rice (page 96)
- Polenta (see page 129)
- Pasta
- Vegetable noodles
- Toast

add a protein
Make it hearty by adding:

- Thawed frozen edamame
- An egg cooked your way (page 139)
- Chopped tofu
- Canned tuna
- Smoked salmon
- Burrata
- Canned beans
- Shredded rotisserie chicken

add a topper
Level up with these savory toppings:

- A drizzle of a store-bought gochujang, or any of our sauces on pages 68–69
- Cheesy Toasted Panko
- Savory Seed Brittle
- Store-bought crispy chickpeas
- Chopped toasted nuts
- Croutons
- Crumbled cheese
- A dollop of hummus or yogurt

savory seed brittle

makes 2 cups

Think of this crunchy, irresistible, slightly sweet showstopper as a savory granola. It adds oomph to sides like Roasted Butternut Squash (page 88) and Roasted Broccoli with Garlic (page 83). Best of all, the brittle can last for up to 1 month, making it perfect to keep on hand as an easy upgrade for bowls or salads, or eaten right out of the container as a snack.

- 2 tablespoons maple syrup
- 1 large egg white
- 1 tablespoon oil
- 1 tablespoon soy sauce
- 1 tablespoon caraway seeds, crushed
- ½ teaspoon table salt
- ¼ teaspoon pepper
- ½ cup old-fashioned rolled oats
- ⅓ cup sunflower seeds
- ⅓ cup pepitas
- 2 tablespoons sesame seeds
- 2 tablespoons nigella seeds

1 Adjust oven rack to upper-middle position and heat oven to 300 degrees. Line 8-inch square baking pan with parchment paper and spray parchment with vegetable oil spray. Whisk maple syrup, egg white, oil, soy sauce, caraway seeds, salt, and pepper together in large bowl. Stir in oats, sunflower seeds, pepitas, sesame seeds, and nigella seeds until well combined.

2 Transfer oat mixture to prepared pan and spread into even layer. Using stiff metal spatula, press oat mixture until very compact. Bake until golden brown and fragrant, 45 to 55 minutes, rotating pan halfway through baking.

3 Transfer pan to wire rack and let brittle cool completely, about 1 hour. Break cooled brittle into pieces of desired size, discarding parchment. (Brittle can be stored in airtight container at room temperature for up to 1 month.)

cheesy toasted panko

makes about 1 cup

Adding crunch is a satisfying way to bring some excitement to your side dish. We like sprinkling this on Lemony Skillet-Charred Green Beans (page 101) and Pan-Roasted Asparagus (page 77).

- 1 cup panko bread crumbs
- 2 tablespoons oil
- 1 ounce Parmesan cheese, grated (½ cup)
- 2 tablespoons minced fresh chives

Toss panko with oil in bowl and season with salt and pepper. Microwave panko, stirring occasionally, until deep golden brown, 2 to 4 minutes; let cool completely. Stir in Parmesan and chives. (Topping can be refrigerated for up to 2 days; bring to room temperature before using.)

take a crack at it

Eggs are delicious any time of the day. Adding an egg is one of the easiest ways to make a side dish seem more meal-worthy, as well as offer appealing richness to a bright dish. Bring brunch vibes to a simple salad or wilted garlicky greens, elevate your stir-fries with an oozy yolk, or chop up or thinly slice hard-cooked eggs and add to sandwiches. And where would ramen be without a soft-cooked egg? Here are the best ways to cook them.

poached egg

1 large egg

1 teaspoon distilled white vinegar

Table salt for cooking egg

1 Bring 2 cups water to boil in small saucepan over high heat. Meanwhile, crack egg into colander. Let sit until loose, watery white drains away from egg, 20 to 30 seconds. Gently transfer egg to 1-cup liquid measuring cup.

2 Add vinegar and ¼ teaspoon salt to boiling water. With lip of measuring cup just above surface of water, gently tip egg into water. Cover saucepan, remove from heat, and let sit until white closest to yolk is just set and opaque, about 3 minutes. If after 3 minutes the white is not set, let sit in water, checking every 30 seconds, until egg reaches desired doneness. (For medium-cooked yolk, let egg sit in pot, covered, for 4 minutes, then begin checking for doneness.)

3 Using slotted spoon, carefully lift and drain egg over saucepan. Season with salt and pepper to taste, and serve.

fried egg

You will need an 8- or 10-inch nonstick skillet with a tight-fitting lid for this recipe.

1 teaspoon oil

1 large egg

Pinch table salt

Pinch pepper

Heat oil in 8- or 10-inch nonstick skillet over medium heat until shimmering. Crack egg into small bowl and sprinkle with salt and pepper. Working quickly, pour egg into pan. Cover and cook for 1 minute. Remove skillet from heat and let sit, covered, for 15 to 45 seconds for runny yolk (white around edge of yolk will be barely opaque), 45 to 60 seconds for soft but set yolk, or about 2 minutes for medium-set yolk. Serve immediately.

hard-cooked eggs

1–6 large eggs

1 Bring 1 inch water to rolling boil in medium or large saucepan over high heat. Place eggs in steamer basket and transfer basket to saucepan. Cover, reduce heat to medium-low, and cook eggs for 13 minutes.

2 When eggs are almost finished cooking, combine 2 cups ice cubes and 2 cups cold water in bowl. Using tongs or slotted spoon, transfer eggs to ice bath and let sit for 15 minutes. Peel before using. (Hard-cooked eggs can be refrigerated, peeled or unpeeled, for up to 3 days.)

soft-cooked eggs

1–6 large eggs

1 Bring 1 inch water to rolling boil in medium or large saucepan over high heat. Place eggs in steamer basket and transfer basket to saucepan. Cover, reduce heat to medium-high, and cook eggs for 6½ minutes.

2 When eggs are almost finished cooking, combine 2 cups ice cubes and 2 cups cold water in bowl. Using tongs or slotted spoon, transfer eggs to ice bath and let sit until just cool enough to handle, about 30 seconds. Peel before using. (Unpeeled soft-cooked eggs can be refrigerated for up to 3 days.)

simple soups
and stews

Soups and stews may conjure images of Dutch ovens or oversize stockpots simmering away for hours on the stove—the quintessential for-a-crowd meal. But scaling down and simplifying these recipes means you don't have to endure excessive leftovers (bonus: there's no giant pot to wash). Soup up your mealtime with easy recipes that don't require a lot of ingredients—a single can of beans gets you most of the way there in our 5-ingredient soups, and calling for just one potato or a couple of carrots means your grocery bags will be light. Even better, use our clean-out-your-fridge guidelines to help you save yourself a trip to the supermarket altogether. And because soups and stews only get better with time, almost all make two servings (but never more)—perfect for lunch the next day.

why this recipe works Sometimes the simpler the recipe, the easier it is to overcomplicate it. Case in point: carrot-ginger soup, whose flavors often get elbowed out with the addition of other vegetables, fruits, or excessive dairy. But this simple, creamy, pared-down version is velvety-smooth with clean carrot flavor and subtle ginger background notes. Carrots are a long-lasting pantry staple, and all it takes are three of them to form the base of this soup. We used ginger as the key aromatic, which eliminated the need to add even onion or shallot, cutting down our ingredient list drastically. A small amount of milk adds subtle richness without dulling the flavors. With the flavors in check, we made a meal out of this warm bowl of comfort by adding some hearty toppings. If you don't have a blender, an immersion blender or a food processor would also work.

gingery carrot soup

total time 40 minutes

makes leftovers

1 tablespoon oil	¼ teaspoon table salt
3 carrots (8 ounces), peeled and cut into 1-inch pieces	1⅓ cups chicken or vegetable broth, plus extra as needed
1 (1-inch) piece fresh ginger, peeled and chopped	⅓ cup milk

1 Heat oil in medium saucepan over medium heat until shimmering. Add carrots, ginger, and salt and cook, stirring occasionally, until lightly browned, about 5 minutes. Stir in broth, scraping up any browned bits. Bring to simmer and cook, covered, over medium-low heat until carrots are very soft, about 15 minutes.

2 Process soup and milk in blender until smooth, about 2 minutes. Return soup to now-empty saucepan and adjust consistency with extra hot broth as needed. Season with salt and pepper to taste. Serve. (Soup can be refrigerated for up to 3 days.)

kitchen improv

level up A handful of store-bought croutons or crispy chickpeas, a sprinkle of chopped cilantro, and/or some sour cream or Greek yogurt add an extra layer of flavor and texture.

creamy curried cauliflower soup

total time 40 minutes

makes leftovers

why this recipe works Fragrant curry powder and nutty cauliflower come together in this easy-to-make, creamy, and highly aromatic soup. After building a flavorful base with shallot, ginger, and curry powder, we added cauliflower and broth and briefly simmered it on the stovetop before blending it all together until smooth. Cauliflower blends beautifully—its low insoluble fiber content gives it a leg up to breaking down compared to other vegetables, contributing to the silky, not chunky, texture. A splash of cream added just the right amount of richness. After cooking, we stirred in cilantro for a fresh finish; a squeeze of lime juice provided a contrasting burst of brightness. You can use any remaining cauliflower to make Cauliflower Rice (page 96) or Skillet-Roasted Cauliflower with Capers and Pine Nuts (page 94). If you don't have a blender, an immersion blender or a food processor would also work.

1 tablespoon oil	2 cups chicken or vegetable broth, plus extra as needed
1 shallot, chopped	
1½ teaspoons curry powder	⅛ teaspoon table salt
1 teaspoon grated fresh ginger or ½ teaspoon ground ginger	¼ cup heavy cream or half-and-half
½ head cauliflower (1 pound), cored and cut into 1-inch florets	1 tablespoon minced fresh cilantro, parsley, or chives
	Lime wedges

kitchen improv

use what you've got You can substitute pre-cut cauliflower florets or uncooked (fresh or frozen) riced cauliflower for the ½ head of cauliflower.

make it vegan Substitute canned coconut milk or plant-based creamer for the cream and use vegetable broth.

make it heartier Add store-bought crispy chickpeas, shredded chicken, or frozen shrimp (be sure to heat until cooked through) along with the cream.

1 Heat oil in medium saucepan over medium-low heat until shimmering. Add shallot and cook until softened and lightly browned, 3 to 5 minutes. Stir in curry powder and ginger and cook until fragrant, about 30 seconds.

2 Stir in cauliflower, broth, and salt, scraping up any browned bits. Bring to simmer and cook until cauliflower is tender, about 15 minutes.

3 Process soup in blender until smooth, about 2 minutes. Return soup to now-empty saucepan, stir in cream, and adjust consistency with extra hot broth as needed. Off heat, stir in cilantro and season with salt and pepper to taste. Serve with lime wedges. (Soup can be refrigerated for up to 3 days.)

creamy butternut squash soup

total time 50 minutes

makes leftovers

why this recipe works If you went through the trouble of lugging a butternut squash home from the supermarket (or perhaps you have a leftover half to use up in your fridge), make it worth your while and turn the cumbersome-yet-delicious vegetable into a creamy, aromatic, and hearty soup. We started by browning squash pieces to caramelize their edges and deepen the flavor—because we only needed a relatively small amount, we found that we could do this on the stovetop (much faster than roasting in the oven). A single shallot proved important, emphasizing the sweet notes of the squash, and cream provided some richness. Sage, a classic pairing with squash, brought piney, herbal notes (using dried is a perfectly acceptable alternative). You could make Roasted Butternut Squash (page 88) with the other half of the squash. If you don't have a blender, an immersion blender or a food processor would also work.

- 1 tablespoon oil
- ½ large butternut squash (1¼ pounds), peeled, seeded, and cut into 1-inch pieces (3 cups)
- 1 shallot, chopped
- 1 garlic clove, minced
- ¼ teaspoon minced fresh sage or thyme or pinch dried

- 2 cups chicken or vegetable broth, plus extra as needed
- ⅛ teaspoon table salt
- 2 tablespoons heavy cream or half-and-half

kitchen improv

use what you've got Substitute store-bought precut butternut squash, just don't use frozen butternut squash as the flavor is often dull.

level up Top with crumbled goat or blue cheese, toasted pepitas, and/or fresh herbs.

make it vegan Substitute canned coconut milk or plant-based creamer for the cream and use vegetable broth.

make it buttery Melt some butter in a skillet, swirling occasionally, until butter is browned and releases a nutty aroma. Drizzle over finished soup.

1 Heat oil in medium saucepan over medium heat until shimmering. Add squash and shallot and cook until vegetables are softened and lightly browned, about 10 minutes. Stir in garlic and sage and cook until fragrant, about 30 seconds.

2 Stir in broth and salt, scraping up any browned bits. Bring to simmer and cook until squash is tender, about 15 minutes.

3 Process soup in blender until smooth, about 2 minutes. Return soup to now-empty saucepan, stir in cream, and adjust consistency with extra hot broth as needed. Off heat, season with salt and pepper to taste. Serve. (Soup can be refrigerated for up to 3 days.)

why this recipe works Miso soup is a nutritious, deeply flavored Japanese soup that is not only the perfect start to a meal, but also a great base for almost any veggies you may have in your crisper drawer. It's also a wonderful medium for poaching fish or shellfish. Miso soup is traditionally made by stirring tangy, nutty, fermented miso paste into dashi, the mother stock of Japanese cuisine, which is traditionally made by cooking katsuobushi (smoked, dried, fermented tuna flakes) and kombu (dried kelp) in water. For a shortcut to a weeknight miso soup, we replaced the dashi with pantry-friendly chicken or vegetable broth, which still allowed the miso to shine and got our soup on the table in just 15 minutes. To make it a meal, we bulked up our soup in the traditional manner, with cubes of tofu (we prefer silken, but soft or firm tofu will also work), and finished with aromatic sliced scallions and briny crumbled toasted nori. You could make our Sriracha-Lime Tofu Bowl (page 214) with the leftover tofu from this recipe. If you plan to store and reheat a portion of this soup, store the scallions and nori separately; sprinkle them over the soup after reheating.

weeknight miso soup
with tofu

total time 15 minutes

makes leftovers

- 2 cups chicken or vegetable broth
- 1 cup water
- 2 tablespoons white miso
- 7 ounces silken, soft, or firm tofu, cut into ½-inch pieces
- 2 scallions, green parts only, sliced thin
- 1 sheet toasted nori, crumbled

Bring broth and water to simmer in medium saucepan. Off heat, whisk in miso then stir in tofu. Sprinkle with scallions and nori and season with salt and pepper to taste. Serve. (Soup can be refrigerated for up to 3 days.)

kitchen improv

level up In place of (or in addition to) the tofu, gently simmer frozen shrimp (be sure to heat until cooked through), pieces of cod or haddock (cooked to 135 degrees), or halibut (cooked to 130 degrees) in the soup before adding the miso.

make it heartier Add sliced shiitake mushrooms, baby greens, shredded carrots or zucchini, and/or any other quick-cooking vegetable you may have on hand.

5-ingredient black bean soup

total time 25 minutes

makes leftovers

pantry recipe

why this recipe works When we set out to develop a group of pantry-friendly soup recipes, we challenged ourselves to see how short we could make the ingredient list, but still create flavorful, crave-worthy soups. And lucky for us (and our taste buds), a single can of beans is so much more than just the beans. The bean liquid did the heavy lifting, providing body, silky texture, and deep flavor—we didn't even need a lot of herbs or aromatics to make these soups sing. For this black bean soup, a base of smoky, fruity chipotle chiles in adobo sauce gave the soup character and depth of flavor in a flash, while lime zest and broth added fresh aroma and subtle complexity. We coarsely mashed the beans after cooking, which helped to thicken the soup, and Greek yogurt brought extra creaminess and tanginess. This soup is hearty enough on its own, but can be bulked up with whatever extra protein you have on hand, from shredded chicken to smoked fish.

1 (15-ounce) can black beans

1 cup chicken or vegetable broth, plus extra as needed

2–3 teaspoons minced canned chipotle chiles in adobo sauce

2 tablespoons plain Greek yogurt

½ teaspoon grated lime zest, plus lime wedges for serving

kitchen improv

level up Garnish with tortilla strips, crumbled cheese (cotija, feta, or goat), fresh herbs like scallions or cilantro, and/or avocado.

make it heartier Stir in shredded chicken, sliced seared steak, smoked fish, or Pan-Seared Shrimp (page 61).

Bring beans and their liquid, broth, and chipotle to simmer in medium saucepan and cook over medium-low heat, stirring occasionally, until beans begin to break down, 5 to 7 minutes. Using potato masher, coarsely mash beans in saucepan. Adjust consistency with extra hot broth as needed. Off heat, stir in yogurt and lime zest, and season with salt and pepper to taste. Serve with lime wedges. (Soup can be refrigerated for up to 3 days.)

why this recipe works Cans of tomato soup concentrate may evoke childhood nostalgia, but the happy memories end there. For a more grown-up version, we found that an unexpected ingredient, canned white beans and their liquid, provided a velvety backdrop and subtle earthiness. And rather than using canned tomatoes, which can taste tinny if they do not cook for an adequate amount of time, we briefly simmered and blended in sweet and tangy sun-dried tomatoes— so potent (and pantry-friendly) that a mere 3 tablespoons were plenty. Parmesan cheese and shredded fresh basil provided rich and aromatic finishes. Creamy white beans brought buttery nuttiness, making this "from-a-can" soup an elegant lunchtime treat. Grilled cheese for dipping is always encouraged. If you don't have a blender, an immersion blender or a food processor would also work.

1   (15-ounce) can small
    white beans

1¼ cups chicken or vegetable
    broth, plus extra as needed

3   tablespoons oil-packed
    sun-dried tomatoes,
    chopped coarse

2   tablespoons grated
    Parmesan cheese,
    plus extra for serving

1   tablespoon shredded
    fresh basil

1   Bring beans and their liquid, broth, and tomatoes to simmer in medium saucepan and cook over medium-low heat, stirring occasionally, until beans begin to break down, 5 to 7 minutes.

2   Process soup and Parmesan in blender until smooth, about 2 minutes. Return soup to now-empty saucepan and adjust consistency with extra hot broth as needed. Season with salt and pepper to taste and sprinkle with basil. Serve with extra Parmesan. (Soup can be refrigerated for up to 3 days.)

5-ingredient sun-dried tomato and white bean soup

total time 25 minutes

makes leftovers

kitchen improv

use what you've got Substitute Pecorino Romano, Grana Padano, Asiago, or Manchego for the Parmesan, or use a semisoft cheese such as cheddar or Monterey Jack.

level up Garnish with toasted nuts, crackers, and/or croutons.

make it a meal For a perfect grilled cheese, brush the outside of the sandwich with butter and cook in a covered skillet over moderate heat, flipping once, until golden.

why this recipe works Through the power of garlic, a can of chickpeas is transformed into a creamy, Mediterranean-inspired soup in 30 minutes flat. To develop deep, nuanced flavor from such simple ingredients, we started by quick-roasting skin-on garlic cloves in a clean, dry saucepan until they turned a beautiful golden color and became intensely fragrant. Roasting the garlic this way yielded mellow, mildly sweet garlic that mimicked the flavor of oven-roasted garlic in a fraction of the time. We peeled the garlic and returned it to the saucepan with some broth and a full can of chickpeas and their liquid (the technique so nice we used it thrice in developing these recipes), and then blended the soup until it was smooth and velvety. A splash of lemon juice and some fresh parsley are more than just finishing elements here—they wake up the flavors by adding bright freshness, and cut through the rich, silky soup. If you don't have a blender, an immersion blender or a food processor would also work.

4 garlic cloves, unpeeled

1 (15-ounce) can chickpeas

1¼ cups chicken or vegetable broth, plus extra as needed

1 tablespoon minced fresh parsley, tarragon, or chives

1 tablespoon lemon juice

1 Toast garlic in medium saucepan over medium heat, stirring occasionally, until fragrant and skins are just beginning to brown, about 5 minutes. Remove garlic from saucepan and let cool slightly. Once cool enough to handle, peel garlic then return to now-empty saucepan along with chickpeas and their liquid and broth. Bring to simmer and cook over medium-low heat, stirring occasionally, until chickpeas begin to break down, 5 to 7 minutes.

2 Process soup in blender until smooth, about 2 minutes. Return soup to now-empty saucepan and adjust consistency with extra hot broth as needed. Off heat, stir in parsley and lemon juice and season with salt and pepper to taste. Serve. (Soup can be refrigerated for up to 3 days.)

5-ingredient creamy chickpea and roasted garlic soup

total time 30 minutes

makes leftovers

kitchen improv

level up Garnish with sun-dried tomatoes, olives, garlic chips (see page 256), roasted red peppers, and/or toasted pine nuts.

make it heartier Stir in roasted butternut squash or chopped greens, or go for broke and top with cooked ground beef or lamb.

why this recipe works Tortellini might be a quick and easy dinner, but we think you deserve more than simply heating them up with some marinara. This hearty soup transforms our favorite pantry-staple cheesy-filled pasta into a whole new meal without much more work. The process starts and ends in the saucepan: We built the base of the soup by first cooking some sausage and then used the fat to cook the aromatics; once we added the liquid and tortellini it was a matter of just simmering the pasta to doneness until our soup was ready. A couple of handfuls of spinach, stirred in at the end to preserve its color and freshness, added green goodness to the simple soup.

1 tablespoon oil

6 ounces hot or sweet Italian sausage, casing removed

1 small onion, chopped fine

2 garlic cloves, minced

1 teaspoon minced fresh rosemary or thyme or ¼ teaspoon dried

2 cups chicken or vegetable broth

1 cup water

3 ounces dried cheese tortellini

3 ounces (3 cups) baby spinach

1 Heat oil in medium saucepan over medium heat until shimmering. Add sausage and cook, breaking up meat with wooden spoon, until lightly browned, 3 to 5 minutes. Stir in onion and cook until softened, about 5 minutes. Stir in garlic and rosemary and cook until fragrant, about 30 seconds.

2 Stir in broth, water, and tortellini, scraping up any browned bits. Bring to simmer and cook until tortellini are tender, 12 to 15 minutes.

3 Stir in spinach 1 handful at a time and let sit off heat until wilted, about 2 minutes. Season with salt and pepper to taste. Serve. (Soup can be refrigerated for up to 3 days.)

sausage and tortellini florentine soup

total time 45 minutes

makes leftovers

kitchen improv

use what you've got Substitute a small amount of finely chopped pancetta or bacon for the sausage. Any dried short pasta like farfalle or penne would work in place of the tortellini, just be sure to adjust the cooking time accordingly. Substitute baby kale for the baby spinach.

level up Garnish with grated Parmesan and a drizzle of oil.

make it vegetarian Omit the sausage and use vegetable broth. Add more pasta to bulk it up.

pantry garlicky chicken and rice soup

total time 40 minutes

makes leftovers

pantry recipe

why this recipe works Whether you're under the weather or just in need of something warming and filling, few things nourish like a well-rounded chicken and rice soup enriched with a hefty dose of sinus-clearing garlic. But while Grandma's big-batch recipe may have you sautéing and simmering for hours, we wanted a simplified and small-batch version that would still be loaded with flavor and complexity. (Plus, if you're really not feeling well, the last thing you want to do is embark on a project.) One shallot replaced the traditional onion, and a garlic press made quick work of mincing the whopping five cloves of garlic (see page 14 for tips on peeling garlic). Some herbes de Provence gave floral brightness (dried thyme is fine, too), and a touch of anchovy paste brought meaty depth without the need to make homemade stock. We added broth, boneless chicken thighs, a single carrot, and rice and simmered it all until everything was perfectly cooked. Convenient frozen peas and a squeeze of lemon juice brought garden freshness. Just what the doctor ordered.

- 1 shallot, minced
- 5 garlic cloves, minced
- 2 teaspoons oil
- ½ teaspoon herbes de Provence or dried thyme
- ½ teaspoon anchovy paste
- 3 cups chicken or vegetable broth
- 6 ounces boneless, skinless chicken thighs, trimmed and cut into ½-inch pieces
- ¼ cup long-grain white rice, rinsed
- 1 carrot, peeled, halved lengthwise, and sliced ¼ inch thick
- ⅛ teaspoon table salt
- ¼ cup frozen peas

  Lemon wedges

kitchen improv

use what you've got Substitute pasta (spaghetti, ditalini, orzo, or egg noodles) for the rice, adjusting cooking time as needed; substitute chicken breasts for the thighs.

level up Fresh herbs, baby greens, tomatoes, beans, harissa, pesto, lime juice, and/or grated cheese all make great stir-ins. Serve with crackers.

spice it up Add minced chipotle chiles in adobo sauce and/or a drizzle of hot sauce or chili oil.

1 Heat shallot, garlic, and oil in medium saucepan over medium-low heat, stirring occasionally, until shallot and garlic are softened and beginning to brown, 3 to 5 minutes. Stir in herbes de Provence and anchovy paste and cook until fragrant, about 30 seconds.

2 Stir in broth, chicken, rice, carrot, and salt, scraping up any browned bits. Bring to simmer and cook until rice is tender, about 12 minutes.

3 Off heat, stir in peas and let sit until warmed through, about 2 minutes. Season with salt and pepper to taste. Serve with lemon wedges. (Soup can be refrigerated for up to 3 days.)

beef and barley soup

total time 1 hour

makes leftovers

why this recipe works Hearty and umami-packed, beef and barley soup is the ultimate winter warmer. To make this classic soup as easy as it is delicious, we employed some shortcuts that still delivered big flavor in a scaled-down version. While standard beef soup recipes often call for a large chuck roast that you cut into cubes, we went with affordable, sized-for-one blade steak, also from the beef shoulder, that would break down just as nicely. (Short ribs are another perfectly portioned option.) We added the beef to the pot all at once (with such a small amount there's no need to brown in batches) and after the moisture evaporated, the meat began to color, yielding a well-browned fond. In lieu of homemade beef broth (store-bought was too weak for this dish), we went with chicken or vegetable broth, which took on meaty flavor from the fond that was then deepened with the addition of a duo of umami bombs, soy sauce and tomato paste, plus plenty of garlic. Pair with a good movie and your coziest socks.

6 ounces beef blade steak, trimmed and cut into ½-inch pieces

⅛ teaspoon table salt

⅛ teaspoon pepper

1 tablespoon oil

4 ounces cremini mushrooms, trimmed and sliced thin

2 carrots, peeled and chopped

1 small onion, chopped fine

1 tablespoon tomato paste

3 garlic cloves, minced

2 teaspoons minced fresh thyme or ½ teaspoon dried thyme or herbes de Provence

3 cups chicken or vegetable broth

1 tablespoon soy sauce

⅓ cup quick-cooking barley, rinsed

2 tablespoons chopped fresh parsley or chives

kitchen improv

use what you've got You can substitute boneless short ribs for the blade steak and pearl couscous or quinoa for the quick-cooking barley.

level up Substitute salsa verde or Chermoula Sauce (page 68) for the parsley for a brighter finish.

1 Pat beef dry with paper towels and sprinkle with salt and pepper. Heat oil in medium saucepan over medium heat until just smoking. Add beef and cook until well browned on all sides, 5 to 7 minutes; transfer to bowl.

2 Pour off all but 1 tablespoon fat (or add oil to equal 1 tablespoon). Add mushrooms, carrots, and onion and cook until vegetables begin to brown, 6 to 8 minutes. Stir in tomato paste, garlic, and thyme and cook until fragrant and beginning to brown, about 1 minute.

3 Stir in broth, soy sauce, and browned beef and any accumulated juices, scraping up any browned bits. Bring to simmer and cook for 15 minutes. Stir in barley and simmer until barley and beef are tender, 10 to 15 minutes. Stir in parsley and season with salt and pepper to taste. Serve. (Soup can be refrigerated for up to 3 days.)

why this recipe works This isn't your dorm room ramen (though it's almost as easy to make). To get all of the flavor of traditionally long-simmered ramen with the ease of the packaged instant versions, we ditched the salty—but otherwise lackluster—flavor packet and kept the noodles. We started by gently browning pieces of sirloin steak tips in a medium saucepan, taking care not to burn the fond that develops as the meat browns—we wanted to keep all that flavor. As the meat rested, we added our broth to the flavorful-fond-coated saucepan, and we further bolstered it with a splash of soy sauce and healthy doses of aromatic ginger and floral lime zest. A single serving of widely available packaged ramen noodles cooked up quickly in this brew. Steak tips, also known as flap meat, can be sold as whole steaks, cubes, or strips. To ensure evenly sized pieces, we prefer to buy whole steaks and cut them ourselves.

almost-instant ginger beef ramen

total time 35 minutes

4 ounces sirloin steak tips, trimmed and cut into 2-inch pieces

⅛ teaspoon table salt

⅛ teaspoon pepper

1 teaspoon oil

1½ cups chicken or vegetable broth

2 teaspoons grated fresh ginger or ½ teaspoon ground ginger

½ teaspoon grated lime zest plus 1 teaspoon juice

1 (3-ounce) package ramen noodles, seasoning packet discarded

2 teaspoons soy sauce

1 scallion, sliced thin

1 Pat beef dry with paper towels and sprinkle with salt and pepper. Heat oil in medium saucepan over medium heat until just smoking. Add beef and cook until well browned all over and registers 120 to 125 degrees (for medium-rare), 4 to 6 minutes, reducing heat if saucepan begins to smoke. Transfer beef to plate, tent loosely with aluminum foil, and let rest until ready to serve.

2 Add broth, ginger, and lime zest to now-empty saucepan; bring to a boil, scraping up any browned bits. Add noodles and cook, stirring often, until tender, about 3 minutes. Off heat, stir in lime juice, soy sauce, scallion, and any accumulated juices from beef, and season with salt and pepper to taste. Transfer soup to serving bowl. Slice steak thin against grain and place on top of noodles. Serve. (Broth and beef can be refrigerated separately for up to 3 days.)

kitchen improv

use what you've got Substitute pork, chicken, shrimp, or tofu for the beef. Substitute spiralized vegetable noodles for the ramen noodles and adjust the cooking time as needed.

level up Sprinkle with crumbled nori or cilantro leaves; drizzle with sesame oil, chili oil, sriracha, or chili-garlic sauce.

make it heartier Stir in baby greens or mustard greens, sliced mushrooms, and/or pickled vegetables, and top with a soft-cooked egg (see page 139).

beef pho

total time 1 hour

makes leftovers

why this recipe works Vietnamese pho is usually made from a long-simmering fragrant broth, but our dead-simple recipe infuses aromatic flavor into store-bought beef broth in a fraction of the time, using ginger, cinnamon, star anise, and cloves—all traditional ingredients in pho. Instead of painstakingly slicing steak, which cooks at the last second in the hot broth, store-bought shaved steak (often used for steak sandwiches) stood in here—a huge time-saver. If you plan to store and reheat a portion of the soup, store the noodles, broth, steak, and garnishes separately; reheat noodles in broth and add steak and garnishes after reheating. You could make a Spicy Peanut Rice-Noodle Bowl (page 273) with the leftover rice noodles and garnish it with leftover bean sprouts.

1 small onion, quartered through root end, divided

3 cups beef broth

1 cup water, plus more as needed

1 tablespoon fish sauce, plus extra for serving

2 teaspoons sugar

1 (1-inch) piece ginger, sliced into thin rounds

1 cinnamon stick

2 star anise pods

4 whole cloves

6 ounces (¼-inch-wide) rice noodles

8 ounces shaved steak

1 ounce (½ cup) bean sprouts

⅓ cup fresh cilantro, Thai basil, or basil

Lime wedges

kitchen improv

use what you've got Substitute trimmed strip steak for the shaved steak. Freeze steak until very firm and slice ⅛ inch thick against the grain. If you don't have fish sauce, you can use a combination of soy sauce and anchovy paste (see page 5 for more information).

spice it up Add thinly sliced chiles and/or finish off the pho with sriracha or Asian chili-garlic sauce.

1 Slice 1 onion quarter as thin as possible; set aside until ready to serve. Bring broth, water, fish sauce, sugar, ginger, cinnamon, star anise, cloves, and remaining 3 onion quarters to boil in medium saucepan, then reduce heat to medium-low and simmer for 30 minutes. While broth simmers, pour 2 quarts boiling water over noodles in bowl and stir to separate. Let noodles soak until soft and pliable but not fully tender, stirring once halfway through soaking, 8 to 10 minutes. Drain noodles and rinse with cold water until water runs clear, shaking to remove excess water. (Noodles can be refrigerated for up to 3 days.)

2 Strain broth through fine-mesh strainer into 4-cup liquid measuring cup, adding water as needed to equal 3 cups. Discard solids. (Strained broth can be refrigerated for up to 3 days.) Combine noodles and broth in now-empty saucepan, return to boil, and cook until noodles are tender, about 1 minute. Season with salt and pepper to taste.

3 Stir in thinly sliced onion and steak. Serve immediately, topping with sprouts, cilantro, and extra fish sauce, and accompanying with lime wedges.

why this recipe works When you want to experience the energetic flavors for which Thai cuisine is famous in one bowl, ladle up the hot-and-sour Thai soup known as tom yum. Jarred Thai curry paste, a wonder ingredient packed with just the right combination of aromatics (lemongrass, ginger, and fresh chiles), gave us a quick pantry-friendly base of flavor. We started by whisking the curry paste and just a hint of sugar into broth, then we staggered the cooking of four key ingredients—mushrooms, fresh chiles, shrimp, and tomato—to be sure they were each cooked perfectly. To finish, we rounded out the flavors with a splash each of briny fish sauce and zesty lime juice, plus a generous hit of fresh herbs. If you plan to store and reheat a portion of the soup, store the fresh herbs and soup separately; stir herbs into soup after reheating.

thai-style hot-and-sour soup

total time 40 minutes

makes leftovers

2 ounces rice vermicelli

3 cups chicken or vegetable broth

2 tablespoons Thai green or red curry paste

1 teaspoon sugar

4 ounces cremini or white mushrooms, trimmed and sliced thin

1 jalapeño chile, stemmed, seeded, and sliced into thin rings

8 ounces extra-large shrimp (21 to 25 per pound), peeled, deveined, and tails removed

1 tomato, cored, seeded, and chopped

1 tablespoon fish sauce

1 tablespoon lime juice

2 tablespoons chopped cilantro, fresh Thai basil, basil, or mint

1 Bring 2 quarts water to boil in medium saucepan. Off heat, add vermicelli and let sit, stirring occasionally, until fully tender, about 5 minutes. Drain, rinse with cold water, drain again, and set aside.

2 Bring broth to simmer in now-empty saucepan over medium-low heat then whisk in curry paste and sugar until dissolved. Add mushrooms and jalapeño and simmer for 1 minute. Stir in shrimp and cook until opaque throughout, about 1 minute. Off heat, stir in tomato, fish sauce, and lime juice and season with salt and pepper to taste. Transfer soup to serving bowl, add noodles, then sprinkle with cilantro. Serve. (Soup can be refrigerated for up to 3 days.)

kitchen improv

use what you've got Substitute (or add in) sliced or shredded cooked chicken, beef, pork, or tofu for the shrimp. If you don't have fish sauce, you can use a combination of soy sauce and anchovy paste (see page 5 for more information).

spice it up Include jalapeño seeds, or substitute a spicier chile like serrano or Thai bird's eye.

why this recipe works You're probably familiar with chili at game-day parties or blue-ribbon cook-offs, with vats of the stuff big enough to feed an army. But there's no reason to wait for a group gathering to enjoy this satisfying and comforting stew. To make a simpler, scaled-down version with the same award-winning flavor, we maximized items that would boost multidimensional flavor and provide great texture in a relatively short time frame. Chili powder and ground cumin added the spicy warmth synonymous with chili— adding the spices right away with the aromatics allowed the flavors to deepen and develop early on. A can of beans and their liquid brought silky texture and richness. And because diced, crushed, or whole canned tomatoes require longer cooking times to dampen their tinny flavor, we instead used a single 8-ounce can of tomato sauce. This enabled us to reduce the cooking time while still adding well-rounded tomato flavor to the beef and beans.

easy beef chili

total time 40 minutes

makes leftovers

1 tablespoon oil

1 red, green, yellow, or orange bell pepper, stemmed, seeded, and chopped

1 shallot, chopped fine

3 garlic cloves, minced

1½–2 tablespoons chili powder

1 teaspoon ground cumin

6 ounces 85 percent lean ground beef

1 (15-ounce) can kidney or pinto beans

1 (8-ounce) can tomato sauce

Lime wedges

1 Heat oil in medium saucepan over medium heat until shimmering. Add bell pepper, shallot, garlic, chili powder, and cumin, and cook, stirring often, until vegetables are softened and spices are fragrant, about 3 minutes.

2 Add ground beef and cook, breaking up meat with wooden spoon, until just beginning to brown, 3 to 5 minutes. Stir in beans and their liquid and tomato sauce. Bring to simmer and cook over medium-low heat until meat is tender and sauce has thickened slightly, about 15 minutes. Season with salt and pepper to taste. Serve with lime wedges. (Chili can be refrigerated for up to 3 days.)

kitchen improv

level up Top with crumbled tortilla chips, grated cheddar cheese, avocado, and/or sour cream.

make it southwestern Substitute a small amount of minced canned chipotle chiles in adobo sauce for the chili powder, and use black beans instead of kidneys or pintos.

make it meatier Add some chopped bacon or chopped salt pork with the vegetables and spices in step 1.

why this recipe works Thai curries are complexly flavored, boasting a balance of aromatic, funky, tangy, and sweet flavors. Curry paste is an ingredient we go back to again and again, and for good reason—we always have it on hand, it's fast, and it packs an aromatic punch. We whisked it into broth to develop a superflavorful base for our curry in a snap. Chicken and a potato gave our curry heft; crunchy bell pepper and snap peas brought texture; sugar, fish sauce, and lime juice provided the balance of flavors we were after; and coconut milk added creamy, slightly sweet richness. Serve on its own or over rice. If you plan to store and reheat a portion of this curry, store the fresh herbs and stew separately; stir herbs into stew after reheating. See page 20 for more information on storing leftover coconut milk.

thai-style coconut chicken curry

total time 35 minutes

makes leftovers

- 1½ cups chicken or vegetable broth
- 2 tablespoons Thai red or green curry paste
- 2 teaspoons sugar
- 8 ounces boneless, skinless chicken thighs, trimmed and cut into 1-inch pieces
- 1 Yukon Gold potato (8 ounces), peeled and cut into 1-inch pieces
- 1 small red, orange, or yellow bell pepper, stemmed, seeded, and chopped
- 4 ounces sugar snap peas, strings removed, cut on bias into ½-inch pieces
- ½ cup canned coconut milk
- 2 tablespoons chopped fresh Thai basil, basil, cilantro, or mint
- 1 tablespoon fish sauce
- 1 tablespoon lime juice

1 Bring broth to simmer in medium saucepan over medium-low heat then whisk in curry paste and sugar until dissolved. Add chicken and potato, bring to simmer, and cook until tender, 8 to 10 minutes. Stir in bell pepper and snap peas and cook until just tender, 3 to 5 minutes.

2 Off heat, stir in coconut milk, basil, fish sauce, and lime juice and season with salt and pepper to taste. Serve. (Curry can be refrigerated for up to 3 days.)

kitchen improv

use what you've got Substitute a sweet potato, chickpeas, or cauliflower florets for the Yukon Gold potato, and snow peas, green beans, or frozen peas for the snap peas. If you don't have fish sauce, you can use a combination of soy sauce and anchovy paste (see page 5 for more information).

level up Sprinkle the finished curry with chopped toasted peanuts or cashews (see page 15).

chicken tagine

total time 40 minutes

makes leftovers

why this recipe works Tagines of North Africa are warmly spiced, assertively flavored stews that typically involve long lists of ingredients (meats, vegetables, fruits, and numerous spices) and are cooked for hours in conical earthenware vessels (also called tagines). They're exceedingly delicious, but can be a lot of work—we'd never think to make one just for ourselves. We judiciously selected ingredients to make sure we were staying true to the flavors while cutting down on work. We relied on ras el hanout, a Moroccan spice blend that captures the heady flavor of many spices in one, to deliver big flavor in a single ingredient. Quick-cooking chicken thighs were our protein of choice. Chickpeas and dried apricots, traditional additions that also happen to be pantry friendly, contributed to the tagine's sweet-savory balance, and just one sweet potato was plenty to amp up the sweetness of the braise. Coarsely mashing the tagine at the end of cooking helped achieve a creamy texture reminiscent of long-cooked stews but in a fraction of the time. Serve over couscous, rice, or other grains. You can use store-bought ras el hanout or make your own (see page 72).

1 tablespoon oil

1 shallot, chopped fine

2 garlic cloves, minced

1½ teaspoons ras el hanout

1 (15-ounce) can chickpeas, rinsed

1½ cups chicken or vegetable broth

8 ounces boneless, skinless chicken thighs, trimmed and cut into 1-inch pieces

1 small sweet potato (8 ounces), peeled and cut into 1-inch pieces

¼ cup dried apricots, quartered

2 tablespoons chopped fresh cilantro

kitchen improv

use what you've got Substitute garam masala or curry powder for the ras el hanout, carrots or parsnips for the sweet potato, and raisins or chopped prunes for the dried apricots.

level up Top with toasted nuts, green olives, pomegranate seeds, and/or thinly sliced preserved lemons.

make it vegan Omit the chicken and use two sweet potatoes.

1   Heat oil in medium saucepan over medium-low heat until shimmering. Add shallot, garlic, and ras el hanout and cook, stirring often, until shallot and garlic are softened and spices are fragrant, about 3 minutes.

2   Stir in chickpeas, broth, chicken, sweet potato, and apricots, scraping up any browned bits. Bring to simmer and cook until chicken and sweet potato are tender, about 15 minutes. Using potato masher or back of large spoon, coarsely mash stew to desired consistency. Off heat, stir in cilantro and season with salt and pepper to taste. Serve. (Tagine can be refrigerated for up to 3 days.)

why this recipe works Gumbo might hail from the Big Easy, but there's nothing "easy" about the typical hours-long process of making the roux, a low-and-slow-cooked mixture of flour and fat that gives gumbo its deep brown color, toasty flavor, and body. To streamline, we cranked up the heat a bit while cooking the roux—we still achieved dark, flavorful, gravy-like results in a mere 15 minutes. The holy trinity (onion, celery, and bell pepper) provided the base, Cajun seasoning gave us complex, authentic flavor with just one ingredient, and a bottle of clam juice brought piquant saltiness without the need to make shrimp stock. Garlicky andouille sausage and quick-cooking shrimp were simple to prepare and rounded out this bayou stew. Serve on its own or with rice.

shrimp and sausage gumbo

total time 1 hour

makes leftovers

¼ cup all-purpose flour

3 tablespoons oil

8 ounces andouille sausage, halved lengthwise and sliced ½ inch thick

1 small onion, chopped fine

1 red bell pepper, stemmed, seeded, and cut into ½-inch pieces

1 celery rib, minced

2 garlic cloves, minced

1 teaspoon Cajun seasoning

½ teaspoon minced fresh thyme or ⅛ teaspoon dried

1 (8-ounce) bottle clam juice

½ cup water

8 ounces extra-large shrimp (21 to 25 per pound), peeled, deveined, and tails removed

2 scallions, sliced thin

1   Whisk flour and oil together in medium saucepan until smooth. Cook over medium heat, whisking occasionally, until mixture is deep brown and fragrant, about 15 minutes.

2   Add andouille, onion, bell pepper, and celery and cook until vegetables are softened and lightly browned, about 10 minutes. Stir in garlic, Cajun seasoning, and thyme and cook until fragrant, about 30 seconds.

3   Slowly whisk in clam juice and water, scraping up any browned bits and smoothing out any lumps. Bring to simmer and cook until vegetables are tender and mixture has thickened, about 10 minutes. Stir in shrimp and continue to simmer until opaque throughout, 2–3 minutes. Stir in scallions and season with salt and pepper to taste. Serve. (Soup can be refrigerated for up to 3 days.)

kitchen improv

use what you've got Any size shrimp works here. If you don't have Cajun seasoning, omit it and add a small amount of cayenne for heat. Substitute kielbasa or chorizo for the andouille.

why this recipe works While "stew" implies long cooking, fish stews are the outlier of the bunch. Because the flavor transfer happens quickly and there's little collagen to break down, fish stews cook in a fraction of the time of heavier, meat-centric varieties. To build an intensely flavorful base, we sautéed an onion and fennel along with smoky chorizo sausage (a hallmark of Spanish dishes) for heartiness and spicy complexity. White wine, diced tomatoes, and a bottle of clam juice gave the broth brightness, welcome acidity, and just the right amount of brininess. The meaty-yet-flaky cod needed just a few minutes of simmering in our highly flavorful broth to cook through. Serve with crusty bread. You could make Arugula and Steak Tip Salad (page 221) with the leftover fennel from this recipe.

spanish-style fish stew

total time 50 minutes

makes leftovers

1	tablespoon oil, plus extra for serving	1	(14.5-ounce) can diced tomatoes
4	ounces Spanish-style chorizo, cut into ½-inch pieces	1	(8-ounce) bottle clam juice
1	small onion, chopped fine	12	ounces skinless cod, 1 to 1½ inches thick, cut into 2-inch pieces
½	fennel bulb, stalks discarded, bulb cored and sliced thin	¼	teaspoon table salt
2	garlic cloves, minced	⅛	teaspoon pepper
⅓	cup dry white wine	1	tablespoon minced fresh parsley or chives

1 Heat oil in medium saucepan over medium heat until shimmering. Add chorizo, onion, and fennel and cook until vegetables are softened, about 8 minutes. Stir in garlic and cook until fragrant, about 30 seconds. Stir in wine, scraping up any browned bits. Stir in tomatoes with their juice and clam juice, bring to simmer, and cook for 10 minutes.

2 Pat cod dry with paper towels then sprinkle with salt and pepper. Nestle cod into tomato mixture, spoon some of sauce over fish, and bring to simmer. Cover and cook over medium-low heat until fish flakes apart when gently prodded with paring knife and registers 135 degrees, about 5 minutes. Gently stir in parsley and season with salt and pepper to taste. Drizzle with extra oil before serving. (Soup can be refrigerated for up to 24 hours.)

kitchen improv

use what you've got Substitute a combination of chicken or vegetable broth and wine vinegar or lemon juice for the wine (see page 5 for more information). You can substitute black sea bass, haddock, or pollock for the cod.

level up Make a quick garnish by stirring together toasted pine nuts, minced fresh mint, and orange zest.

clam and cannellini bean stew

with sausage

total time 35 minutes

makes leftovers

why this recipe works No need to wait for a clambake to get your fix of these briny mollusks—buying them at the seafood counter makes them easy to portion for one. This easy-to-make yet complexly flavored stew combines the salty brightness of fresh littleneck clams with the earthy, aromatic qualities of fennel-scented sweet Italian pork sausage and the heartiness of cannellini beans and Swiss chard. To keep things simple for the solo cook, we came up with a concise and readily available combination of ingredients (white wine, tomato paste, shallot, and garlic) to tie the flavors together. If you plan to store and reheat a portion of this stew, discard the clam shells and nestle the clams into the soup. If you'd like to accentuate the briny flavor of the clams, substitute up to ½ cup of clam juice for an equal measure of the broth. We call for 2 ounces of sausage in this recipe, but you can use more without negatively impacting the recipe. You could use the leftover Swiss chard to substitute for the spinach in Stovetop Spinach Macaroni and Cheese (page 261).

1 teaspoon oil

2 ounces sweet Italian sausage, casing removed

1 shallot, minced

3 ounces Swiss chard, stems chopped fine, leaves chopped coarse

2 garlic cloves, minced

1 teaspoon tomato paste

¼ cup dry white wine

1 cup chicken or vegetable broth

1 cup water

1 (15-ounce) can cannellini beans, rinsed

1 pound littleneck or cherrystone clams, scrubbed

Lemon wedges

kitchen improv

use what you've got Substitute mussels or shrimp for the clams, adjusting the cooking time as needed. Substitute kale, collard greens, broccoli rabe, or broccolini for the chard. You can use a combination of chicken or vegetable broth and wine vinegar or lemon juice to replace the wine (see page 5 for more information).

level up Finish with a sprinkling of grated hard cheese, such as Parmesan, Asiago, Pecorino Romano, or Manchego.

1 Heat oil in medium saucepan over medium heat until shimmering. Add sausage and cook, breaking up meat with wooden spoon, until no longer pink, about 3 minutes. Add shallot and chard stems and cook until softened, about 3 minutes.

2 Stir in garlic and tomato paste and cook until fragrant, about 30 seconds. Stir in wine and cook, scraping up any browned bits, until reduced by half, 30 to 60 seconds.

3 Stir in broth, water, and beans, bring to boil, then add clams and chard leaves. Cover and cook over medium-high heat until clams open, 4 to 8 minutes. Remove from heat and discard any clams that refuse to open. Season with salt and pepper to taste. Serve with lemon wedges. (Soup and shelled clams can be refrigerated for up to 24 hours.)

mexican street-corn chowder

total time 45 minutes

makes leftovers

why this recipe works We love the salty, spicy, tangy, rich flavors of elote, the popular (and messy) Mexican street corn—so much so that we turned it into an easy-to-eat soup that feels like a treat. Because this snack is all about the toppings, we doubled down— first sautéing poblano chiles for vegetal depth, and then cooking up Mexican chorizo until it turned deliciously crispy and rendered some flavorful fat, which we used to toast our corn. After adding aromatics and broth to the corn, we pureed most of it until creamy, leaving some corn kernels whole for a pleasant chunky texture. If you don't have a blender, an immersion blender or a food processor would also work.

1 tablespoon oil, divided	4 ears corn, kernels cut from cobs, or 3½ cups frozen
2 poblano chiles, stemmed, seeded, and sliced thin	⅛ teaspoon table salt
4 garlic cloves, minced, divided	1½ cups chicken or vegetable broth
1¼ teaspoons chili powder, divided	¼ cup chopped fresh cilantro or parsley
2 ounces Mexican-style chorizo sausage, casings removed	Lime wedges

kitchen improv

use what you've got If you can't find Mexican-style chorizo sausage, you can use Spanish-style chorizo, or make your own using ground pork and chili powder (or cayenne if your chili powder is mild).

level up For a creamy topping and even more brightness, make a crema by mixing together sour cream or yogurt and lime juice.

make it vegetarian Omit the chorizo and add oil as needed in step 2; use vegetable broth.

1   Heat 1 teaspoon oil in medium saucepan over medium heat until shimmering. Add poblanos and cook until just tender, 3 to 5 minutes. Stir in one-fourth of garlic and ¼ teaspoon chili powder and cook until fragrant. Transfer to bowl, cover with aluminum foil, and set aside until ready to serve. In now-empty saucepan, heat remaining 2 teaspoons oil over medium heat until shimmering. Add chorizo and cook until browned, about 3 minutes, breaking up meat with wooden spoon. Using slotted spoon, transfer chorizo to bowl with poblanos, covering with foil to keep warm.

2   Pour off all but 1 teaspoon fat from pan. (If necessary, add oil to equal 1 teaspoon.) Add corn and cook over medium heat, stirring occasionally, until lightly browned, about 5 minutes. Stir in remaining garlic, ¾ teaspoon of remaining chili powder, and salt and cook until fragrant, 30 seconds. Stir in broth, scraping up browned bits. Bring to simmer and cook until corn is tender, 2 minutes.

3   Process 2 cups soup in blender until very smooth, about 2 minutes. Stir pureed soup into remaining soup in saucepan, adjusting consistency with hot water as needed, and season with salt and pepper to taste. Off heat, top with poblano-chorizo mixture, cilantro, and remaining ¼ teaspoon chili powder. Serve with lime wedges. (Soup can be refrigerated for up to 3 days.)

why this recipe works While we love a hearty, meat-based stew, it's rare to see a good-for-you grain stew, rarer still one built on a protein-rich ancient grain. But quinoa is the star of this South American–inspired stew, and our version just so happens to rely mainly on pantry ingredients. In fact, it's hardly more work than cooking quinoa itself: After sautéing aromatics, adding liquid, and cooking a single chopped red potato in it, we simply stirred in the quinoa (followed by quicker cooking vegetables) and simmered until tender. The result? A cozy, warmly spiced soup that will keep you full well into the evening. We like the convenience of prewashed quinoa; rinsing removes quinoa's bitter protective coating (called saponin). If you buy unwashed quinoa, rinse it and pat it dry.

quinoa and vegetable stew

total time 45 minutes

makes leftovers

1 tablespoon oil	1 red potato (6 ounces), unpeeled, cut into ½-inch pieces
1 small onion, chopped	
1 small red bell pepper, cut into ½-inch pieces	½ cup water
2 garlic cloves, minced	⅓ cup prewashed white quinoa
1 teaspoon paprika	⅓ cup fresh or frozen corn
¾ teaspoon ground coriander	3 tablespoons minced fresh cilantro, parsley, basil, or chives
½ teaspoon ground cumin	
2 cups chicken or vegetable broth	

1 Heat oil in medium saucepan over medium heat until shimmering. Add onion, bell pepper, garlic, paprika, coriander, and cumin. Cook, stirring often, until vegetables are softened and spices are fragrant, about 5 minutes. Stir in broth, potato, and water, scraping up any browned bits, then bring to simmer and cook for 10 minutes.

2 Stir in quinoa and simmer for 8 minutes. Stir in corn and continue to simmer until vegetables and quinoa are just tender, 6 to 8 minutes. Season with salt and pepper to taste and sprinkle with cilantro. Serve. (Soup can be refrigerated for up to 3 days.)

kitchen improv

use what you've got Any type of bell pepper could work here.

level up Lime wedges, diced avocado, and/or crumbled queso fresco or cotija cheese would all make great toppings.

make it heartier Crack an egg over the top of the stew before sprinkling with cilantro in step 2; cover and let egg poach off heat until whites have set but yolks are still soft, about 4 minutes.

clean-out-your-fridge soup

Even if you follow our shopping tips (see pages 16–17), leftover ingredients can sometimes be inevitable. But waste not. Follow along with each step to create a soup using whatever ingredients you have on hand. Each ingredient category lists suggestions, with cooking instructions at the bottom of each column so you can turn past-their-prime vegetables into a comforting, hearty soup in six easy steps.

1. start with... →

1 teaspoon oil

+

1 ounce mushrooms, trimmed and chopped fine (optional)

white, portobello caps, or shiitakes

+

1 ounce pork, chopped fine (optional)

bacon, chorizo, pancetta, salt pork, or sausage

+

3 tablespoons minced hearty aromatics

shallot, onion, leek whites, scallion whites, celery, fennel, sweet or hot peppers

Cook in medium saucepan over medium-low heat until vegetables have softened and pork is lightly browned, about 3 minutes.

2. build your base with... →

2 teaspoons minced garlic

+

1 teaspoon minced fresh hearty herb or ¼ teaspoon dried

thyme, herbes de Provence, marjoram, oregano, rosemary, or sage

+

½ teaspoon umami booster (optional)

anchovy paste or tomato paste

Add to saucepan and cook until fragrant, about 30 seconds.

3. give it body with... →

3 cups chicken or vegetable broth

+

8 ounces root vegetable, cut into ½-inch pieces

carrot, eggplant, parsnip, sweet potato, potato, or winter squash

+

1 flavor infuser

1 strip citrus zest, 1 lemongrass stalk (bruised), 2 slices fresh ginger, 1 tablespoon miso, 1 tablespoon soy sauce, 1 tablespoon fish sauce, 2 tablespoons Thai red or green curry paste, Parmesan cheese rind, or bay leaf

+

⅛ teaspoon table salt

Stir into vegetable mixture, scraping up any browned bits. Bring to simmer and cook until root vegetable is tender, 6 to 8 minutes.

4. make it hearty with...

8 ounces fresh vegetable, cut into 1-inch pieces

green beans, asparagus, bok choy, broccoli, Brussels sprouts, cabbage, cauliflower, hearty greens (collard greens, kale, mustard greens, and/or Swiss chard), snap peas, or summer squash

Stir into soup and cook until just tender, 1 to 5 minutes.

→

5. finish the flavor with...

¼ cup chopped quick-cooking vegetable

frozen peas, artichoke hearts, bamboo shoots, canned beans, fresh or frozen corn, edamame, tender greens (arugula, baby kale, spinach, and/or watercress), roasted red peppers, fresh or sun-dried tomatoes, or water chestnuts

+

1 tablespoon minced fresh herb

parsley, cilantro, tarragon, basil, scallions, chives, or dill

Stir into soup, remove saucepan from heat, and let sit until warmed through, about 1 minute.

→

6. level up and add a...

brightener

lemon or lime wedges, capers, olives, pickles, or vinegar

+

garnish (optional)

croutons, crackers, tortilla chips, garlic chips, kale chips, crumbled nori sheets, toasted nuts or seeds, Parmesan crisps, or radishes

Season soup with salt and pepper to taste. Finish with brightener and garnish (if using). Serve.

sandwiches and salads

We've got the antidotes to your mundane midweek meals with these make-ahead sandwiches and salads that are bursting with fresh flavor. We all love a big salad (but nobody loves leftover wilted greens), so we developed recipes that store well and are flexible depending on your appetite—eat it all as one meal, or if you plan to save the rest for the next day, we included storage information. Shake it up with bold flavors and unexpected ingredients, or keep it classic with creamy deli salads that are just as delicious sandwiched between rye toast as they are over a bed of greens. With this colorful array of options, there's no excuse for lackluster lunches.

why this recipe works Avocados are a tricky ingredient for the for-one cook—it's a race against the clock once you cut into it, and you can only eat so much guacamole. Luckily, avocado toast is the ideal way to use up that extra half of an avocado; it's healthy, delicious, and one of the simplest things to make for a quick breakfast or lunch. But despite its name, this good-for-you snack is more than just avocado on toast. (At least it should be.) We took ours up a notch by whisking together a lemony vinaigrette and mixing it in as we mashed a quarter of an avocado, giving our dish a distinct citrusy punch. Smeared on toasted rustic country bread, topped with more sliced avocado, then sprinkled with a little coarse sea salt and red pepper flakes, our version is an elevated option for a simple meal, or the base for any number of toppings for something a bit more filling. You could make a Sweet Potato–Bacon Wrap (page 192) with the leftover avocado, or use it as a taco topping (see page 200). See page 20 for more information about storing avocados.

avocado toast

total time 15 minutes

1 tablespoon oil

½ teaspoon grated lemon zest plus 1½ teaspoons juice

⅛ teaspoon flake sea salt, divided

Pinch pepper

½ ripe avocado, halved and pitted, ¼ avocado chopped and ¼ avocado sliced thin, divided

1 (½-inch-thick) slice crusty bread, toasted

Pinch red pepper flakes (optional)

1 Whisk oil, lemon zest and juice, pinch salt, and pepper together in small bowl. Add chopped avocado and coarsely mash with fork.

2 Spread mashed avocado mixture evenly on toast, then arrange avocado slices evenly over top. Sprinkle with remaining pinch salt and pepper flakes, if using. Serve.

kitchen improv

use what you've got We like the coarse texture of flake sea salt here, but you could use table salt or kosher salt if you prefer. Use any bread you have on hand.

level up Add crumbled feta or queso fresco, an extra squeeze of lemon, fresh herbs, and/or a sprinkle of store-bought dukkah.

make it a meal Add a fried egg (see page 139), tomato slices, and/or crisped bacon. Or, double the recipe, using 2 slices of bread and the full avocado.

why this recipe works Making breakfast sandwiches for a crowd is no easy task—they're best when every element is hot, so it's imperative you work quickly. (There's a reason they're usually made to order.) Better to make one just for yourself, so you can focus your attention on one sandwich. We started by cooking a strip of bacon in a skillet and using the flavorful drippings to toast our English muffin. Next we gently fried our egg in the same skillet; after a minute over the heat, the egg got topped with the crispy bacon, a handful of shredded cheddar cheese, and some fresh baby spinach. We covered the pan and let it sit until the egg white was cooked through, the cheese was melted, and the spinach was slightly wilted. A spicy mayonnaise added richness and a kick of heat to this crispy, gooey sandwich that, despite the name, is irresistible any time of the day. You will need an 8- or 10-inch nonstick skillet with a tight-fitting lid for this recipe.

breakfast sandwich

total time 30 minutes

1 tablespoon mayonnaise

½ teaspoon hot sauce or sriracha

1 slice bacon, cut in half crosswise

1 English muffin, split

½ teaspoon oil or unsalted butter

1 large egg

Pinch table salt

Pinch pepper

1 ounce sharp cheddar, Monterey Jack, or American cheese, shredded (¼ cup)

½ ounce (½ cup) baby spinach

1 Combine mayonnaise and hot sauce in bowl; set aside. Cook bacon in 8- or 10-inch nonstick skillet over medium heat until fat begins to render, about 2 minutes. Flip bacon and cook until crispy, about 4 minutes, flipping as needed. Transfer to paper towel–lined plate to drain.

2 Place muffin split side down in fat left in skillet (add 1 teaspoon oil if skillet looks dry). Cook over medium heat until muffin is golden brown, about 1 minute; transfer muffin to plate and wipe skillet clean with paper towel.

3 Heat oil in skillet over medium heat until shimmering. Meanwhile, crack egg into small bowl and sprinkle with salt and pepper. Once oil is shimmering, pour egg into skillet; cover and cook for 1 minute. Working quickly, top egg with bacon, cheddar, and spinach. Cover skillet, remove from heat, and let sit until cheddar is melted and spinach is wilted slightly, about 2 minutes.

4 Spread mayonnaise mixture on split sides of muffin. Place topped egg on muffin bottom and top with muffin top. Serve.

kitchen improv

use what you've got Substitute ham, a sausage patty, or Canadian bacon for the bacon, or arugula or watercress for the spinach.

level up Add a slice of tomato, avocado, and/or herbs.

make it vegetarian Omit the bacon and add oil in step 2. Substitute leftover mushrooms (see page 102) or sautéed onion instead.

sweet potato– bacon wrap

total time 45 minutes

why this recipe works Making your work lunch in the morning can be a drag. We wanted a sandwich that could be made the night before that was filling—and not a soggy mess. Sturdy sweet potatoes are the delicious (and unexpected) star of this make-ahead wrap. We added salty, crispy bacon to contrast the tender sweet potato, and found that peppery arugula and a mashed avocado dressed up with vinegar and fresh herbs gave us punch and necessary tang. The vinegar also prevented the avocado from oxidizing. To keep the sogginess at bay, it was all about careful construction. While we typically would spread the avocado directly on the wrap, crispy bacon is the first line of defense here, followed by the arugula. The avocado dressing was then dolloped on top, followed by potatoes—which we cooled to room temperature before assembling—and finally, the second piece of bacon. With a lunch like this, your emails can wait. You could make Roasted Sweet Potato Wedges (page 113) with the extra sweet potato from this recipe. See page 20 for more information about storing avocados.

¼ ripe avocado

1½ teaspoons white wine vinegar, white vinegar, or apple cider vinegar

½ teaspoon minced fresh dill or cilantro

¼ teaspoon table salt, divided

¼ teaspoon pepper, divided

2 slices bacon

¼ sweet potato (4 ounces), peeled or unpeeled, cut into ½-inch pieces

1 (10- or 12-inch) flour tortilla

½ cup baby arugula, baby spinach, or baby kale

kitchen improv

use what you've got Skip the mashed avocado mixture and substitute your favorite dressing (like ranch or blue cheese).

level up Add shredded cheddar, crumbled blue cheese, or any of your favorite cheeses.

make it vegetarian Omit the bacon and add oil in step 2. Cook the sweet potato with a little smoked paprika to mimic the smoky meatiness. Add rinsed canned beans to bulk it up.

1 Using fork, coarsely mash avocado, vinegar, dill, ⅛ teaspoon salt, and ⅛ teaspoon pepper together in bowl; set aside. Cook bacon in 10-inch skillet over medium heat until fat is beginning to render, about 2 minutes. Flip bacon and cook until crispy, about 6 minutes, flipping as needed. Transfer to paper towel–lined plate to drain.

2 Pour off all but 1 tablespoon fat from skillet (or add oil to equal 1 tablespoon). Add potato, remaining ⅛ teaspoon salt, and remaining ⅛ teaspoon pepper to skillet and cook over medium-low heat until tender throughout and lightly browned, about 8 minutes. Transfer to paper towel–lined plate with bacon and let cool completely, about 10 minutes.

3 Place 1 piece bacon in center of tortilla. Top bacon with arugula, then dollop with avocado mixture and sprinkle sweet potatoes over top. Place remaining piece bacon over top. Fold sides of tortilla over filling, fold bottom of tortilla over sides and filling, and roll tightly. Serve. (Wrap can be refrigerated for up to 24 hours.)

why this recipe works This lively sandwich combines savory hummus, crunchy-tart pickles, fresh tomato, and rich eggs in a soft pita. This might sound like a moisture-induced recipe for disaster, but we found that construction is the key to avoiding sogginess—as we learned with the Sweet Potato–Bacon Wrap (page 192). The trick to this sandwich was not cutting the pita open and putting the ingredients on the inside, but rather on the outside and folding the pita over. The double wall of pita prevented the exterior from getting unpleasantly mushy, so you can make the night before for lunch the next day. In fact, not only was this suitable, the sandwich actually benefited from the rest—the flavors start to meld and become more potent, transforming it into a more cohesive sandwich. See page 21 for more information about storing tomatoes.

packable pita sandwich

total time 35 minutes

- 1 (8-inch) pita bread or wrap
- 2 tablespoons hummus
- ¼ cup chopped dill pickle chips
- ¼ teaspoon ground dried Aleppo pepper, ⅛ teaspoon pepper, or pinch red pepper flakes (optional)
- ½ cup baby arugula, baby spinach, or baby kale
- 2 thin tomato slices
- ⅛ teaspoon table salt, divided
- 2 Hard-Cooked Eggs (page 139), peeled and sliced thin
- 1 teaspoon chopped fresh cilantro, parsley, dill, or mint

Lay pita flat and spread hummus over top, leaving ½-inch border along edge. Sprinkle hummus with pickles and Aleppo pepper (if using). Sprinkle arugula over one half of pita, then shingle tomato slices over top and sprinkle with pinch salt. Shingle egg on top of tomato and sprinkle with cilantro and remaining pinch salt. Fold in half and serve. (Sandwich can be refrigerated for up to 24 hours.)

kitchen improv

use what you've got Substitute any green, such as romaine, baby kale, or mixed greens for the arugula.

level up Substitute pepperoncini for the pickles and sprinkle crumbled feta along with the cilantro.

make it sabich-style Try leftover Broiled Eggplant with Honey-Lemon Vinaigrette (page 99) in place of or in addition to the egg to mimic the flavors of the popular Middle-Eastern sandwich.

lamb pita sandwiches

with tzatziki

total time 30 minutes

makes leftovers

why this recipe works We wanted a shawarma-style sandwich with straight-off-the-rotisserie flavor, but without constructing an actual at-home vertical rotisserie (or ordering takeout). Our solution? Creating cinnamon- and garlic-spiked lamb patties that we seared in a hot nonstick skillet. This cooking method developed a flavorful crust on both sides, mimicking the deeply savory exterior achieved from a restaurant-style roaster. A quick tzatziki sauce of rich Greek yogurt, cooling cucumber, tangy lemon juice, garlic, and fresh herbs completed this stunner. Our flavorful patties, tzatziki, and vegetables were then stuffed into a pita to make a sandwich you'll want to get your hands around. This recipe makes enough for two sandwiches. Reheat patties before assembling second sandwich.

¼ cup plain Greek yogurt

½ cucumber, ¼ cucumber grated and ¼ cucumber sliced thin, divided

½ teaspoon minced fresh mint or dill

1 garlic clove, minced, divided

⅛ teaspoon plus ½ teaspoon table salt, divided

12 ounces ground lamb

½ teaspoon ground cinnamon

⅛ teaspoon pepper

1 teaspoon oil

2 (8-inch) pita breads

½ romaine lettuce heart (3 ounces), sliced thin

4 thin slices tomato

kitchen improv

use what you've got Substitute any mixed greens, arugula, or other lettuce for the romaine lettuce heart, or substitute chopped cherry or grape tomatoes for the regular tomato.

make it dairy-free Substitute a drizzle of tahini or dollop of hummus in place of the tzatziki.

1   Combine yogurt, grated cucumber, mint, half of garlic, and ⅛ teaspoon salt in bowl; cover and refrigerate tzatziki until ready to serve. Break up ground lamb into small pieces in bowl then add cinnamon, pepper, remaining garlic, and remaining ½ teaspoon salt. Lightly knead with hands until combined. Pinch off and shape mixture into six ½-inch-thick patties.

2   Heat oil in 12-inch nonstick skillet over medium-high heat until just smoking. Add patties and cook until well browned on first side, about 4 minutes. Flip patties, reduce heat to medium, and cook until well browned on second side and tender throughout, about 4 minutes. Transfer to paper towel–lined plate.

3   Cut top 2 inches from 1 pita; discard or reserve for other use. Place pita on plate, cover, and microwave until warm, about 30 seconds. Spread half of tzatziki inside pita, then fill with half of lettuce, sliced cucumber, tomato, and lamb patties. Serve. (Remaining lamb patties, tzatziki, and prepped vegetables can be refrigerated, separately, for up to 24 hours.)

zucchini quesadilla

total time 30 minutes

why this recipe works Sure you can increase the filling factor of a simple quesadilla by adding shredded chicken, but we wanted something a little different for a grown-up spin on this ultraconvenient meal for one. We went with zucchini sautéed with garlic and cumin, which gave it earthy, toasty, Southwestern flavor. We sandwiched it in a tortilla and added Monterey Jack cheese for its gooey meltability and pickled jalapeños for a little briny kick. We lightly coated the filled tortilla with oil and warmed it in the skillet until it was well browned and the cheese was fully melted. A sprinkle of salt on the exterior of the tortilla added an unexpected layer of flavor to the part of the quesadilla usually ignored. Use a light hand when seasoning with salt, as the cheese itself is rather salty. Let the quesadilla cool slightly before cutting and serving; straight from the skillet, the cheese is molten and will ooze out. Cook the other half of the zucchini and use it as an omelet filling (see page 66).

2 teaspoons oil, divided

½ zucchini, trimmed and cut into ½-inch pieces (1 cup)

⅛ teaspoon table salt

⅛ teaspoon pepper

1 small garlic clove, minced

¼ teaspoon ground cumin

1½ ounces Monterey Jack, cheddar, or Colby Jack cheese, shredded (⅓ cup)

1–2 teaspoons minced jarred jalapeños

1 (10- or 12-inch) flour tortilla

kitchen improv

use what you've got Substitute sliced bell pepper or poblano pepper for zucchini.

level up Sour cream, salsa, and avocado would all make great toppings for this quesadilla.

make it heartier Add cooked shredded chicken and/or canned beans to the quesadilla with the zucchini.

1 Heat 1½ teaspoons oil in 12-inch nonstick skillet over medium-high heat until shimmering. Add zucchini, salt, and pepper and cook, stirring occasionally, until zucchini is browned and tender, about 5 minutes. Add garlic and cumin and cook until fragrant, about 30 seconds; transfer to bowl. Wipe out skillet with paper towels.

2 Sprinkle zucchini mixture, Monterey Jack, and jalapeños over half of tortilla, leaving ½-inch border around edge. Fold other half of tortilla over top and press to flatten. Brush one side with ¼ teaspoon oil and season lightly with salt.

3 Place quesadilla in now-empty skillet, oiled side down. Cook over medium heat until crispy and well browned, about 2 minutes. Brush top of quesadilla with remaining ¼ teaspoon oil and season lightly with salt, then flip quesadilla and cook until second side is crispy and browned, 1 to 2 minutes. Transfer quesadilla to cutting board and let cool for 3 minutes. Serve.

simplest ground beef tacos

total time 15 minutes

makes leftovers

why this recipe works Consider this taco Tuesday for one, but without the overly salty, stale-tasting supermarket seasoning packets that are designed for pounds of ground beef. We wanted to spice up, speed up, and pare down the well-loved weeknight staple. We started by quickly sautéing a shallot and garlic with a pantry-friendly combination of chili powder and tomato paste; this provided both savory and spicy notes and delivered all of the flavor (and more) that a spice packet would. Using 85 percent lean ground beef prevented greasiness but still gave us the richness we were after. This recipe makes enough for four tacos. Reheat filling before assembling remaining tacos.

1 teaspoon oil

3 garlic cloves, minced

2 teaspoons tomato paste

2 teaspoons chili powder

¼ teaspoon table salt

1 shallot, minced, divided

8 ounces 85 percent lean ground beef

4 taco shells

Shredded Monterey Jack, cheddar, pepper Jack, or Colby Jack cheese

Jarred jalapeños

kitchen improv

use what you've got Substitute soft tortillas for the hard taco shells; substitute ground pork or ground turkey for the ground beef.

level up Shredded lettuce, chopped tomatoes, diced avocado, cilantro, Mexican crema or sour cream, queso fresco, red onion (fresh or pickled), lime wedges, and/or any of your favorite toppings would work here.

spice it up Add ground cumin, ground coriander, and/or dried oregano to the aromatics in step 1.

1   Heat oil in medium saucepan or 10-inch skillet over medium heat until shimmering. Add garlic, tomato paste, chili powder, salt, and half of shallot and cook until fragrant, about 1 minute.

2   Stir in ground beef and cook, breaking up meat with wooden spoon, until no longer pink, 2 to 4 minutes. Divide half of filling evenly among 2 taco shells and top with cheese, jalapeños, and remaining shallot. Serve. (Remaining filling and toppings can be refrigerated, separately, in airtight container for up to 2 days.)

why this recipe works It's easy to default to chicken or beef for taco night, but tender and juicy shrimp are just as, if not more, convenient—defrost just what you need from your freezer to instantly be transported to a sunny, breezy taco stand. Tossed in a potent and pantry-friendly spice rub, they cook in a snap, and are the perfect companion to our mixture of lightly charred sautéed corn and tomatoes. After assembling the tacos, we finish them with a drizzle of a zesty, creamy lime sauce, which contrasts with the spices and adds a tangy finish. See page 11 for more information about frozen shrimp. You will need a 10-inch skillet with a tight-fitting lid for this recipe.

chipotle shrimp tacos

total time 30 minutes

2 tablespoons sour cream or Greek yogurt	¼–½ teaspoon chipotle chile powder
¼ teaspoon grated lime zest plus 1½ teaspoons juice, plus lime wedges for serving	¼ teaspoon dried oregano
	¼ teaspoon garlic powder
1 tablespoon oil, divided	8 ounces extra-large shrimp (21 to 25 per pound), peeled, deveined, tails removed, and halved crosswise
¼ cup fresh or frozen corn	
¼ cup chopped cherry or grape tomatoes	
¼ teaspoon table salt, divided	2 (6-inch) corn tortillas, warmed
	1 tablespoon chopped fresh cilantro

1 Combine sour cream and lime zest and juice in bowl; set aside until ready to serve. Heat 1 teaspoon oil in 10-inch skillet over medium heat until shimmering. Add corn and cook until softened and beginning to brown, about 2 minutes. Stir in tomatoes and ⅛ teaspoon salt and cook until tomatoes are softened, about 1 minute. Transfer to second bowl and wipe out skillet with paper towels.

2 Combine chile powder, oregano, garlic powder, and remaining ⅛ teaspoon salt in medium bowl. Pat shrimp dry with paper towels then add to chile mixture and toss to coat. Heat remaining 2 teaspoons oil in now-empty skillet over medium-high heat until just smoking. Add shrimp to skillet in single layer and cook until spotty brown and edges begin to turn pink, about 1 minute. Off heat, flip shrimp, cover, and cook second side using residual heat of skillet until shrimp are opaque throughout, 1 to 2 minutes.

3 Evenly divide corn-tomato mixture between tortillas, top with shrimp, drizzle with sour cream mixture, and sprinkle with cilantro. Serve with lime wedges.

kitchen improv

use what you've got Substitute flour tortillas or hard taco shells for the corn tortillas; substitute smoked paprika, regular paprika, or regular chili powder for the chipotle chile powder.

level up Add shredded jícama, chopped onion, sliced avocado, and/or thinly sliced radishes; char the tortillas over a gas flame before filling.

make it spicy Use the greater amount of chile powder and/or substitute chopped poblano peppers for the tomatoes.

asian barbecue chicken lettuce cups

total time 30 minutes

makes leftovers

why this recipe works Lettuce is one of the easiest ingredients to use up—and not just in salads. Here, we make a dead-simple dish out of buttery, crunchy Bibb lettuce leaves encasing chicken thighs that we poached in sweet, tangy, umami-rich hoisin thinned with a little water. That's it! (Bonus: It's all cooked in a single skillet.) While keeping it simple, we elevated the dish with a few flavorful additions: Scallions, toasted sesame seeds, and lime wedges added depth, crunch, and tanginess. We also like to keep a bottle of sriracha well within reach for an extra hit of spice. You will need an 8-inch skillet with a tight-fitting lid for this recipe—any larger and there will be too much evaporation. If you plan to store and reheat a portion of this recipe, store the lettuce, chicken, and garnishes separately; assemble lettuce cups after reheating filling.

1 teaspoon oil

1 scallion, white part minced, green part sliced thin

3 tablespoons hoisin sauce

1 tablespoon water

2 (3- to 4-ounce) boneless, skinless chicken thighs, trimmed

1 teaspoon toasted sesame seeds

4 Bibb, Boston, iceberg, or green leaf lettuce leaves

Lime wedges

Sriracha

kitchen improv

use what you've got Substitute one boneless, skinless chicken breast for the thighs; cook chicken to 160 degrees, adjusting cooking time as needed.

make it a bbq chicken sandwich Substitute your favorite barbecue sauce for the hoisin and water; serve chicken in hamburger buns and top with coleslaw.

1 Heat oil in 8-inch skillet over medium-low heat until shimmering. Add scallion white and cook, stirring occasionally, until softened, about 2 minutes. Stir in hoisin and water, scraping up any browned bits. Nestle chicken into sauce, cover, and simmer for 5 minutes. Flip chicken and continue to simmer, covered, until chicken registers 175 degrees, 5 to 7 minutes.

2 Transfer chicken to plate and let cool slightly; remove skillet with sauce from heat. Using 2 forks, shred chicken into bite-size pieces. Return shredded chicken to skillet and stir to coat with sauce.

3 Cook chicken and sauce over medium heat until sauce is thickened slightly, 2 to 4 minutes. Sprinkle with sesame seeds and scallion greens. Serve filling in lettuce leaves with lime wedges and sriracha. (Filling can be refrigerated in airtight container for up to 2 days.)

creamy deli salads

No counter service necessary to get your fix of this well-loved deli fare. These classic standbys are easy to make ahead for a quick bite or grab-and-go lunch. Turn them into sandwiches or wraps, scoop them over salads or onto a bagel, or make lettuce cups.

classic egg salad

makes 2 servings

Be sure to use red onion; yellow onion is too harsh.

- 3 Hard-Cooked Eggs (page 139), peeled and diced
- 2 tablespoons mayonnaise
- 1 tablespoon minced red onion
- 1½ teaspoons minced fresh parsley
- 2 tablespoons minced celery
- 1 teaspoon Dijon mustard
- 1 teaspoon lemon juice

Mix all ingredients together in bowl and season with salt and pepper to taste. Serve. (Salad can be refrigerated for up to 2 days.)

variations

curried egg salad
Substitute minced fresh cilantro for parsley and add ¾ teaspoon curry powder.

egg salad with capers and anchovies
Add ¼ teaspoon minced garlic, 1 tablespoon rinsed and minced capers, and 1 small rinsed and minced anchovy fillet.

chickpea salad

makes 2 servings

Use vegan mayonnaise to make it vegan.

- 1 (15-ounce) can chickpeas, rinsed, divided
- ¼ cup mayonnaise
- 2 tablespoons water
- 1½ teaspoons lemon juice
- ¼ teaspoon table salt
- 1 celery rib, minced
- 2 tablespoons finely chopped dill pickles
- 1 scallion, sliced thin
- 1 tablespoon minced fresh parsley, dill, or tarragon

1 Process ½ cup chickpeas, mayonnaise, water, lemon juice, and salt in food processor until smooth, about 30 seconds, scraping down sides of bowl as needed.

2 Add remaining chickpeas to food processor and pulse until coarsely chopped with some larger pieces remaining, about 4 pulses.

3 Combine chickpea mixture, celery, pickles, scallion, and parsley in large bowl and season with salt and pepper to taste. Serve. (Salad can be refrigerated for up to 2 days.)

variation

curried chickpea salad
Add 1½ teaspoons curry powder to chickpea mixture in food processor in step 1. Substitute ¼ cup golden raisins for pickles.

classic tuna salad

makes 2 servings

Microwaving the shallot in oil tames the shallot and infuses the oil with additional flavor.

- 2 tablespoons minced shallot
- 1 tablespoon oil
- 2 (5-ounce) cans solid white tuna in water
- ¼ cup mayonnaise
- 1 small celery rib, minced
- 1 teaspoon lemon juice
- Pinch sugar

1 Combine shallot and oil in small bowl and microwave until shallot begins to soften, about 2 minutes; set aside to cool for 5 minutes. Drain tuna in fine-mesh strainer then press dry with paper towels. Transfer tuna to medium bowl and mash with fork until finely flaked.

2 Add mayonnaise, celery, lemon juice, sugar, and shallot mixture to tuna and mix until well combined. Season with salt and pepper to taste. Serve. (Salad can be refrigerated for up to 2 days.)

variations
curried tuna salad

Add ½ teaspoon curry powder to bowl with shallot and oil before microwaving. Add ½ cup green grapes, halved, to salad in step 2.

tuna salad with apples, walnuts, and tarragon

Add ½ apple, cored and cut into ½-inch pieces; ¼ cup walnuts, toasted and chopped coarse; and 1½ teaspoons minced fresh tarragon to salad in step 2.

tuna salad with cornichons and whole-grain mustard

Add ¼ cup finely chopped cornichons, 1½ teaspoons minced fresh chives, and 1½ teaspoons whole-grain mustard to salad in step 2.

chopped chicken salad

with fennel and apple

total time 35 minutes

makes leftovers

kitchen improv

use what you've got You could use green leaf lettuce, baby arugula, or mesclun in place of the romaine lettuce heart.

level up Add chopped toasted walnuts.

make it vegetarian You could substitute sautéed tofu or chickpeas for the chicken, or omit it.

make it easier Substitute shredded rotisserie chicken for the chicken breast.

why this recipe works Chopped salads are a great way to clear out your crisper drawer (here, refreshing cucumber, licorice-y fennel, sweet apple, and romaine) and make a crunchy and surprisingly hearty meal. With a couple more protein-rich additions like chicken breast and goat cheese, you can have a bistro-worthy salad to savor. Don't skimp on the cucumber draining time or the salad will taste watery. You will need an 8- or 10-inch skillet with a tight-fitting lid for this recipe.

½ cucumber, peeled, halved lengthwise, seeded, and sliced crosswise ½ inch thick

¼ teaspoon plus ⅛ teaspoon table salt, divided

1 (6- to 8-ounce) boneless, skinless chicken breast, trimmed

⅛ teaspoon pepper

1 tablespoon oil, divided

2 tablespoons water

1 ounce goat cheese, crumbled (¼ cup)

2 tablespoons cider vinegar or white wine vinegar

2 tablespoons minced fresh tarragon or parsley

1 apple, cored, quartered, and sliced crosswise ¼ inch thick

1 small fennel bulb, stalks discarded, bulb halved, cored, and sliced ¼ inch thick

1 large shallot, minced

½ romaine lettuce heart (3 ounces), chopped

1   Toss cucumber and ¼ teaspoon salt together and let drain in colander for 15 minutes.

2   Meanwhile, place chicken on cutting board and cover with plastic wrap. Using meat pounder, gently pound chicken to even thickness. Pat chicken dry with paper towels and sprinkle with remaining ⅛ teaspoon salt and pepper.

3   Heat 1 teaspoon oil in 8- or 10-inch skillet over medium heat until just smoking. Add chicken and cook until well browned on first side, about 3 minutes. Flip chicken, add water, and cover skillet. Reduce heat to low and continue to cook until chicken registers 160 degrees, about 3 minutes. Transfer chicken to cutting board and let cool slightly. Using 2 forks, shred chicken into bite-size pieces.

4   Whisk goat cheese, vinegar, tarragon, and remaining 2 teaspoons oil together in medium bowl until smooth to make dressing. Add drained cucumber, shredded chicken, apple, fennel, and shallot and toss to combine. Let sit until flavors meld, about 5 minutes. Add lettuce and gently toss to coat. Season with salt and pepper to taste and serve. (Dressing and salad can be refrigerated separately for up to 2 days.)

moroccan chicken salad

total time 35 minutes

makes leftovers

why this recipe works Spice up your standard lunchtime chicken and green salad go-to with a warmly spiced dressing made by blooming garam masala and coriander in the microwave to intensify the flavors. Chickpeas lend heartiness, while dried apricots add sweetness to balance the dressing. Tossing half the dressing with our greens and drizzling the rest on just before serving ensures that the flavors are evenly distributed. You will need an 8- or 10-inch skillet with a tight-fitting lid for this recipe.

1 (6- to 8-ounce) boneless, skinless chicken breast, trimmed

⅛ teaspoon plus ¼ teaspoon table salt, divided

⅛ teaspoon plus ¼ teaspoon pepper, divided

2 teaspoons plus 3 tablespoons oil, divided

2 tablespoons water

½ teaspoon garam masala

¼ teaspoon ground coriander

2 tablespoons lemon juice

1 teaspoon honey

1 romaine lettuce heart (6 ounces), chopped

2 ounces (2 cups) watercress

1 tablespoon minced fresh parsley

1 small shallot, sliced thin

½ cup canned chickpeas, rinsed

¼ cup dried apricots, chopped coarse

kitchen improv

use what you've got You can substitute baby spinach or baby arugula for the watercress, or simply use all romaine lettuce; substitute dried figs or golden raisins for the dried apricots.

level up Add green olives and/or capers for a briny kick.

make it vegetarian Omit the chicken and double up on chickpeas.

make it easier Substitute shredded rotisserie chicken for the chicken breast.

1 Place chicken on cutting board and cover with plastic wrap. Using meat pounder, gently pound chicken to even thickness. Pat chicken dry with paper towels and sprinkle with ⅛ teaspoon salt and ⅛ teaspoon pepper. Heat 1 teaspoon oil in 8- or 10-inch skillet over medium heat until just smoking. Brown chicken well on first side, about 3 minutes.

2 Flip chicken, add water, and cover skillet. Reduce heat to low and continue to cook until chicken registers 160 degrees, about 3 minutes. Transfer chicken to plate and let cool slightly. Using 2 forks, shred chicken into bite-size pieces.

3 Microwave 1 teaspoon oil, garam masala, and coriander in medium bowl until fragrant, about 30 seconds. Whisk lemon juice, honey, remaining ¼ teaspoon salt, and remaining ¼ teaspoon pepper into spice mixture until combined. While whisking constantly, drizzle in remaining 3 tablespoons oil until combined.

4 Toss romaine, watercress, parsley, and shallot with half of vinaigrette to coat, then season with salt and pepper to taste. Top with shredded chicken, chickpeas, and apricots and drizzle with remaining vinaigrette. Serve. (Salad and vinaigrette can be refrigerated separately for up to 2 days.)

why this recipe works Get your glow on with this good-for-you salad full of healthful, verdant ingredients like baby spinach, convenient frozen edamame, buttery avocado, and chopped pistachios, as well as shredded chicken. For our brighter spin on the often mayo-heavy green goddess dressing, we used yogurt, lemon, garlic, parsley, and, most importantly, tarragon, which gives the dressing its distinctive flavor. You will need an 8- or 10-inch skillet with a tight-fitting lid for this recipe. You could make Avocado Toast (page 189) with the leftover avocado. See page 20 for more information about storing avocados.

green goodness salad

total time 35 minutes

makes leftovers

1 (6- to 8-ounce) boneless, skinless chicken breast, trimmed

¼ teaspoon table salt, divided

¼ teaspoon pepper, divided

1 teaspoon oil

3 tablespoons water, divided

¼ teaspoon grated lemon zest plus 1½ teaspoons juice

1 small garlic clove, minced

¼ cup plain yogurt

2 tablespoons chopped fresh parsley or chives

1 teaspoon minced fresh tarragon

4 ounces (4 cups) baby spinach

¼ cup frozen shelled edamame, thawed and patted dry

½ ripe avocado, sliced thin

2 tablespoons chopped toasted pistachios

1 Place chicken on cutting board and cover with plastic wrap. Using meat pounder, gently pound chicken to even thickness. Pat chicken dry with paper towels and sprinkle with ⅛ teaspoon salt and ⅛ teaspoon pepper. Heat oil in 8- or 10-inch skillet over medium heat until just smoking. Brown chicken well on first side, about 3 minutes.

2 Flip chicken, add 2 tablespoons water, and cover skillet. Reduce heat to low and continue to cook until chicken registers 160 degrees, about 3 minutes. Transfer chicken to plate and let cool slightly. Using 2 forks, shred chicken into bite-size pieces.

3 Combine lemon zest and juice and garlic in medium bowl and let sit for 5 minutes. Stir in yogurt, remaining 1 tablespoon water, parsley, tarragon, remaining ⅛ teaspoon salt, and remaining ⅛ teaspoon pepper; set aside. (Dressing should be loose; adjust consistency with extra water as needed.)

4 Toss spinach with half of dressing to coat, then season with salt and pepper to taste. Top with shredded chicken, edamame, avocado, and pistachios and drizzle with remaining dressing. Serve. (Salad and dressing can be refrigerated separately for up to 2 days. Prep avocado just before serving.)

kitchen improv

use what you've got Substitute arugula or romaine for the spinach.

make it vegetarian Omit the chicken and double up on the edamame and pistachios.

make it easier Use your favorite creamy store-bought dressing and/or rotisserie chicken.

sriracha-lime tofu bowl

total time 45 minutes

makes leftovers

kitchen improv

use what you've got You could use Pan-Seared Shrimp (page 61) in place of or in addition to the tofu; any type of bell pepper would work here.

level up Sprinkle with chopped peanuts.

why this recipe works This slaw-like salad, sturdy enough to stand up to an overnight rest in the fridge, features napa cabbage, scallion, red bell pepper, and shredded carrot and delivers big flavor (and texture). But the real stunner here is the dressing: a spicy-sweet-sour combo of lime juice, honey, fish sauce, fresh ginger, sriracha, and oil. Tofu brings some protein, and pressing it to drain before browning in a hot nonstick skillet ensures each piece turns out creamy and custard-like, but with a slightly crispy exterior. A sprinkling of grassy cilantro and sweet, floral Thai basil provides herbaceous accents. You can make the Weeknight Miso Soup with Tofu (page 149) with the leftover tofu and the Skillet Roasted Cabbage with Mustard and Thyme (page 90) with the leftover cabbage.

7 ounces firm or extra-firm tofu, cut into ¾-inch pieces

⅛ teaspoon table salt

Pinch pepper

4 teaspoons oil, divided

1 tablespoon lime juice, plus lime wedges for serving

2½ teaspoons honey

2½ teaspoons fish sauce

1 teaspoon grated fresh ginger

1 teaspoon sriracha, plus extra for serving

½ head napa cabbage, cored and shredded (6 cups)

1 carrot, peeled and shredded

½ red bell pepper, stemmed, seeded, and sliced thin

¼ cup fresh cilantro leaves

¼ cup chopped fresh Thai basil, basil, or mint

1   Spread tofu over paper towel–lined baking sheet, let drain for 20 minutes, then gently press dry with paper towels. Sprinkle with salt and pepper.

2   Heat 1 teaspoon oil in 10-inch nonstick skillet over medium-high heat until shimmering. Add tofu and cook until lightly browned, 6 to 8 minutes; transfer to bowl.

3   Whisk lime juice, honey, fish sauce, ginger, and sriracha together in second bowl. While whisking constantly, slowly drizzle in remaining 1 tablespoon oil until combined. Toss cabbage with half of vinaigrette to coat, then season with salt and pepper to taste. Top with tofu, carrot, bell pepper, cilantro, and basil and drizzle with remaining vinaigrette. Serve with lime wedges and drizzle with extra sriracha. (Tofu, vinaigrette, and vegetables can be refrigerated separately for up to 2 days.)

why this recipe works This healthful take on hearty and satisfying fall comfort food features caramelized roasted sweet potatoes and crunchy, tart apples for a salad that fills you up and stores well. (Plus, it's made from long-lasting ingredients that store well themselves.) To carry the harvest theme all the way through, we whisked up a cider and caraway vinaigrette, toasting and cracking the seeds but leaving them whole for appealing texture. For toppings, feta cheese added briny contrast and dried cranberries contributed color and more tartness, helping you turn lunchtime into an autumnal affair. To crack caraway seeds, rock the bottom edge of a skillet over the toasted seeds on a cutting board until they crack.

harvest salad

total time 35 minutes

makes leftovers

1 small sweet potato (8 ounces), unpeeled, halved lengthwise, and sliced crosswise ¼ inch thick

1½ teaspoons plus 2 tablespoons oil, divided

¼ teaspoon table salt, divided

4 teaspoons cider vinegar

1 tablespoon water

2 teaspoons Dijon mustard

1 teaspoon caraway seeds, toasted and cracked

⅛ teaspoon pepper

4 ounces (4 cups) baby kale

½ Granny Smith apple, cored and cut into ½-inch pieces

2 ounces feta cheese or goat cheese, crumbled (½ cup)

2 tablespoons dried cranberries

1 Adjust oven rack to middle position and heat oven to 400 degrees. Toss potatoes, 1½ teaspoons oil, and ⅛ teaspoon salt together in bowl, then spread in even layer on aluminum foil–lined rimmed baking sheet. Roast until potatoes are beginning to brown, 15 to 20 minutes, flipping slices halfway through roasting. Let potatoes cool for 5 minutes then season with salt and pepper to taste. (Sweet potatoes can be refrigerated for up to 2 days.)

2 Whisk vinegar, water, mustard, caraway seeds, remaining ⅛ teaspoon salt, and pepper together in bowl. While whisking constantly, slowly drizzle in remaining 2 tablespoons oil until combined. Toss kale with half of vinaigrette to coat, then season with salt and pepper to taste. Top with sweet potatoes, apple, feta, and dried cranberries and drizzle with remaining dressing. Serve. (Salad and vinaigrette can be refrigerated separately for up to 2 days.)

kitchen improv

use what you've got Substitute leftover Roasted Butternut Squash (page 88), or Roasted Carrots (page 93) for the sweet potatoes; substitute blue cheese for the feta or goat cheese.

make it heartier You could add wild rice or any of your favorite grains (sees page 124–125) to this salad to bulk it up.

why this recipe works In Mexico, vendors sell a messy, cheesy, utterly delicious grilled corn from street carts—we love it so much that we turned it into a chowder (page 180). But the flavor combination also makes for a great salad, with charred kernels tossed with the garnishes. You get the ideal ratio of flavors and textures in every bite but with the convenience of a fork. We toasted corn on the stovetop, and then used the hot skillet to bloom chili powder and lightly cook minced garlic to temper its bite. We added lettuce, and dressed the salad with a creamy and tangy mixture of sour cream and lime juice. Letting the corn cool before adding chopped cilantro and spicy chiles preserved the bright colors and fresh flavors. You will need a 10-inch nonstick skillet with a tight-fitting lid for this recipe.

mexican street-corn salad

total time 35 minutes

makes leftovers

- 1 teaspoon grated lime zest plus 1 tablespoon juice, plus lime wedges for serving
- 1 tablespoon sour cream or Greek yogurt
- ½ jalapeño or serrano chile, stemmed, seeded, and sliced thin (optional)
- ¼ teaspoon table salt, divided
- 4 teaspoons oil, divided
- 3 ears corn, kernels cut from cobs, or 2¼ cups frozen

- 1 garlic clove, minced
- ½ teaspoon chili powder
- 2 ounces cotija cheese, queso fresco, or feta cheese, crumbled (½ cup), divided
- ⅓ cup coarsely chopped fresh cilantro, divided
- 1 romaine lettuce heart (6 ounces), chopped
- 1 radish, trimmed and sliced thin

1 Combine lime zest and juice, sour cream, jalapeño (if using), and ⅛ teaspoon salt in medium bowl; set aside. Heat 1 tablespoon oil in 10-inch nonstick skillet over medium-high heat until shimmering. Add corn and remaining ⅛ teaspoon salt, cover, and cook, without stirring, until corn is charred, 3 to 4 minutes. Remove skillet from heat and let sit, covered, until any popping subsides, about 1 minute. Transfer corn to bowl with sour cream mixture and wipe out skillet with paper towels.

2 Add remaining 1 teaspoon oil, garlic, and chili powder to now-empty skillet and cook over medium heat until fragrant, about 30 seconds; transfer to bowl with corn mixture and toss to combine. Let cool completely, about 10 minutes.

3 Add ⅓ cup cotija, ¼ cup cilantro, and romaine to corn mixture, toss to combine, and season with salt and pepper to taste. Top with radish, remaining cotija, and remaining cilantro. Serve with lime wedges. (Corn-dressing mixture and salad can be refrigerated separately for up to 2 days.)

kitchen improv

level up Crumbled tortilla chips or corn chips add nice texture to this salad.

make it heartier Top with shrimp (see page 61), shredded chicken, or thinly sliced steak.

SANDWICHES AND SALADS

219

why this recipe works Steak and arugula is a well-loved classic that seems to hit the spot no matter the time of day—brunch, lunch, or dinner, it's all on the table. We dressed ours up a bit with a potent combination of pomegranate molasses and ground allspice, which added warm spice notes that brought out the fruitiness of the pomegranate molasses. We sprinkled rich steak tips (once again our choice for their convenience) with additional allspice before searing them and slicing them thin. Fennel gave the salad crunch and subtle anise notes. Pomegranate seeds brought the whole salad together, while shaved Pecorino added a salty bite. You can make the Spanish-Style Fish Stew (page 177) with the leftover fennel from this recipe, and use extra pomegranate molasses in the Pomegranate-Glazed Salmon with Black-Eyed Peas and Walnuts (page 252). Steak tips, also known as flap meat, can be sold as whole steaks, cubes, or strips. To ensure evenly sized pieces, we prefer to buy whole steaks and cut them ourselves.

arugula and steak tip salad

total time 30 minutes

- 6 ounces sirloin steak tips, trimmed and cut into 2-inch pieces
- ½ teaspoon plus pinch ground allspice, divided
- ⅛ teaspoon table salt, divided
- ⅛ teaspoon pepper, divided
- 1 tablespoon oil, divided
- 1½ teaspoons pomegranate molasses
- ¾ teaspoon cider vinegar, white wine vinegar, or red wine vinegar

- 1 cup baby arugula or baby spinach
- ¼ small fennel bulb, stalks discarded, cored, and sliced thin
- 1 tablespoon pomegranate seeds
- 2 tablespoons shaved Pecorino Romano or Parmesan cheese

1 Pat steak tips dry with paper towels and sprinkle with ½ teaspoon allspice, pinch salt, and pinch pepper. Heat 1½ teaspoons oil in 10-inch skillet over medium heat until just smoking. Add steak tips and cook until well browned all over and register 120 to 125 degrees (for medium-rare), 7 to 10 minutes, flipping steak tips every minute and reducing heat if skillet begins to smoke. Transfer steak tips to cutting board and let rest for 5 minutes. Slice steak tips thin against grain.

2 Whisk remaining 1½ teaspoons oil, pomegranate molasses, vinegar, remaining pinch allspice, remaining pinch salt, and remaining pinch pepper together in medium bowl. Add arugula and fennel and toss to coat, then season with salt and pepper to taste. Sprinkle with pomegranate seeds and Pecorino and top with steak. Serve.

kitchen improv

use what you've got Substitute blue cheese, feta, or goat cheese for the Pecorino; use your favorite vinaigrette instead of the pomegranate vinaigrette.

level up Top with a runny egg (see page 139) and/or a sprinkle of chopped toasted walnuts (see page 15).

make it fruity Try sliced pear, segmented orange, or sliced apple in place of pomegranate seeds.

SANDWICHES AND SALADS

221

seared scallop salad

with snap peas and radishes

total time 30 minutes

why this recipe works Scallops often conjure up images of candlelit white tablecloth dinners, the mollusks served with a browned butter sauce atop a fussy puree. But there's no need to save scallops for a special occasion—purchasing them by the piece (rather than the pound) at the fish counter makes them easy to portion for one. For a fresh preparation, we like this weeknight-friendly but still-special main dish salad. And as fancy as this seafood and snap pea salad may look, it comes together in a, well, snap. Turn on your stove just briefly for the quick-cooking scallops; we found that they should be browned on only one side to prevent overcooking, and they take just a few seconds once flipped to cook through. These morsels are a light-yet-buttery companion to a salad bursting with fresh, crunchy spring vegetables like sweet sugar snap peas and thinly sliced peppery radishes brightened with a punchy Dijon dressing. We recommend buying "dry" scallops, which don't have chemical additives and taste better than "wet." Dry scallops will look ivory or pinkish; wet scallops are bright white.

6 ounces large sea scallops, tendons removed

⅛ teaspoon table salt

Pinch pepper

2 tablespoons oil, divided

1½ teaspoons red wine vinegar

¼ teaspoon Dijon mustard

3 ounces sugar snap peas, strings removed, halved crosswise

2 ounces (2 cups) mesclun

2 radishes, trimmed and sliced thin

1 small shallot, sliced thin

kitchen improv

use what you've got You can use Pan-Seared Shrimp (page 61) in place of the scallops in this recipe; substitute arugula for the mesclun.

make it easier Use your favorite store-bought vinaigrette.

1 Place scallops on large plate lined with clean dish towel. Place second clean dish towel on top of scallops and press gently on towel to blot liquid. Let scallops sit at room temperature for 10 minutes while towels absorb moisture.

2 Sprinkle scallops with salt and pepper. Heat 1 tablespoon oil in 8- or 10-inch nonstick skillet over medium heat until just smoking. Add scallops in single layer, flat side down, and cook, without moving, until well browned, 1½ to 2 minutes. Flip scallops and continue to cook until sides of scallops are firm and centers are opaque, 30 to 90 seconds (remove smaller scallops as they finish cooking). Transfer scallops to plate.

3 Combine vinegar and mustard in large bowl. Whisking constantly, drizzle remaining 1 tablespoon oil into vinegar mixture in slow, steady stream. Add snap peas, mesclun, radishes, and shallot and gently toss to coat. Season with salt and pepper to taste. Arrange scallops over salad. Serve.

why this recipe works Tuna salad is a good go-to for a quick pantry-friendly meal (see page 207). But we don't always want the traditional creamy deli-style version; this salad shows the versatility of tuna with fresh, bright flavors and a lemon vinaigrette. We bypassed the mayo and instead opened a jar of oil-packed sun-dried tomatoes. Their concentrated sweetness enhanced the plain canned tuna, but we also used some of the oil from the jar to prepare the vinaigrette and imbue every bite of our salad with warm Mediterranean flavor. Meaty cannellini beans and briny olives over a bed of tender Bibb lettuce brought salty, savory balance to the tart dressing. And what is tuna salad without some crisp celery? For prominent celery flavor we doubled up and used both the celery ribs and the leaves. You can use extra sun-dried tomatoes in the Garam Masala Pork Chop with Couscous and Spinach (page 247) or Italian Pasta Salad (page 226).

tuscan tuna salad bowl

total time 20 minutes

- 1 small shallot, sliced thin
- 1 small garlic clove, minced
- 1 teaspoon Dijon mustard
- ¾ teaspoon lemon juice
- ⅛ teaspoon table salt
- ⅛ teaspoon pepper
- 1 tablespoon oil-packed sun-dried tomatoes, minced, plus 1½ tablespoons sun-dried tomato oil
- 1 (5-ounce) can solid white tuna in water, drained and flaked
- ¼ head Bibb lettuce (2 ounces), torn into 1-inch pieces
- ¼ cup canned cannellini beans, rinsed
- 1 celery rib, sliced thin on bias, plus 2 tablespoons celery leaves
- 2 tablespoons thinly sliced pitted kalamata olives

1 Whisk shallot, garlic, mustard, lemon juice, salt, and pepper together in bowl. While whisking constantly, slowly drizzle in sun-dried tomato oil until combined; set aside for 5 minutes.

2 Toss sun-dried tomatoes and tuna with ½ tablespoon vinaigrette to coat. In separate bowl, toss lettuce with ½ tablespoon vinaigrette to coat, then season with salt and pepper to taste. Top with tuna mixture, beans, sliced celery, and olives. Drizzle with remaining 1 tablespoon vinaigrette and sprinkle with celery leaves. Serve.

kitchen improv

use what you've got Chickpeas would work in place of the cannellini beans.

level up Sprinkle a handful of pomegranate seeds or pine nuts over the top for extra crunch.

italian pasta salad

total time 20 minutes

makes leftovers

why this recipe works Pasta salad is a crowd-pleasing, easily portable dish that checks all the cheesy, meaty, tangy, and carb-y boxes—if you've ever been to a graduation party or potluck, you've probably eaten your fair share. But it's also perfect for a casual solo meal (and is a great excuse to clean out your fridge). Even better, it improves the longer it sits and the flavors have the chance to mingle—certainly something to look forward to for lunch the next day. Here we were inspired by the cured meats and vegetables of Italian antipasto platters, but the beauty of this salad is that it's easy to switch up depending on what you have on hand. The only constant is slightly overcooking the pasta so it maintains its tender texture as it firms up when it cools. We prefer a small, individually packaged, dry Italian-style salami such as Genoa or soppressata, but unsliced deli salami can be used. You can use extra pepperoncini instead of pickles in the Packable Pita Sandwich (page 195).

6 ounces fusilli	½ cup chopped fresh basil
Table salt for cooking pasta	4 ounces fresh mozzarella cheese, chopped coarse and patted dry
2 tablespoons oil	
1 garlic clove, minced	2 ounces salami, chopped coarse
⅛ teaspoon red pepper flakes	
½ cup pepperoncini, stemmed, plus 1 tablespoon brine	¼ cup oil-packed sun-dried tomatoes, sliced thin
	¼ cup pitted kalamata olives, quartered
1 cup baby arugula	

kitchen improv

use what you've got Substitute any short pasta for the fusilli; substitute baby kale or baby spinach for the arugula.

level up If you've got them, capers and anchovies would give the pasta salad a briny boost; toasted pine nuts or walnuts (see page 15) would add crunch.

make it vegetarian Omit the salami and add chickpeas.

make it greek Substitute crumbled feta for the mozzarella, shredded chicken for the salami, and chopped dill for the basil, and add cucumbers and red onion.

1 Bring 2 quarts water to boil in large saucepan. Add pasta and 1½ teaspoons salt and cook, stirring often, until pasta is tender throughout, 2 to 3 minutes past al dente. Drain pasta and rinse under cold water until chilled. Drain well and transfer to bowl.

2 Meanwhile, combine oil, garlic, and pepper flakes in liquid measuring cup. Cover and microwave until bubbling and fragrant, 30 to 60 seconds; set aside. Slice half of pepperoncini into thin rings and set aside. Mince remaining pepperoncini then add to dressing along with pepperoncini brine.

3 Add dressing to pasta and toss to combine. Add arugula, basil, mozzarella, salami, sun-dried tomatoes, olives, and reserved pepperoncini and toss well. Season with salt and pepper to taste. Serve. (Salad, arugula, and basil can be refrigerated separately for up to 2 days.)

warm spiced couscous salad

total time 35 minutes

makes leftovers

why this recipe works Grain salads are a heartier alternative to lettuce-based ones, but often require more time and work. Not so here. In this bright-yet-smoky, sweet-yet-tart riff on a grain salad, we used quick-cooking pearl couscous and toasted it with chorizo and a carrot, then stirred in broth with some smoked paprika and cumin. We added pantry-friendly chickpeas for heft, and parsley (or cilantro) added a punch of freshness. Dried fruit gave additional textural contrast as well as a bit of sweetness, and a squeeze of lemon juice brightened everything up. You can make the Spanish-Style Fish Stew (page 177) with the leftover chorizo from this recipe, and use leftover pearl couscous in place of barley in the Beef and Barley Soup (page 160).

½ cup pearl couscous

3 ounces Spanish-style chorizo, cut into ½-inch pieces

1 carrot, peeled and chopped

4 teaspoons oil, divided

⅛ teaspoon table salt

⅔ cup chicken or vegetable broth

½ teaspoon smoked paprika

¼ teaspoon ground cumin

1 cup canned chickpeas, rinsed and patted dry

⅓ cup chopped fresh parsley or cilantro

¼ cup raisins, chopped dried apricots, chopped dates, or chopped dried figs

2 teaspoons lemon juice plus lemon wedges for serving

kitchen improv

level up Sprinkle with pomegranate seeds.

make it heartier Baby spinach or baby arugula would be a nice addition.

make it vegetarian Omit the chorizo, add extra oil as needed in step 1, use vegetable broth, and double the amount of chickpeas.

1 Combine couscous, chorizo, carrot, 1 teaspoon oil, and salt in medium saucepan and cook over medium heat, stirring frequently, until half of grains are golden, about 5 minutes. Stir in broth, paprika, and cumin. Bring to simmer, cover, and simmer over low heat, stirring occasionally, until broth is absorbed, 10 to 15 minutes. Let sit off heat, covered, for 3 minutes.

2 Stir in chickpeas, parsley, raisins, lemon juice, and remaining 1 tablespoon oil. Season with salt and pepper to taste. Serve with lemon wedges. (Salad can be refrigerated for up to 2 days.)

why this recipe works Though actually a seed, quinoa is often referred to as a "supergrain" because it's a nutritionally complete protein (translation: it'll keep you full well past lunchtime). We started by using our pilaf method to cook the grains until just tender. Then we spread the cooked quinoa out on a plate to cool it to room temperature quickly, so it wouldn't wilt the arugula. Crisp, sweet bell pepper, jalapeño, and fresh cilantro provided a sweet and spicy contrast to the hearty, chewy quinoa. We tossed the vegetables and grains with a bright dressing flavored with lime juice, mustard, garlic, and cumin. Feta cheese brought a briny, creamy element, and roasted pepitas added crunch. We like the convenience of prewashed quinoa; rinsing removes the quinoa's bitter protective coating (called saponin). If you buy unwashed quinoa, rinse it and pat it dry.

quinoa salad
with red bell pepper and cilantro

total time 55 minutes

makes leftovers

- ⅔ cup prewashed white quinoa
- 1 cup water
- ⅛ teaspoon table salt
- 2 teaspoons lime juice
- 1 teaspoon Dijon mustard
- 1 small garlic clove, minced
- ¼ teaspoon ground cumin
- 2 tablespoons oil
- 1 cup baby arugula
- 1 small red bell pepper, stemmed, seeded, and chopped fine
- 1 small jalapeño chile, stemmed, seeded, and minced
- 1 ounce feta cheese, crumbled (¼ cup)
- 2 tablespoons roasted pepitas
- 2 tablespoons minced fresh cilantro

1 Toast quinoa in small saucepan over medium heat, stirring often, until lightly toasted and aromatic, about 5 minutes. Stir in water and salt and bring to simmer. Reduce heat to low, cover, and simmer until quinoa has absorbed most of water and is just tender, 12 to 14 minutes. Spread quinoa on plate lined with paper towels and let cool for about 20 minutes.

2 Whisk lime juice, mustard, garlic, and cumin together in medium bowl. While whisking constantly, slowly drizzle in oil until combined. Add cooled quinoa, arugula, bell pepper, jalapeño, feta, pepitas, and cilantro and toss to coat. Serve. (Salad can be refrigerated for up to 2 days.)

kitchen improv

use what you've got Any type of bell pepper would work here; substitute baby spinach for the arugula and roasted sunflower seeds or walnuts for the pepitas.

level up Finish with avocado, crumbled cheese, and/or crushed tortilla chips.

make it heartier Stir in canned beans or shredded chicken.

chilled soba noodle salad

total time 20 minutes

why this recipe works Chewy, nutty soba noodles can be slurped up along with hot broth, but we love them in this casual noodle salad that is fleshed out with crisp vegetables and a flavorful miso-based dressing that clings to the noodles. Cooking the noodles until they were tender but still resilient, and rinsing them under cold running water removed excess starch and prevented sticking. We cut a mix of vegetables into varying sizes so they'd incorporate nicely into the noodles while adding crunch and color. Strips of toasted nori added more texture and a subtle briny taste. And like our Italian Pasta Salad (page 226), this salad is easily customizable—bulk it up with whatever proteins you have on hand, and substitute (or add in) any thinly sliced crunchy vegetables you need to use up.

2 ounces dried soba noodles

1 teaspoon oil (optional)

½ (8-inch square) sheet nori (optional)

1½ teaspoons toasted sesame oil

¾ teaspoon white, yellow, red, or brown miso

¾ teaspoon mirin

¾ teaspoon water

¾ teaspoon sesame seeds

¼ teaspoon grated fresh ginger

⅛ teaspoon red pepper flakes

¼ English cucumber, quartered lengthwise, seeded, and sliced thin on bias

1 ounce snow peas, strings removed, cut lengthwise into matchsticks

1 radish, trimmed, halved, and sliced thin

1 scallion, sliced thin on bias

kitchen improv

use what you've got Substitute any thinly sliced crunchy vegetable like celery or bell pepper for the radish (or add in); substitute pretoasted seaweed snacks for the toasted nori strips.

level up Drizzle the salad with chili oil or sriracha.

make it heartier Add salmon, shrimp, tofu, or chicken to make this a heartier meal.

1   Bring 2 quarts water to boil in large saucepan. Add noodles and cook, stirring often, until cooked through but still retaining some chew. Drain and rinse under cold water until chilled. Drain well.

2   Meanwhile, if using nori, heat oil in 8- or 10-inch nonstick skillet over medium heat until just shimmering. Using paper towels, wipe out oil, leaving thin film in pan. Place nori sheet in skillet and cook until fragrant and shrunken slightly, about 3 minutes, flipping every 30 seconds. Remove and let cool slightly; then, using scissors, cut nori into 1-inch strips.

3   Combine sesame oil, miso, mirin, water, sesame seeds, ginger, and pepper flakes in bowl and whisk until smooth. Add drained noodles to dressing and toss to combine. Add cucumber, snow peas, radish, scallion, and nori, if using, and toss well to evenly distribute. Season with salt to taste, and serve.

one-pan dinners

No more keeping tabs on multiple pots and pans on the stove—enjoy streamlined meals in whatever form you're after, whether it's cheesy, saucy comfort food, or bright, fresh flavors. Make just enough for dinner (no more excessive leftovers) or choose a recipe that makes an extra serving. Then, follow our tips on packing lunch and reheating leftovers at the end of the chapter, so the next day is just as good as the first. And when you're solo you're always stuck with cleanup—make it easier on yourself. With these one-pan meals, you'll never dread dish duty again.

skillet-roasted chicken and potatoes

total time 1 hour

makes leftovers

why this recipe works No need to dig out a heavy roasting pan when you're looking for comfort in the form of crispy-skinned chicken and buttery roasted potatoes. For this scaled-down recipe, we used leg quarters—arguably the most succulent part of a roast chicken—and started by browning them skin side down in a skillet to jump-start the crisping of the skin. Next, we made a "roasting rack" for the chicken out of sliced Yukon Gold potatoes and halved shallots. This put the vegetables in contact with the hot skillet so they could get supremely golden brown while simultaneously elevating the chicken so the drippings could work their way into the potatoes, infusing the spuds with deep, savory flavor. For a final flourish, we combined parsley, lemon zest, and garlic for an easy gremolata, a mixture Italian cooks use to brighten roasted meats. Some leg quarters are sold with the backbone attached. Be sure to remove it before cooking.

- 2 (10-ounce) chicken leg quarters, trimmed
- 1 teaspoon minced fresh thyme
- ¾ teaspoon plus pinch table salt, divided
- ½ teaspoon pepper, divided
- 2 Yukon Gold potatoes (1 pound), peeled and sliced into ½-inch-thick rounds
- 2 shallots, halved through root end
- 2 tablespoons oil, divided
- 1 tablespoon chopped fresh parsley, chives, or tarragon
- ½ teaspoon grated lemon zest, plus lemon wedges for serving
- ½ teaspoon minced garlic

kitchen improv

use what you've got Substitute two bone-in split chicken breasts (cook to 160 degrees) for the leg quarters.

spice it up Rub the chicken with a store-bought (sugar-free) spice rub or any of our spice rubs from page 72.

get saucy Omit the parsley, lemon zest, and garlic and instead drizzle with a sauce from pages 68–69.

1 Adjust oven rack to middle position and heat oven to 400 degrees. Pat chicken dry with paper towels and sprinkle with thyme, ½ teaspoon salt, and ¼ teaspoon pepper. Toss potatoes, shallots, 1 tablespoon oil, ¼ teaspoon salt, and remaining ¼ teaspoon pepper together in bowl. Combine parsley, lemon zest, garlic, and remaining pinch salt in separate bowl; set aside.

2 Heat remaining 1 tablespoon oil in 12-inch ovensafe nonstick skillet over medium heat until shimmering. Add chicken, skin side down, and cook until well browned, about 5 minutes. Transfer chicken to plate, skin side up.

3 Place potatoes and shallots in single layer in now-empty skillet. Cook over medium heat, without moving vegetables, until bottoms of potatoes are golden brown, about 5 minutes. Place chicken, skin side up, on top of vegetables and transfer skillet to oven. Roast until chicken registers 175 degrees and potatoes are tender, about 30 minutes. Sprinkle with parsley mixture. Serve with lemon wedges. (Chicken, vegetables, and parsley mixture can be refrigerated for up to 2 days.)

weeknight chicken cacciatore

total time 45 minutes

makes leftovers

why this recipe works Long-simmering braises, like chicken cacciatore (also called "hunter-style chicken") aren't generally our go-to weeknight recipes when cooking for ourselves. But this isn't your nonna's recipe; we've adapted the classic Italian American dish of mushrooms, chicken, and tomatoes to come together quickly in one skillet. To build flavor in the much faster cooking time, we seared quick-cooking chicken breasts, developing tasty bits of fond that would add depth to our sauce. Adding a single sliced portobello mushroom cap, red bell pepper, shallot, and a can of diced tomatoes created a savory sauce and kept the chicken tender and moist. Serve this with crusty bread today, and the leftovers over pasta or even mashed potatoes (see page 106) to sop up every last drop of the robust, hearty sauce. You will need a 12-inch nonstick skillet with a tight-fitting lid for this recipe.

- 2 (6- to 8-ounce) boneless, skinless chicken breasts, trimmed
- ¼ teaspoon plus ⅛ teaspoon table salt, divided
- ¼ teaspoon plus ⅛ teaspoon pepper, divided
- 4 teaspoons oil, divided
- 1 portobello mushroom cap (2 ounces), gills removed, sliced ½-inch thick
- 1 small red bell pepper, stemmed, seeded, and cut into ½-inch-wide strips
- 1 shallot, sliced thin
- 2 garlic cloves, minced
- 1 teaspoon minced fresh rosemary, marjoram, oregano, sage, or thyme
- 1 (14.5-ounce) can diced tomatoes

kitchen improv

use what you've got Substitute any mushroom you have on hand for the portobello.

level up Sprinkle the finished dish with grated Parmesan and/or garlic chips (see page 256).

make it meatier Brown pancetta or bacon in the skillet and cook the chicken in the rendered fat (omit the oil). Sprinkle the cooked pancetta or bacon over the finished dish.

1 Place chicken on cutting board and cover with plastic wrap. Using meat pounder, gently pound chicken to even thickness. Pat chicken dry with paper towels and sprinkle with ¼ teaspoon salt and ¼ teaspoon pepper. Heat 2 teaspoons oil in 12-inch nonstick skillet over medium heat until just smoking. Add chicken and cook until well browned on first side, about 4 minutes. Transfer chicken to plate, browned side up.

2 Heat remaining 2 teaspoons oil in now-empty skillet over medium heat until shimmering. Add mushroom, bell pepper, shallot, remaining ⅛ teaspoon salt, and remaining ⅛ teaspoon pepper and cook, stirring occasionally, until mushrooms are lightly browned, 6 to 7 minutes.

3 Stir in garlic and rosemary and cook until fragrant, about 30 seconds. Stir in tomatoes and their juice, scraping up any browned bits. Bring to simmer, cover, and cook for 5 minutes, stirring occasionally. Nestle chicken, browned side up, into sauce and bring to simmer. Cover skillet and cook until chicken registers 160 degrees and sauce has thickened slightly, 6 to 8 minutes. Serve. (Chicken and sauce can be refrigerated for up to 2 days.)

why this recipe works While making hash for a crowd might mean endless chopping, all it takes is one single potato to get this scaled-down version going. To drastically cut down the cooking time, we microwaved the cut-up potato to give it a head start. Store-bought chicken sausage is filled with flavors and spices, so we didn't have to add many ingredients to the dish by way of seasonings. Brussels sprouts (it's easy to buy just a few) brought together a classic combination of cabbage and potatoes. To ensure everything was evenly cooked, we sautéed each component in stages, then added it all back to the pan, covered it to steam briefly, and then uncovered it and cooked until the edges were crispy. This not only gave a savory depth to the dish, but also made the mixture more cohesive. Then we cleared a small well in the center of the skillet and cracked an egg in the middle for a poached/fried hybrid that delivered a luxuriously oozy yolk (if desired). You will need an 8- or 10- inch nonstick skillet with a tight-fitting lid for this recipe.

chicken sausage hash

total time 40 minutes

1 small Yukon Gold potato, peeled and cut into ½-inch pieces

1 tablespoon oil, divided

⅛ teaspoon table salt, divided

⅛ teaspoon pepper, divided

4 ounces chicken sausage, casing removed

2 ounces brussels sprouts, trimmed and quartered

1 tablespoon water

1 large egg

1 Toss potato, 1 teaspoon oil, pinch salt, and pinch pepper together in bowl. Cover and microwave until tender, 3 to 5 minutes, stirring once halfway through microwaving; set aside. Heat 1 teaspoon oil in 8- or 10-inch nonstick skillet over medium heat until shimmering. Add sausage and cook, breaking up meat with wooden spoon, until sausage is lightly browned, 3 to 5 minutes; add sausage to bowl with potatoes.

2 Heat remaining 1 teaspoon oil in now-empty skillet over medium heat until shimmering. Add brussels sprouts and cook, stirring occasionally, until browned, 3 to 5 minutes. Stir in water and sausage-potato mixture. Reduce heat to medium-low, cover, and cook until brussels sprouts are tender, 2 minutes longer, stirring once halfway through. Flip hash, 1 scoop at a time, then lightly repack hash into pan. Repeat flipping and repacking hash every minute until potatoes are well browned, about 4 minutes.

3 Off heat, make one shallow well in hash with back of spoon. Break egg into well in hash, sprinkle with remaining pinch salt and remaining pinch pepper, then cover skillet and place over medium-low heat. Cook to desired doneness: 4 to 5 minutes for runny yolks or 6 to 7 minutes for set yolks. Season with salt and pepper to taste and serve.

kitchen improv

use what you've got You can use any sausage in place of the chicken sausage; substitute half of a sweet potato or any squash you have on hand for the Yukon Gold and/or sliced cabbage or thinly sliced fennel in place of the brussels sprouts.

level up Sprinkle with fresh herbs, crumbled cheese, and/or a drizzle of your favorite hot sauce or herb sauce (see pages 68–69).

spice-rubbed flank steak

with celery root and lime yogurt sauce

total time 40 minutes

makes leftovers

why this recipe works For this subtly sweet, smoky, and spiced sheet pan dinner, we roasted earthy celery root along with flank steak that we rubbed with chili powder and sugar. We removed the cooked steak, and then added scallions and tossed the vegetables in the juices on the sheet, ensuring the flavor from the steak permeated each element. A lime-spiked yogurt sauce added creamy brightness. Leftovers are perfect on a salad or folded into a taco the next day.

- ¼ cup plain yogurt
- 2 tablespoons minced fresh cilantro, divided
- ½ teaspoon grated lime zest plus 2 teaspoons juice
- ¾ teaspoon table salt, divided
- 1 celery root (14 ounces), peeled, halved, and sliced ¼-inch thick
- 1 tablespoon plus ¼ teaspoon oil, divided
- ¼ teaspoon plus pinch pepper, divided
- 1 (12-ounce) flank steak, 1 inch thick, trimmed
- 1 tablespoon chili powder
- 2 teaspoons packed brown sugar
- 6 scallions, trimmed
- 2 tablespoons roasted pepitas

kitchen improv

use what you've got Substitute carrots, a turnip, a sweet potato, or a potato for the celery root, adjusting cooking times as necessary; substitute sunflower seeds for the pepitas; sour cream would also work instead of the yogurt.

1   Adjust oven rack to upper-middle position and heat oven to 475 degrees. Line rimmed baking sheet with aluminum foil and place sheet on rack. Whisk yogurt, 1 tablespoon cilantro, lime zest and juice, and ⅛ teaspoon salt together in bowl; set aside.

2   Toss celery root, 1 tablespoon oil, ¼ teaspoon salt, and ¼ teaspoon pepper together in bowl then arrange in single layer on one side of hot sheet. Roast celery root until just tender and spotty brown, about 10 minutes.

3   Pat steak dry with paper towels and sprinkle with chili powder, sugar, and ¼ teaspoon salt. Lay steak on opposite side of hot sheet and roast until steak registers 120 to 125 degrees (for medium-rare), about 10 minutes.

4   Transfer steak to cutting board, tent loosely with aluminum foil, and let rest for 5 minutes. Meanwhile, toss scallions with remaining ¼ teaspoon oil, remaining ⅛ teaspoon salt, and remaining pinch pepper. Add to pan, toss with celery root and any accumulated juice, and redistribute in even layer. Return to oven and roast until celery root is tender and scallions begin to wilt, about 5 minutes.

5   Slice steak thin against grain. Transfer to plate with celery root and scallions. Drizzle with yogurt sauce and sprinkle with pepitas and remaining 1 tablespoon cilantro. Serve. (Steak, vegetables, yogurt sauce, and garnishes can be refrigerated separately for up to 2 days.)

beef and broccoli stir-fry

total time 40 minutes

makes leftovers

why this recipe works Why order takeout when you can make a homemade version of this Chinese restaurant favorite before delivery even arrives? For our sauce, we relied on a few key Asian flavor boosters: Oyster sauce gave us the perfect thick, clingy texture, and sweet chili sauce offered complex flavor with its sweet, spicy, and bright notes. Using toasted sesame oil to quickly marinate the beef added a layer of nutty flavor and richness, and we also added some toasted sesame oil to the sauce to ensure its rich flavor shone through in the final dish. Thin flank steak cooked quickly and offered big, beefy flavor, and crunchy vegetables contributed color and fresh brightness. You will need a 12-inch nonstick skillet with a tight-fitting lid for this recipe. Serve with rice (see page 119). See Roasted Broccoli with Garlic (page 83) for ideas for using up any extra broccoli.

½ cup water, divided

¼ cup Asian sweet chili sauce

2 tablespoons oyster sauce

2 tablespoons toasted sesame oil, divided

1 (12-ounce) flank steak, trimmed and sliced thin against grain

6 ounces broccoli florets, cut into 1-inch pieces

1 small red bell pepper, stemmed, seeded, and sliced thin

2 scallions, white parts minced, green parts sliced thin

kitchen improv

use what you've got Any type of bell pepper would work here.

make it vegetarian Substitute tempeh or tofu for the beef and mushroom oyster sauce for the oyster sauce.

1 Whisk ¼ cup water, chili sauce, oyster sauce, and 1 tablespoon sesame oil together in bowl. Combine 1 tablespoon chili sauce mixture, steak, and remaining 1 tablespoon sesame oil in separate bowl, then cover and let sit for 10 minutes.

2 Combine broccoli, bell pepper, and remaining ¼ cup water in 12-inch nonstick skillet, cover, and cook over high heat until vegetables begin to soften, about 3 minutes. Uncover and continue to cook until water has evaporated and vegetables are crisp-tender, about 2 minutes; transfer to clean bowl.

3 Add beef mixture to now-empty skillet, breaking up any clumps, and cook over high heat until lightly browned all over, about 6 minutes. Push beef to sides of skillet. Add scallion whites and cook, mashing whites into skillet, until fragrant, 15 to 30 seconds. Stir beef into scallion whites.

4 Stir in cooked vegetable mixture. Whisk sauce to recombine, then add to skillet. Cook, stirring constantly, until sauce is thickened, about 1 minute. Sprinkle with scallion greens. Serve. (Stir-fry can be refrigerated for up to 2 days.)

why this recipe works When you want to ramp up the flavor of a dish without using (or buying) every spice on the shelf, look to spice blends like garam masala, an Indian mix of warm spices—including cinnamon, cumin, coriander, and cardamom—all in one jar. Rubbed on a pork chop, garam masala added aroma and flavor to the mild pork, as well as to the couscous that we cooked in the same skillet while the pork chop rested. Pantry-friendly power ingredient sun-dried tomatoes added bites of sweet, intense tomato flavor to counter the savory pork and couscous, and we even used the oil to cook the chop. Tender spinach brought freshness and color (and a dose of veggies). You will need a 10-inch nonstick skillet with a tight-fitting lid for this recipe. If you do not have enough oil from your sun-dried tomatoes to make 1 tablespoon, you can use a cooking oil to make up the difference.

garam masala pork chop
with couscous and spinach

total time 30 minutes

- 1 (8- to 10-ounce) bone-in pork rib chop, ¾ to 1 inch thick, trimmed
- ½ teaspoon garam masala
- ¼ teaspoon table salt, divided
- ⅛ teaspoon plus pinch pepper, divided
- 1 tablespoon chopped oil-packed sun-dried tomatoes plus 1 tablespoon sun-dried tomato oil
- ⅓ cup couscous
- 1 cup baby spinach
- 1 garlic clove, minced
- ½ cup water

1 Pat chop dry with paper towels and sprinkle with garam masala, ⅛ teaspoon salt, and ⅛ teaspoon pepper. Heat sun-dried tomato oil in 10-inch nonstick skillet over medium heat until just smoking. Add chop and cook until it's well browned all over and registers 140 degrees, 8 to 10 minutes, flipping chop occasionally and reducing heat if skillet begins to smoke. Transfer to plate and let rest for 5 minutes.

2 While chop rests, toast couscous in now-empty skillet over medium heat for 1 minute. Stir in spinach and continue to cook until couscous is just beginning to brown and spinach has wilted, about 3 minutes. Stir in sun-dried tomatoes and garlic and cook until fragrant, about 30 seconds. Stir in water, remaining ⅛ teaspoon salt, and remaining pinch pepper, cover, and remove skillet from heat. Let sit until couscous is tender, about 5 minutes. Fluff grains with fork and season with salt and pepper to taste. Serve with pork.

kitchen improv

use what you've got Bone-in center or blade-cut chops as well as boneless pork chops will work here; instead of sun-dried tomatoes, use other pantry-friendly staples like chopped roasted red peppers, olives, or artichoke hearts and their oil.

level up To couscous, add chopped toasted nuts, chopped fresh herbs (parsley, mint, cilantro, chives, or scallions), and/or crumbled or shaved cheese (feta, goat, or Parmesan).

crispy sesame pork chops

with wilted napa cabbage salad

total time 40 minutes

why this recipe works For pan-fried crispy pork chops that are a far cry from the Shake 'n Bake norm, we coated them in panko mixed with sesame seeds, which added nutty flavor and extra crunch. For a slaw-like salad, we briefly wilted napa cabbage to soften it slightly while the heat allowed the flavors of garlic and ginger to bloom. Don't let the pork chops drain on the paper towels for longer than 30 seconds, or the heat will steam the crust and make it soggy. Serve with lime wedges. You can make Skillet-Roasted Cabbage with Mustard and Thyme (page 90) with the extra cabbage.

2 tablespoons all-purpose flour

1 large egg

5 tablespoons panko bread crumbs

3 tablespoons sesame seeds

2 (3-ounce) boneless pork chops, ½ to ¾ inch thick, trimmed

⅛ teaspoon table salt

Pinch pepper

1 tablespoon oil

¾ teaspoon toasted sesame oil

1 garlic clove, minced

¼ teaspoon grated fresh ginger or pinch ground ginger

¼ small head napa cabbage, cored and shredded (2 cups)

1 carrot, peeled and shredded

1½ teaspoons rice vinegar, plus extra for seasoning

⅓ cup oil for frying

kitchen improv

use what you've got Omit the sesame seeds and substitute extra panko.

get saucy Drizzle everything with sriracha or Asian chili-garlic sauce; serve with a swipe of hoisin.

make it heartier You could add any quick-cooking vegetable to this salad, like baby spinach, green beans, and/or bell pepper. Substitute savoy cabbage for the napa cabbage.

1   Set wire rack in rimmed baking sheet. Spread flour in shallow dish. Beat egg in second shallow dish. Combine panko and sesame seeds in third shallow dish.

2   Pat chops dry with paper towels and sprinkle with salt and pepper. Working with 1 chop at a time, dredge chop in flour, dip in egg, then coat with panko mixture, pressing gently to adhere; transfer to prepared rack.

3   Heat 1 tablespoon oil and sesame oil in 12-inch nonstick skillet over medium heat until shimmering. Add garlic and ginger and cook until fragrant, about 30 seconds. Stir in cabbage and carrot and cook until just wilted, about 1 minute. Off heat, add rice vinegar and toss to combine. Transfer to serving bowl and season with salt, pepper, and extra vinegar to taste. Wipe out skillet with paper towels.

4   Line large plate with triple layer of paper towels. Heat ⅓ cup oil in now-empty skillet over medium-high heat until shimmering. Carefully lay chops in skillet and cook until golden brown and crisp on both sides and meat registers 140 degrees, 2 to 5 minutes per side. Drain chops briefly on paper towel–lined plate. Serve with cabbage salad.

why this recipe works Fennel-studded Italian sausage is often used as a flavoring element, but the links are perfect to keep in the freezer (or, better yet, bought just a few at a time) for the center of a hearty, satisfying meal. In this sheet pan dinner, crispy yet tender broccoli rabe and caramelized sweet potato slices (made from a single sweet potato) are slathered with a tangy and rich mustard-chive butter, which offsets broccoli rabe's bitter edge with its richness. The leaves of the broccoli rabe crisp up like chips in the oven, creating a perfect foil for the soft sweet potato, only made better by the textural pops of mustard seeds in the compound butter. There's hardly any prep work involved—you don't even have to peel the sweet potato. The weight of individual sausage links can vary; you could add more to suit your appetite. See Sweet Potato–Bacon Wrap on page 192 and Broiled Broccoli Rabe on page 85 for ideas for using up any extra sweet potato and broccoli rabe. Melt the extra compound butter over a steak (see page 45) or dollop on a baked potato (see page 105).

sheet pan sausages

with sweet potatoes, broccoli rabe, and mustard-chive butter

total time 35 minutes

1 sweet potato, unpeeled, halved lengthwise, and sliced ½ inch thick

1 tablespoon oil, divided

¼ teaspoon table salt, divided

¼ teaspoon pepper, divided

4 ounces broccoli rabe, trimmed and cut into 1½-inch pieces

6 ounces sweet Italian sausage

2 tablespoons Mustard-Chive Compound Butter (page 71), softened

1 Adjust oven rack to lowest position and heat oven to 450 degrees. Line rimmed baking sheet with aluminum foil and place sheet on rack.

2 Toss sweet potato, 1 teaspoon oil, ⅛ teaspoon salt, and ⅛ teaspoon pepper together in bowl then arrange in single layer over one-third of hot sheet. Toss broccoli rabe, remaining 2 teaspoons oil, remaining ⅛ teaspoon salt, and remaining ⅛ teaspoon pepper in now-empty bowl then arrange broccoli rabe in single layer over opposite third of hot sheet. Place sausage in center of hot sheet then roast until sausage registers 160 degrees and broccoli rabe stems are tender, 10 to 15 minutes.

3 Remove sheet from oven and transfer sausage and broccoli rabe to plate; tent loosely with foil to keep warm. Return sheet with sweet potato to oven and continue to roast until sweet potato is tender and golden brown, 5 to 7 minutes. Transfer sweet potato to plate with broccoli rabe then dollop with mustard butter. Serve.

kitchen improv

use what you've got You can use a regular potato in place of the sweet potato if you prefer.

level up You can use any compound butter on pages 70–71 in place of the mustard-chive butter.

ONE-PAN DINNERS

251

pomegranate-glazed salmon

with black-eyed peas and walnuts

total time 25 minutes

why this recipe works For a hands-free way of cooking foolproof salmon with a nicely browned exterior and a silky, moist interior, we developed a hybrid roasting method, preheating the oven to 500 degrees but then turning down the heat to 275 just before placing the fish in the oven. The initial blast of high heat firmed the exterior and rendered some excess fat from the skin. The fish gently cooked in the oven and stayed moist as the temperature slowly dropped. Pomegranate molasses, a sweet-and-sour syrup, does double-duty here, acting as both a glaze for the salmon itself as well as a main ingredient in our black-eyed pea salad dressing, tying the two elements together. The fresh, sweet, acidic, and nutty components perfectly complement the richness of the salmon.

1 (6- to 8-ounce) skin-on salmon fillet, 1 inch thick

¼ teaspoon plus 1 tablespoon oil, divided

2 teaspoons plus 1 tablespoon pomegranate molasses, divided

¼ teaspoon table salt, divided

¼ teaspoon pepper, divided

2 teaspoons lemon juice

¾ cup canned black-eyed peas, rinsed and drained well

2 tablespoons minced fresh parsley, mint, or chives

2 tablespoons pomegranate seeds

2 tablespoons toasted chopped walnuts, pecans, or pistachios

kitchen improv

use what you've got Substitute chickpeas, navy beans, or cannellini beans for the black-eyed peas; if you don't have pomegranate molasses, combine 2 parts balsamic vinegar with 1 part honey.

make it heartier Add a handful of baby spinach or baby arugula to the salad.

1 Adjust oven rack to lowest position and heat oven to 500 degrees. Line rimmed baking sheet with aluminum foil and place sheet on rack. Pat salmon dry with paper towels. Brush with ¼ teaspoon oil and 1 teaspoon pomegranate molasses then sprinkle with ⅛ teaspoon salt and ⅛ teaspoon pepper.

2 Once oven reaches 500 degrees, reduce oven temperature to 275 degrees. Remove sheet from oven and carefully place salmon, skin side down, on hot sheet. Roast salmon until center is still translucent when checked with tip of paring knife and registers 125 degrees (for medium-rare), 9 to 13 minutes.

3 Meanwhile, whisk lemon juice, 1 tablespoon pomegranate molasses, remaining 1 tablespoon oil, remaining ⅛ teaspoon salt, and remaining ⅛ teaspoon pepper together in bowl until combined. Add black-eyed peas, parsley, pomegranate seeds, and walnuts and toss to combine. Season salad with salt and pepper to taste.

4 Remove salmon from oven and brush with remaining 1 teaspoon pomegranate molasses. Transfer salmon to plate and serve with black-eyed pea salad.

why this recipe works You can enjoy fresh, bright flavors regardless of the season with this sweet and slightly acidic tomato-mango salad (cherry or grape tomatoes are our go-to for their year-round sweetness) dressed with a honey-lime vinaigrette that's the perfect complement to rich coriander-dusted salmon. Giving salmon a spiced coating is an easy and pantry-friendly way to switch up the flavor profile. And while we love the hands-off nature of roasted salmon (see page 252), pan-searing the spice-crusted fish ensures the spices bloom properly, and the crispy skin is a beautiful textural contrast to the salad. Frozen mango works just as well if you're unable to find fresh (or as an excuse to use it for more than your morning smoothie), just be sure to thaw and drain before using.

spiced crispy-skinned salmon

with tomato-mango salad

total time 30 minutes

1 tablespoon oil

1 small shallot, sliced thin

1 teaspoon grated lime zest plus 2 teaspoons juice

1 teaspoon honey

¼ teaspoon table salt, divided

¼ teaspoon pepper, divided

3 ounces cherry or grape tomatoes, halved (½ cup)

¼ cup chopped mango

2 tablespoons minced fresh cilantro, basil, or mint, divided

1 (6- to 8-ounce) skin-on salmon fillet, 1 inch thick

¾ teaspoon ground coriander

1 tablespoon roasted pepitas

1 Whisk oil, shallot, lime zest and juice, honey, ⅛ teaspoon salt, and ⅛ teaspoon pepper together in bowl. Add tomatoes, mango, and 1 tablespoon cilantro and toss to combine; set salad aside.

2 Pat salmon dry with paper towels and sprinkle with coriander, remaining ⅛ teaspoon salt, and remaining ⅛ teaspoon pepper. Place salmon, skin side down, in cold 8- or 10-inch nonstick skillet and place over medium heat. Cook fillet, without moving it, until skin is golden brown and bottom ¼ inch of fillet turns opaque, 6 to 8 minutes.

3 Using 2 spatulas, flip fillet skin side up and continue to cook without moving it until golden brown and bottom ¼ inch of fillet turns opaque, about 3 minutes. Flip fillet onto one side and cook until golden, about 1 minute. Flip fillet onto final side and cook, continuing to flip as needed until salmon registers 125 degrees (for medium-rare), about 1 minute. Serve with salad, sprinkling with remaining 1 tablespoon cilantro and pepitas.

kitchen improv

use what you've got Substitute sunflower seeds for the roasted pepitas; if you don't have ground coriander, cumin would work in a pinch, or omit the coriander.

couscous with shrimp, cilantro, and garlic chips

total time 25 minutes

why this recipe works When you're making a quick weeknight meal for yourself, it's easy to overlook garnishes or deem them fussy or unnecessary. But in this simple, one-saucepan dish, the garlic chips—thinly sliced garlic cooked in oil until just lightly golden and crispy—bring a simple elegance. We relied on couscous and shrimp, both quick-cooking and easy-to-riff-upon pantry staples, to create our meal. We started by making the garlic chips so they could cool while we used the flavorful garlic oil to sauté pieces of shrimp until just pink, and then added couscous, broth, and tomatoes, turned off the heat, and covered the pan. In just 5 minutes, the couscous was fluffy and the shrimp had finished cooking. We stirred in the last bit of garlic oil, lots of fresh chopped cilantro, and a squeeze of lime to brighten everything up. And then the final (and essential) flourish: A generous sprinkling of toasty garlic chips brought crunch and concentrated garlic flavor.

2 tablespoons oil

2 garlic cloves, sliced thin

6 ounces extra-large shrimp (21 to 25 per pound), peeled, deveined, tails removed, and cut into 1-inch pieces

⅛ teaspoon table salt

⅛ teaspoon pepper

⅓ cup couscous

⅓ cup chicken or vegetable broth

1 ounce cherry or grape tomatoes, quartered (¼ cup)

2 tablespoons chopped fresh cilantro or parsley

1 teaspoon lime juice

kitchen improv

use what you've got Chopped scallops could be used instead of the shrimp.

level up Sprinkle with crumbled queso fresco or cotija cheese, thinly sliced scallions, toasted pepitas, sliced pickled jalapeños, minced red onion, and/or chunks of avocado.

1 Heat oil and garlic in medium saucepan over medium heat, stirring constantly once garlic starts to sizzle. Cook until garlic is light golden brown, about 3 minutes. Using slotted spoon, transfer garlic to paper towel–lined plate and season with salt to taste.

2 Pour off oil from saucepan and set aside (you should have about 2 tablespoons oil; add oil to equal 2 tablespoons if needed). Pat shrimp dry with paper towels then sprinkle with salt and pepper. Wipe out now-empty saucepan with paper towels and heat 1 tablespoon reserved oil over medium heat until shimmering. Add shrimp and cook until edges begin to turn pink, 30 seconds to 1 minute. Stir in couscous and broth, then sprinkle tomatoes over top. Cover saucepan and let sit off heat until couscous is tender and shrimp are opaque throughout, about 5 minutes.

3 Stir in cilantro, lime juice, and remaining 1 tablespoon reserved oil. Season with salt and pepper to taste and sprinkle with garlic chips. Serve.

risotto primavera

total time 55 minutes

makes leftovers

why this recipe works Most risotto recipes require constant stirring while adding hot broth by the ladleful from a nearby saucepan. We eliminated the extra saucepan by heating the broth in the microwave. We let the rice (half a cup was plenty) simmer hands-off until partially tender and then stirred for 6 minutes while it finished cooking. This method released enough starch to give us remarkably creamy risotto. Springtime vegetables and meaty mushrooms added heft, and lemon juice and fresh herbs brought brightness.

1¾	cups chicken or vegetable broth	3	ounces asparagus, trimmed and cut into ½-inch pieces
½	cup water	¼	cup frozen peas
4	teaspoons oil, divided	¼	cup grated Parmesan cheese, plus extra for serving
3	ounces cremini or white mushrooms, trimmed and sliced thin	2	tablespoons chopped fresh basil or parsley
½	teaspoon table salt, divided	1	tablespoon unsalted butter
1	small onion, chopped fine	2	teaspoons lemon juice
½	cup Arborio rice		

kitchen improv

use what you've got Substitute Pecorino Romano for the Parmesan and green beans for the asparagus.

level up Add a pinch of saffron to the broth before microwaving.

1 Combine broth and water in 4-cup liquid measuring cup or medium bowl and microwave until simmering, about 5 minutes. Cover and keep warm.

2 Meanwhile, heat 2 teaspoons oil in medium saucepan over medium heat until shimmering. Add mushrooms and ¼ teaspoon salt and cook, covered, until just starting to brown, about 4 minutes; transfer to bowl. Heat remaining 2 teaspoons oil in now-empty saucepan over medium heat until shimmering. Add onion and remaining ¼ teaspoon salt and cook until just beginning to soften, about 3 minutes. Add rice and cook, stirring constantly, until grains are translucent around edges, about 1 minute.

3 Stir in 1½ cups warm broth-water mixture, reduce heat to medium-low, cover, and simmer until almost all liquid is absorbed, about 12 minutes. Stir in asparagus, cover, and cook for 2 minutes. Add ½ cup broth-water mixture and cook, stirring constantly, until liquid is absorbed, about 3 minutes. Add remaining broth-water mixture and peas and cook, stirring constantly, until rice is creamy and tender, about 3 minutes.

4 Off heat, stir in cooked mushrooms, cover, and let sit until warmed through, about 2 minutes. Stir in Parmesan, basil, butter, and lemon juice. Season with salt and pepper to taste. Serve, sprinkling with extra Parmesan if desired. (Risotto can be refrigerated for up to 2 days.)

why this recipe works When you get a craving for macaroni and cheese (and who doesn't?) it seems you have two options: Reach for the boxed stuff with its powdery, lackluster "cheese" packet, or make a big batch in the oven that will last you far beyond your current craving. Not anymore. Our single-serving stovetop version delivers rich, cheesy goodness in one pot—and you don't even have to drain it. We cooked the pasta in water and milk, and then stirred in the cheese. We used American cheese for its emulsifying qualities, and pitched up the flavor of the mild cheese with an equal portion of extra-sharp cheddar. You could omit the spinach, but we added some to make this an adult mac and cheese with a welcome fresh element. Real American cheese is key here for its meltability—imitation American cheeses are loaded with stabilizers and thickeners that make them seem like plastic. Use a block of American cheese from the deli counter rather than the presliced cheese.

stovetop spinach macaroni and cheese

total time 30 minutes

⅔ cup water

½ cup milk

¾ cup elbow macaroni

2 ounces American cheese, shredded (½ cup)

¼ teaspoon Dijon mustard

2 ounces (2 cups) baby spinach or stemmed Swiss chard, chopped

2 ounces extra-sharp cheddar cheese, shredded (½ cup)

1 tablespoon panko bread crumbs

½ teaspoon oil

1 Bring water and milk to boil in small saucepan over medium high heat. Stir in macaroni and reduce heat to medium-low. Cook, stirring frequently, until macaroni is soft (slightly past al dente), 6 to 8 minutes. Add American cheese and mustard and cook, stirring constantly, until cheese is completely melted, about 1 minute. Stir in spinach, 1 handful at a time, until just beginning to wilt. Off heat, stir in cheddar until evenly distributed. Cover saucepan and let sit for 5 minutes.

2 Meanwhile, toss panko with oil in bowl. Microwave, stirring frequently, until golden brown, 1 to 3 minutes.

3 Stir macaroni mixture until sauce is smooth (sauce may look loose but will thicken as it cools) and season with salt and pepper to taste. Sprinkle with toasted panko and serve immediately.

kitchen improv

use what you've got Substitute any short pasta for the elbow macaroni.

level up Substitute Gruyère, Manchego, or Cambozola for the cheddar cheese.

make it cheesier Substitute Cheesy Toasted Panko (page 137) for the panko in step 2.

lemony spaghetti

with garlic and pine nuts

total time 30 minutes

why this recipe works No more pulling out two pots (not to mention washing them) just to get pasta on your plate—this bright, fresh, single serving of lemony pasta is made in a single skillet (not even a heavy pot), cooking liquid and all. We built in flavor from the beginning by toasting our garlic low and slow until the natural sugars created sticky, almost candy-like flavor. When the pasta was nearly ready, we uncovered the skillet and reduced the liquid, which melded with the starch from the pasta resulting in a luscious sauce that coated the noodles perfectly. Lots of lemon, savory Parmesan, and crunchy pine nuts transformed this quick weeknight meal into a sophisticated dish you'll be making time and time again. You can use just about any shape pasta you prefer in this dish, though covered cooking times will vary slightly. You will need a 12-inch nonstick skillet with a tight-fitting lid for this recipe.

2 garlic cloves, minced

2 tablespoons oil, divided

2 cups chicken or vegetable broth

3 ounces spaghetti

⅛ teaspoon red pepper flakes

¼ cup chopped fresh basil or parsley

2 tablespoons Parmesan cheese, grated

2 tablespoons toasted pine nuts

½ teaspoon grated lemon zest plus 2 teaspoons juice

kitchen improv

use what you've got Substitute whatever toasted nut you have on hand for the pine nuts and any hard cheese for the Parmesan.

make it heartier Stir in baby spinach or peas.

Cook garlic and 1 tablespoon oil in 12-inch nonstick skillet over low heat, stirring frequently, until garlic is pale golden brown, 7 to 10 minutes. Stir in broth, spaghetti, and pepper flakes and bring to boil. Cover and simmer vigorously over medium-high heat, stirring occasionally, until pasta is nearly tender, about 10 minutes. Uncover and continue to cook, stirring occasionally, until sauce is thickened slightly, 3 to 6 minutes. Off heat, stir in remaining 1 tablespoon oil, basil, Parmesan, pine nuts, and lemon zest and juice. Season with salt and pepper to taste. Serve.

why this recipe works We loved our Lemony Spaghetti with Garlic and Pine Nuts (page 262) so much that we decided to use the same single-skillet concept to create a rich, luxurious—but single-serve portion—of carbonara with ingredients we had in our pantry. We started by cooking some bacon (nearly as good as hard-to-find traditional guanciale) in the skillet, and then set it aside. We added broth and angel hair to some of the rendered fat and let that cook, covered, before removing the lid and simmering until the sauce had thickened slightly. We then stirred in an egg yolk–cheese mixture that emulsified with the starchy broth into a silky-smooth sauce. Bacon and eggs never had it so good. You will need a 12-inch nonstick skillet with a tight-fitting lid for this recipe.

fastest-ever carbonara

total time 20 minutes

3 tablespoons grated Pecorino Romano or Parmesan cheese, plus extra for serving

1 large egg yolk

1 tablespoon water

Pinch pepper

2 slices bacon, chopped

1½ cups chicken or vegetable broth

3 ounces angel hair pasta

Whisk Pecorino, egg yolk, water, and pepper together in bowl; set aside. Cook bacon in 12-inch nonstick skillet over medium heat until crispy, 5 to 7 minutes. Using slotted spoon, transfer bacon to paper towel–lined plate. Pour off all but 2 teaspoons fat from skillet (or add oil to equal 2 teaspoons). Stir in broth and pasta and bring to boil. Cover and simmer vigorously over medium-high heat, stirring occasionally, until pasta is nearly tender, about 3 minutes. Uncover and continue to cook, stirring occasionally, until sauce is thickened slightly, about 2 minutes. Off heat, stir in egg mixture and crisped bacon. Season with salt and pepper to taste. Serve with Pecorino.

kitchen improv

use what you've got Substitute pancetta for the bacon.

make it heartier Add peas or baby greens and finish with Cheesy Toasted Panko (page 137).

why this recipe works Our spaghetti with meat sauce captures the fragrance and flavor of a huge pot of red sauce bubbling on the stove, but is sized for a solo diner and speedy enough to pull together just after you walk in the door on a weeknight. To amp up the heartiness of our sauce, we started by sautéing earthy cremini mushrooms with bacon for smoky complexity. After lightly browning ground beef, we used our single-skillet method and added tomato sauce, pasta, and enough water to cook the pasta to the perfect tenderness right in the same pan. You can use just about any shape pasta you prefer in this dish, though covered cooking times will vary slightly. You will need a 12-inch nonstick skillet with a tight-fitting lid for this recipe. See Weeknight Chicken Cacciatore on page 238 for an idea for using up any extra mushrooms.

weeknight pasta
with meat sauce

total time 45 minutes

1 teaspoon oil	2 garlic cloves, minced
2 ounces cremini mushrooms, trimmed, halved, and sliced thin	3 ounces 85 percent lean ground beef
1 shallot, minced	1½ cups water
1 slice bacon, chopped fine	1 (8-ounce) can tomato sauce
⅛ teaspoon table salt	3 ounces spaghetti
Pinch pepper	Shaved Parmesan cheese

1 Heat oil in 12-inch nonstick skillet over medium heat until shimmering. Add mushrooms, shallot, bacon, salt, and pepper and cook until mushrooms are lightly browned, 6 to 8 minutes. Stir in garlic and cook until fragrant, about 30 seconds. Stir in beef, breaking up meat with wooden spoon, and cook until no longer pink, 2 to 3 minutes.

2 Stir in water, tomato sauce, and spaghetti and bring to boil. Cover, reduce heat to low, and simmer, stirring occasionally, until pasta is tender, 15 to 17 minutes. Uncover and continue to cook, stirring occasionally, until sauce is thickened slightly, about 1 minute. Serve with Parmesan.

kitchen improv

use what you've got Substitute pancetta for bacon; substitute meatloaf mix, ground pork, or ground turkey for ground beef; any type of mushrooms would work here.

level up Sprinkle with fresh basil and drizzle with extra-virgin olive oil.

spice it up Add red pepper flakes with mushrooms and bacon in step 1.

make it vegetarian Substitute additional minced mushrooms (cremini, portobello, and/or shiitake) for the beef and bacon, adding oil as needed.

vegetarian fideos

total time 35 minutes

why this recipe works A cousin of paella, fideos ("noodles" in Spanish) is a one-skillet dish of short, thin noodles that are toasted and simmered in a flavorful broth with additions, most frequently meat or seafood. But fideos are so flavorful that the dish is also a great option for a vegetarian meal (plus, it's a whole lot easier). We first toasted the fideos, which gave nuttiness and color to the noodles, then added smoked paprika, shallots, and garlic to create a flavorful and smoky broth. Our well-stocked pantry (see pages 10–11) yielded canned chickpeas and roasted red peppers, which contributed the heft we were after. Baby greens, stirred in at the end, brought freshness and color. We like extra-virgin olive oil as a finishing drizzle to add richness and authentic flavor.

2 ounces (½ cup) fideo pasta

2 teaspoons oil, divided, plus extra for drizzling

1 shallot, minced

¼ teaspoon table salt, divided

1 garlic clove, minced

½ teaspoon smoked paprika

⅛ teaspoon pepper

1½ cups water

½ cup canned chickpeas, rinsed

⅓ cup jarred roasted red peppers, rinsed, patted dry, and chopped

2 ounces (2 cups) baby kale or baby spinach

kitchen improv

use what you've got Substitute thin spaghetti broken into 1- to 2-inch pieces for the fideo pasta (wrap bundle of pasta in a clean dish towel before breaking).

level up Sprinkle with grated or crumbled cheese (Manchego, Parmesan, feta, or goat), chopped herbs (parsley or chives), and chopped olives and/or tomatoes.

make it meaty Add chopped chorizo or other cured sausage in step 2 with the shallot.

1 Toss pasta with ½ teaspoon oil in 10-inch skillet until evenly coated. Toast over medium heat, stirring often, until browned and pasta has nutty aroma, 3 to 4 minutes; transfer to bowl.

2 Heat remaining 1½ teaspoons oil in now-empty skillet over medium-low heat until shimmering. Add shallot and ⅛ teaspoon salt and cook until softened and lightly browned, 3 to 5 minutes. Stir in garlic, paprika, and pepper and cook until fragrant, about 30 seconds.

3 Stir in toasted pasta, water, chickpeas, red peppers, and remaining ⅛ teaspoon salt. Bring to simmer, then reduce heat to medium-low and simmer, stirring occasionally, until most of liquid has been absorbed and pasta is tender, 12 to 14 minutes. Off heat, stir in kale until wilted. Drizzle with extra oil and serve.

why this recipe works These are without a doubt the punchiest sesame noodles you've ever had. Sesame seeds are rarely more than a final sprinkle over a finished dish, but here they're the star of the show. With a whopping 3 tablespoons of sesame seeds throughout the dish, they provide ample crunch (and of course toasty flavor) with every bite. And a healthy dose of black pepper brings extra heat. We sought out the fresh Chinese egg noodles for their unique chewiness and textural contrast to the crunchy topping. For the sauce, a little soy, garlic, and robust toasted sesame oil were key, but the kicker was to add a splash of zippy lime juice that awoke the flavors and kept the dish from tasting one-note or too spicy. Bok choy was a wonderful pairing here, not only for its natural grassy freshness, but also for the subtle crunch it provided. We think the texture of fresh Chinese noodles makes a difference in this recipe, but in a pinch you could substitute dried linguine. See Sautéed Baby Bok Choy with Umami Garlic Sauce on page 80 for an idea for using up any extra baby bok choy. Extra uncooked noodles can be stored in the freezer for up to one month.

peppery sesame noodles
with bok choy

total time 35 minutes

- 4 ounces fresh Chinese egg noodles
- 1 tablespoon oil
- 1 head baby bok choy (4 ounces), halved, cored, and sliced thin (1½ cups)
- 3 tablespoons toasted sesame seeds, divided
- 2 teaspoons soy sauce
- 2 teaspoons lime juice
- 1 teaspoon toasted sesame oil
- 1 garlic clove, minced
- ¼ teaspoon pepper

1 Bring 2 quarts water to boil in medium saucepan. Add noodles and cook, stirring often, until tender but still chewy. Drain noodles in colander and rinse well with cold water; set aside to drain.

2 Heat oil in now-empty saucepan over medium heat until shimmering. Add bok choy and cook, stirring occasionally, until tender, about 5 minutes. Stir in noodles, 2 tablespoons sesame seeds, soy sauce, lime juice, sesame oil, garlic, and pepper. Reduce heat to low and cook, turning constantly with tongs, until noodles are evenly coated, about 1 minute. Season with salt and pepper to taste. Sprinkle with remaining 1 tablespoon sesame seeds and serve.

kitchen improv

use what you've got You can use Swiss chard, napa cabbage, or even baby spinach or baby kale in place of baby bok choy, adjusting cooking times as necessary.

level up Finish with a sprinkling of sliced scallion.

spice it up Add a drizzle of sriracha or chili oil to turn up the heat.

why this recipe works We combined tender rice noodles with savory edamame and crunchy cabbage, and draped it all with a rich peanut sauce that's a little spicy, a little sweet, and a little acidic—something to hit every taste bud. While we soaked our rice noodles, we whisked together the simple peanut sauce (only six ingredients if you count the water) and sautéed the edamame just until it was speckled brown but still maintained a tender-crisp texture and fresh flavor. After removing the edamame from the skillet, we finished cooking the noodles in the same pan with our sauce and some store-bought coleslaw mix until the noodles were perfectly tender and chewy. When making a big batch of noodles, this step can be a bit unwieldy because the pan gets overcrowded, but with just 3 ounces of noodles it's a whole lot more manageable. We finished it with lots of fresh herbs, and an extra drizzle of sriracha for an added kick.

spicy peanut rice-noodle bowl

total time 30 minutes

3 ounces (¼-inch-wide) rice noodles

2 tablespoons creamy or crunchy peanut butter

2 teaspoons lime juice, plus lime wedges for serving

2 teaspoons soy sauce

1 teaspoon sriracha, plus extra for serving

½ teaspoon brown sugar

2 teaspoons oil, divided

¼ cup frozen edamame

½ cup (1½ ounces) coleslaw mix

1 tablespoon chopped fresh basil, cilantro, or scallions

1   Pour 2 quarts boiling water over noodles in bowl and stir to separate. Let noodles soak until soft and pliable but not fully tender, stirring once halfway through soaking, 8 to 10 minutes. Drain noodles and rinse with cold water until water runs clear, shaking to remove excess water.

2   Whisk peanut butter, lime juice, soy sauce, sriracha, brown sugar, and 3 tablespoons water together in bowl; set aside. Heat 1 teaspoon oil in 10-inch nonstick skillet over medium heat until shimmering. Add edamame and cook until spotty brown, about 2 minutes; transfer to clean bowl. Heat remaining 1 teaspoon oil in now-empty skillet over medium heat until shimmering. Add drained noodles, coleslaw mix, and peanut sauce and cook until noodles are well coated and tender, about 1 minute, adjusting consistency with water, 1 teaspoon at a time, as needed.

3   Off heat, sprinkle noodles with edamame and basil. Serve with lime wedges and drizzle with extra sriracha if desired.

kitchen improv

use what you've got Substitute almond butter or tahini for the peanut butter; substitute shredded cabbage and/or carrot for coleslaw mix.

level up Top with chopped peanuts, pickled carrots, and/or bean sprouts.

make it heartier Add shredded chicken, cooked shrimp (see page 61), or tofu.

why this recipe works Spiralized zucchini noodles are a fresher, brighter alternative to pasta, but there's no need to treat them as an even swap—they're made from a vegetable, after all. Instead of pairing them with heavy sauces we wanted to lean into the lightness. We quickly sautéed them with garlic, shallot, and chopped artichokes before tossing them with a lemony dressing and a generous amount of herbs. A sprinkle of crumbled cheese and toasted nuts gave them crunch and a hit of bold flavor. If you're spiralizing the zucchini yourself, you will need about 8 ounces of zucchini (just one medium zucchini) to get 6 ounces of spiralized noodles; you can also use store-bought zucchini noodles. Cook the zucchini to your desired level of doneness but be careful not to overcook or the zoodles will be mushy.

lemon-herb zoodles

with artichokes, feta, and walnuts

total time 20 minutes

4   teaspoons oil, divided

½   teaspoon grated lemon zest plus 1 teaspoon juice

⅛   teaspoon table salt, divided

⅛   teaspoon pepper, divided

1   shallot, minced

6   ounces spiralized zucchini noodles, cut into 6-inch lengths

½   cup jarred artichoke hearts packed in water, drained, patted dry, and chopped

1   garlic clove, minced

2   tablespoons chopped fresh dill, mint, basil, or parsley

1   tablespoon crumbled feta or goat cheese

1   tablespoon chopped toasted walnuts, almonds, hazelnuts, pine nuts, or pistachios

1   Combine 2 teaspoons oil, lemon zest and juice, pinch salt, and pinch pepper together in bowl; set aside.

2   Heat remaining 2 teaspoons oil in 10-inch nonstick skillet over medium-low heat until shimmering. Add shallot and cook until softened and lightly browned, 3 to 5 minutes. Stir in zucchini noodles, artichoke hearts, garlic, remaining pinch salt, and remaining pinch pepper and cook, tossing frequently, until noodles are crisp-tender, 1 to 2 minutes. Off heat, stir in lemon mixture and dill. Sprinkle with feta and walnuts. Serve.

kitchen improv

use what you've got Substitute other pantry-friendly ingredients like chopped roasted red peppers, olives, and/or sun-dried tomatoes for the artichoke hearts.

level up Sprinkle with store-bought croutons, crumbled pita chips, and/or store-bought crispy chickpeas for additional texture.

make it heartier Add a handful of baby spinach or kale with the zoodles.

dal with tofu and spinach

total time 40 minutes

makes leftovers

why this recipe works Dal is an Indian dish of red lentils simmered to a porridgelike consistency and seasoned with spices, tomatoes, and onions. Traditional recipes call for a laundry list of spices, and while that's delicious, we wanted to streamline this meal for the solo cook. We found that we got a similarly complex flavor with just garam masala and ginger. It took some trial and error to get the consistency of the dal just right—too much water and it wound up thin and soupy; too little and it was thick and pasty. Two cups of broth to ½ cup of lentils turned out to be just right. Tofu and spinach rounded out the meal and tomatoes, lime juice, and fresh herbs brightened everything up. Serve with naan or pita. See Sriracha-Lime Tofu Bowl on page 214 for an idea for using up any extra tofu.

2 tablespoons oil, divided

1 small onion, chopped fine

2 garlic cloves, minced

1¼ teaspoons garam masala

1 teaspoon grated fresh ginger or ⅛ teaspoon ground ginger

Pinch cayenne pepper

2 cups chicken or vegetable broth

½ cup red lentils, picked over and rinsed

3 ounces cherry or grape tomatoes, quartered (½ cup)

2 tablespoons minced fresh cilantro or parsley

1 teaspoon lime juice

7 ounces firm tofu, cut into ¾-inch pieces

1 cup baby spinach

kitchen improv

level up Dollop with yogurt or sprinkle with sliced scallions, pickled jalapeños, and/or toasted cashews.

make it heartier Add roasted vegetables like cauliflower (see page 94), potatoes, and/or squash.

1 Heat 1 tablespoon oil in medium saucepan over medium heat until shimmering. Add onion and cook until softened, about 5 minutes. Stir in garlic, garam masala, ginger, and cayenne and cook until fragrant, about 30 seconds. Stir in broth and lentils, bring to simmer, and cook over low heat until lentils are tender and resemble thick, coarse puree, 12 to 15 minutes. Season with salt and pepper to taste.

2 Meanwhile, combine tomatoes, cilantro, lime juice, and remaining 1 tablespoon oil in bowl. Season with salt and pepper to taste; set aside until ready to serve.

3 Stir tofu and spinach into lentils and cook until spinach is wilted and tofu is warmed through, 2 to 3 minutes. Top dal with tomato mixture. (Dal and tomato mixture can be refrigerated separately for up to 2 days.)

why this recipe works In less time than it takes to receive delivery pizza, you could make our fresh, tangy, and savory skillet flatbread (and you won't be stuck eating leftover pizza). Starting with store-bought naan meant we didn't need to wait for dough to rise or warm up, and we cooked it on the stovetop so we didn't even have to turn on the oven for at-home pizza. Creamy, tangy goat cheese, brightened with lemon zest, pepper, and a little bit of sun-dried tomato oil made a perfect base for our fresh, no-prep toppings of arugula and prosciutto, and they didn't sog out the naan as tomato sauce would. We got plenty of intense tomato flavor with the chopped sun-dried ones, anyway. You will need a 12-inch skillet with a tight-fitting lid for this recipe. If you do not have enough oil from your sun-dried tomatoes to make 1 tablespoon, you can use any cooking oil to make up the difference.

skillet flatbread
with goat cheese, sun-dried tomatoes, and prosciutto

total time 20 minutes

2 ounces (½ cup) goat cheese, softened

2 tablespoons chopped oil-packed sun-dried tomatoes, plus 1 tablespoon oil, divided

1 small garlic clove, minced

½ teaspoon grated lemon zest

⅛ teaspoon table salt, divided

⅛ teaspoon pepper

1 naan bread

½ cup baby arugula

½ teaspoon balsamic vinegar

1 ounce thinly sliced prosciutto, torn into 2-inch pieces

1 Using fork, mash goat cheese, 2 teaspoons sun-dried tomato oil, garlic, lemon zest, pinch salt, and pepper together in bowl until smooth and spreadable. Spread cheese mixture on naan and sprinkle with sun-dried tomatoes. Place naan in 12-inch skillet, cover, and cook over medium-low heat until naan is golden brown and goat cheese is softened, 6 to 7 minutes.

2 Combine arugula, remaining 1 teaspoon sun-dried tomato oil, balsamic vinegar, and remaining pinch salt in bowl. Off heat, arrange arugula and prosciutto over goat cheese. Serve.

kitchen improv

use what you've got Substitute marinated goat cheese, shredded mozzarella, or torn or sliced fresh mozzarella for the goat cheese.

level up Add thin slices of pear and/or quartered figs with the sun-dried tomatoes. Use flavored or spiced naan (garlic or onion).

tex-mex cheese enchiladas

total time 50 minutes

makes leftovers

pantry recipe

why this recipe works No need for a giant 13 by 9-inch casserole (not to mention endless leftovers). These scaled-down enchiladas come together in a single pan. We created a smoky, gravy-like sauce by combining chili powder, tomato paste, shallots, flour (for thickening), and broth for some sweet and earthy flavors. We made the sauce in the skillet, set aside a portion of it, and then built the whole dish on top of the remaining sauce, nestling cheese-filled tortillas into the thick, spicy goodness. We poured the reserved sauce over the top, sprinkled it all with more cheese, and popped it in the oven until it was bubbly. You will need a 10-inch ovensafe skillet with a tight-fitting lid for this recipe.

sauce

- 2 tablespoons oil
- 2 large shallots, chopped fine
- 1½ tablespoons chili powder
- 1½ tablespoons all-purpose flour
- 2 teaspoons tomato paste
- 2 garlic cloves, minced
- 1½ cups chicken or vegetable broth

enchiladas

- 6 (6-inch) corn tortillas
- 8 ounces Monterey Jack or cheddar cheese, shredded (2 cups), divided
- 1 shallot, chopped fine
- Lime wedges

kitchen improv

level up Sprinkle with chopped cilantro, sliced scallions, sliced olives, chopped tomatoes, pickled jalapeños, and/or diced avocado.

spice it up Use pepper Jack cheese if you like more heat.

make it heartier Add leftover canned beans, wilted greens, and/or shredded chicken to the cheese filling.

1 for the sauce Adjust oven rack to middle position and heat oven to 450 degrees. Heat oil in 10-inch ovensafe skillet over medium heat until shimmering. Add shallots and cook until softened, about 3 minutes. Stir in chili powder, flour, tomato paste, and garlic and cook until fragrant, 30 seconds to 1 minute. Gradually whisk in broth and bring to simmer. Cook until thickened slightly, about 4 minutes. Remove from heat. Measure out 1 cup sauce and set aside, leaving remaining sauce in skillet.

2 for the enchiladas Stack tortillas and wrap in damp dish towel. Microwave until pliable, 30 seconds to 1 minute. Working with one tortilla at a time, place ¼ cup Monterey Jack across center of 1 tortilla, tightly roll tortilla around cheese, and place seam side down in sauce in skillet. Repeat with remaining 5 tortillas and 1¼ cups Monterey Jack, arranging enchiladas side by side in single row in skillet.

3 Pour reserved sauce over enchiladas and sprinkle with remaining ½ cup Monterey Jack. Bake, covered, until cheese is melted, about 10 minutes. Uncover and continue to bake until sauce is bubbling around edges, about 5 minutes. Sprinkle with shallot and serve with lime wedges. (Enchiladas can be refrigerated for up to 2 days.)

asparagus and goat cheese frittata

total time 30 minutes

makes leftovers

why this recipe works While the idea of saving scrambled eggs for later may sound far from appealing, frittatas are ideal leftovers. With soft, tender eggs just firm enough to hold plentiful fillings in place, they're just as delicious reheated the next day as they are eaten cold straight from the fridge. The key to a perfect frittata is to chop the ingredients into small pieces to avoid breaking up the frittata's structure so it won't fall apart. We cooked the asparagus and lemon zest and juice (a bright, springlike combination) in the skillet, and then added cheese, herbs, and the egg mixture and cooked it until the eggs were partially done. We popped it into the oven until it puffed up and was tender inside. Enjoy the frittata as a light dinner paired with a green salad and a glass of wine, and turn the leftovers into an elegant breakfast sandwich or protein-packed midday snack. This recipe works best with thin and medium-size asparagus spears. See Pan-Roasted Asparagus on page 77 for an idea for using up any extra asparagus.

- 6 large eggs
- 2 tablespoons milk
- ¼ teaspoon plus ⅛ teaspoon table salt, divided
- 1½ teaspoons oil
- 8 ounces asparagus, trimmed and cut into ¼-inch lengths
- ¼ teaspoon grated lemon zest plus ¼ teaspoon juice
- ⅛ teaspoon pepper
- 2 ounces goat cheese or feta, crumbled (½ cup)
- 1 tablespoon chopped fresh mint, chives, parsley, or tarragon

kitchen improv

use what you've got Any melty cheese (like grated cheddar or Manchego) would work in place of the goat cheese. Substitute sautéed broccoli, bell pepper, and/or baby spinach for the asparagus.

1 Adjust oven rack to middle position and heat oven to 350 degrees. Whisk eggs, milk, and ¼ teaspoon salt in bowl until well combined; set aside. Heat oil in 8-inch ovensafe nonstick skillet over medium-high heat until shimmering. Add asparagus, lemon zest and juice, pepper, and remaining ⅛ teaspoon salt and cook until asparagus is crisp-tender, 3 to 4 minutes.

2 Stir in goat cheese, mint, and egg mixture and cook, using rubber spatula to stir and scrape bottom of skillet, until large curds form and spatula leaves trail through eggs but eggs are still very wet, 30 seconds. Smooth curds into even layer and cook, without stirring, for 30 seconds. Transfer skillet to oven and bake until frittata is slightly puffy and surface bounces back when lightly pressed, 6 to 9 minutes. Using rubber spatula, loosen frittata from skillet and transfer to cutting board. Let stand for 5 minutes before slicing and serving. (Frittata can be refrigerated for up to 2 days.)

better brown bagging

Just because you're eating at your desk doesn't mean you can't treat yourself. A lot of these one-pan dinners make enough for two servings, so you'll have lunch for the next day. Bringing leftovers for lunch saves you money, helps reduce food waste, and is always going to be more delicious than anything you were contemplating at the salad bar. Here are our tips for making a meal's second life just as good as its first.

eating

Sick of relying on single-use containers and cutlery to eat your bland and boring lunches? A desk pantry can help with that. Use it to liven up your lunch beyond the mini salt and pepper packets, and make your midday meal something to look forward to.

small cutting board

Use it to cut up an apple, slice cheese, open an avocado—the sky's the limit.

something crunchy

Aside from making the perfect afternoon snack, nuts, seeds, or protein-rich garnishes like store-bought crispy chickpeas are great for sprinkling over anything that needs a bit of crunch.

mini containers of olive oil and hot sauce

A finishing drizzle of olive oil or hot sauce adds richness and flavor to your meal, making it feel more complete.

reusable plate, bowl, set of silverware

Make your lunch feel a bit more special by eating the way you'd eat at home. (It's also better for the environment.)

citrus

A squeeze of lemon or lime brings brightness and wakes up the flavors of a second-day meal.

packing

See page 13 for container recommendations.

keep garnishes separate When packing up your leftovers for tomorrow's lunch, keep anything you don't want heated up (like raw vegetables and cold sauces) in a smaller, separate container.

assemble simple sandwiches when you're ready to eat them Some of our sandwiches were designed to withstand an overnight rest in the fridge (see pages 192–195), but when you're making your own, consider packing the bread separate from the fillings. This works especially well for sandwiches like egg salad (see page 206) or the Lamb Pita Sandwiches with Tzatziki (page 196), but also can mean waiting until lunchtime to add the sliced tomato and spread of hummus to your turkey sandwich.

pack it right away Make it easier to grab-and-go in the morning by combining packing your lunch with cleaning up after dinner—put the leftovers you want to eat for lunch right into a single-serving storage container once you're finished eating.

reheating

Here are some best practices when reheating leftovers in the microwave. See pages 14–15 for more information about microwaves.

cause a stir Avoid the dreaded cold spots in food by stirring or flipping occasionally to even out where the heat is concentrated.

cover up Use a plate or inverted bowl to cover the food. This traps steam, which provides more cooking via conduction.

give it a rest Let food rest for a few minutes after cooking to allow hot and cool spots to even out.

loosen up You may need to add a little liquid (like extra sauce, soy sauce, or water) to things like a stir fry (see page 244) or risotto (see page 258) to keep it from clumping together and drying out.

know when to avoid the microwave altogether Some things just aren't the same reheated (looking at you, salmon). So why bother? Instead, flake salmon over salad; shred chicken breast and mix it with avocado, fresh herbs, and a squeeze of lime and scoop it up with tortilla chips; or enjoy your pasta cold or at room temperature.

something sweet

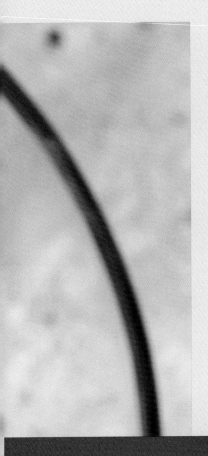

Leftovers can be a double-edged sword when you're cooking for one, particularly when it comes to dessert: too much of a good thing, as they say. But with personal-size desserts, you only prep and eat what you need at one sitting, no pan of brownies or big batch of cookies that get tiresome after a week (or more!). Whip up two perfectly baked, gooey chocolate chip cookies just for yourself, or use your microwave to make a single-serving mug cake or fruit crisp. Want something even easier? Create your own ice cream sundae with homemade toppings, or use our unexpected pantry suggestions for unique flavor combinations. From fruit-forward to chocolaty, sweet-and-salty to creamy, these desserts are perfect for when you just want something sweet—not a project.

solo sundae

Vanilla ice cream is the best thing to keep stashed away in your freezer for when you want an easy-to-portion dessert with minimal effort. Plus, it's a blank slate that welcomes a wide variety of toppings that can elevate it from a convenient dessert to a standout treat. Level up your scoops with a simple microwaved fruit topping, shake up some single-serving whipped cream in a mason jar, or dig into your pantry for some unexpected flavor combos.

strawberry-balsamic topping with pepper

makes ½ cup

- 2 teaspoons packed brown sugar
- 1 teaspoon balsamic vinegar
  Pinch pepper
- ½ cup chopped hulled strawberries

Microwave sugar, vinegar, and pepper in small bowl until just steaming, about 30 seconds. Stir to dissolve sugar then add strawberries and toss to coat. Serve warm or at room temperature.

honey-ginger fig topping

makes ½ cup

Feel free to use apple, pear, persimmon, or any stone fruit instead of the fresh figs.

- 2 teaspoons honey
- 1 teaspoon lemon juice
- ⅛ teaspoon grated fresh ginger or pinch ground ginger
- ½ cup chopped stemmed figs

Microwave honey, lemon, and ginger in small bowl until just steaming, about 30 seconds. Stir to dissolve honey then add figs and toss to coat. Serve warm or at room temperature.

classic hot fudge sauce

makes 2 cups

This is a great recipe to make in a big batch and keep in your fridge for whenever the mood strikes.

- 1¼ cups (8¾ ounces) sugar
- ⅔ cup whole milk
- ¼ teaspoon table salt
- ⅓ cup (1 ounce) unsweetened cocoa powder, sifted
- 3 ounces unsweetened chocolate, chopped fine
- 4 tablespoons unsalted butter, cut into 8 pieces and chilled
- 1 teaspoon vanilla extract

1 Heat sugar, milk, and salt in medium saucepan over medium-low heat, whisking gently, until sugar has dissolved and liquid starts to bubble around edges of saucepan, about 6 minutes. Reduce heat to low, add cocoa, and whisk until smooth.

2 Off heat, stir in chocolate and let sit for 3 minutes. Whisk sauce until smooth and chocolate is fully melted. Whisk in butter and vanilla until fully incorporated and sauce thickens slightly. Serve. (Sauce can be refrigerated for up to 1 month; gently warm in microwave, stirring every 10 seconds, until pourable, before using.)

whipped cream for one

makes ⅓ cup
total time 5 minutes

- ¼ cup heavy cream, chilled
- ½ teaspoon sugar
- ¼ teaspoon vanilla extract

Combine all ingredients in 1- or 2-cup mason jar. Close lid tightly, then shake jar until cream is thickened and holds shape on spoon, about 2 minutes. Serve.

blueberry compote

makes ½ cup

You can use fresh blueberries, though you'll need to crush one-third of them against the side of the saucepan with a wooden spoon after adding them to the butter to achieve the desired consistency.

- 1 tablespoon unsalted butter
- 5 ounces (1 cup) frozen blueberries
- 1 tablespoon sugar, plus extra for seasoning
  Pinch table salt
- ¼ teaspoon lemon juice

Melt butter in small saucepan over medium heat. Add blueberries, sugar, and salt and bring to boil. Reduce heat and simmer, stirring occasionally, until sauce is thickened and about one-quarter of juice remains, 8 to 10 minutes. Remove pan from heat and stir in lemon juice. Season with extra sugar to taste. (Compote can be refrigerated for up to 4 days.)

pantry-friendly ice cream toppings

keep it simple

- granola + honey
- Toasted Nuts (page 15) + espresso powder
- flaked coconut + mango
- crumbled cookies + whipped cream
- jam + peanuts
- marshmallow crème + peanut butter
- orange zest + Classic Hot Fudge Sauce

get creative

- matcha powder + honey
- bourbon + cinnamon
- balsamic glaze + gorgonzola
- crumbled nori + sesame seeds
- extra-virgin olive oil + flaky sea salt
- M&M's + crumbled potato chips
- cayenne + chopped chocolate
- maple syrup + crumbled bacon
- Savory Seed Brittle (page 137) + maple syrup
- pomegranate seeds + white chocolate chips
- toasted cashews (see page 15) + curry powder
- chopped crystallized ginger + shaved chocolate

why this recipe works Consider this your own personal chocolate fondue. We were inspired by thick, creamy European-style hot dipping chocolates (known in Italy as cioccolata calda and in Spain as chocolate a la taza) meant for dunking cookies or churros. Unlike a super-rich, butter-charged fudge sauce that is better enjoyed in smaller doses, this almost pudding-like treat is just decadent enough. We tested our way through versions made from melted dark, milk, and white chocolates, but found too much variability depending on brands and styles. For a basic recipe that worked every time and that lent itself to endless improvisation, we opted for a simple combination of cocoa powder, sugar, and cream. This luscious dessert is also a delicious base, when thinned with milk, for a comforting mug of drinkable hot chocolate. Serve with fresh fruit, cookies, pretzels, doughnut holes, or crackers. We slightly prefer natural cocoa powder to Dutch-processed, but you can use either in this recipe. See page 15 for more information about microwaves.

¼ cup heavy cream or half-and-half

2 tablespoons unsweetened cocoa powder

2 tablespoons sugar

Stir all ingredients together in small bowl until evenly combined. Microwave at 50 percent power for 30 seconds, then whisk until few lumps remain. Microwave at 50 percent power for 30 seconds longer, then whisk until smooth. Serve.

dipping hot chocolate

total time 5 minutes

pantry recipe

kitchen improv

spice it up Add a pinch of a warm spice or spice blend (such as cinnamon, allspice, or ras el hanout), citrus zest, or a splash of aromatic extract (such as vanilla, almond, orange, or anise).

make it boozy Whisk in your favorite liqueur (try orange, almond, or raspberry).

make it drinkable Add warm milk to reach the desired consistency.

why this recipe works Turn your snack drawer into a composed dessert with these sweet, salty, crunchy, and (best of all) easy-to-make treats. Named for their telltale shape, these cookies are made from little more than pretzels, peanuts, and melted chocolate chips. Melting chocolate with a little oil helped to create a thinner coating so it was easier to cover every inch of the pretzel and peanut mixture. After forming the mixture into mounds and letting them rest in the refrigerator for just 15 minutes, the chocolate solidified and became snappy, with an appealing sheen. You can use milk, white, or any dark chocolate in this recipe. See page 15 for more information about microwaves.

¼   cup (1½ ounces)
      chocolate chips

½   teaspoon oil

¼   cup pretzel sticks,
      broken in half

2   tablespoons dry-roasted
      peanuts

Line large plate with parchment paper. Microwave chocolate chips and oil in bowl at 50 percent power, stirring occasionally, until melted and smooth, about 2 minutes. Using rubber spatula, fold in pretzels and peanuts until evenly coated. Drop 4 heaping 1-tablespoon portions of pretzel mixture onto prepared plate in mounds and refrigerate until set, about 15 minutes. Serve. (Haystacks can be stored at room temperature for up to 2 days.)

chocolate haystacks

total time 25 minutes

makes leftovers

kitchen improv

use what you've got You could use your favorite breakfast cereal in place of the pretzels; any nut (chopped, if necessary) in place of the peanuts; and any type of chocolate (chopped bar or chips) that you have on hand.

level up Stir in peanut butter, dried fruit, mini marshmallows, and/or butterscotch chips.

cinnamon–sugar pita chips

total time 35 minutes

pantry recipe

why this recipe works You may associate pitas with stuffable sandwiches or savory chips for scooping up hummus, but they can also be turned into a quick, satisfying, buttery-sweet dessert. Pitas often come in bags of four, and there's always that one bread that starts to lose its freshness before you can make it into a sandwich: This is a great way to use it up. First, we separated an 8-inch pita into its two component layers. We seasoned the split rounds with butter, cinnamon, and sugar before stacking them and cutting them into wedges—much easier than seasoning each individual chip. Many recipes instruct you to flip each chip halfway through for better browning. Don't bother. We found that the heat from the baking sheet browned the bottoms nicely while the tops naturally got golden from the oven. This no-flip method is not only less work, but it also ensures all of that cinnamon-sugar goodness stays on the pita, not on the baking sheet. After about 15 minutes in the oven, the chips are crisped and ready to be crumbled over ice cream, dipped into a chocolate concoction (see pages 289 and 291), or eaten as-is.

1 (8-inch) pita bread

1 tablespoon sugar

1 teaspoon ground cinnamon

Pinch table salt

2 tablespoons unsalted butter, melted

kitchen improv

level up Serve with ice cream, Dipping Hot Chocolate (page 291), or cream cheese drizzled with a little maple syrup.

spice it up Add chipotle chile powder or a pinch of cayenne for kick, or substitute pumpkin pie spice for the cinnamon.

make it savory Omit cinnamon and sugar, substitute olive oil for butter, and sprinkle with minced fresh herbs and grated Parmesan.

1   Adjust oven rack to upper-middle position and heat oven to 350 degrees. Using kitchen shears, cut around perimeter of pita and separate into 2 thin rounds. Combine sugar, cinnamon, and salt in bowl.

2   Brush rough sides of pita with melted butter and sprinkle evenly with cinnamon mixture. Stack rounds on top of one another and, using chef's knife, cut pita stack into 8 wedges. Spread wedges, cinnamon side up and in single layer, on rimmed baking sheet. Bake until wedges are golden brown and crisp, about 15 minutes. Let cool before serving. (Pita chips can be stored at room temperature for up to 3 days.)

paper bag popcorn

total time 15 minutes

why this recipe works In about the amount of time it takes to watch the opening credits of your favorite film, this lightly buttered, salty-sweet microwave popcorn is ready to join you on the couch. No fancy gadgets here: We used a paper lunch bag and some popcorn kernels lightly coated in oil, and after just 3 minutes in the microwave, the kernels were perfectly popped. As the popcorn cooled just a little in its bag (the steam that escapes from the bag upon opening can be quite hot), we microwaved a mixture of butter, brown sugar, and cinnamon and then drizzled it over the popcorn and finished with a sprinkle of salt. We love this caramelly sweet and salty combo, but mix-in ideas abound, from chocolate candies that melt ever-so-slightly, to nuts for the ultimate snack mix. Microwaves vary in strength so rather than watching the clock, listen for the popping sounds: When they slow down, the popcorn is ready. This recipe works best in a microwave with a wattage of 900 or higher. See page 15 for more information about microwaves.

2 tablespoons popcorn kernels	1½ teaspoons packed brown sugar
¼ teaspoon oil	¼ teaspoon ground cinnamon
½ tablespoon unsalted butter	¼ teaspoon table salt

kitchen improv

level up Mix in chocolate chips, peanuts, shredded coconut, and/or M&M's.

make it savory In place of the cinnamon and sugar, try Parmesan and black pepper or a barbecue spice blend (see page 72). Or, omit the cinnamon and sugar and finish with a drizzle of truffle oil.

1 Place popcorn kernels in clean brown paper lunch bag and drizzle with oil. Fold over top of bag three times to seal (do not tape or staple) and shake bag to coat kernels with oil. Place bag on its side in microwave, shaking kernels into even layer in bag. Microwave bag until popping slows to one or two pops at a time, about 3 minutes. Remove bag from microwave and set aside to cool slightly.

2 Meanwhile, microwave butter, sugar, and cinnamon in medium bowl at 50 percent power until butter is melted, 30 to 60 seconds. Stir to dissolve sugar.

3 Carefully open paper bag and pour popcorn into bowl with melted butter mixture. Use rubber spatula to toss popcorn with butter, then sprinkle with salt. Serve.

why this recipe works These make-ahead sweet treats are an elegant indulgence that is simple to whip up. We kept it classic with peanut butter and chocolate and lightened the peanut butter filling by mixing it with butter and confectioners' sugar. We coated the peanut butter mixture in chocolate we had tempered in the microwave to achieve a glossy sheen. A quick rest in the fridge hardened the chocolate coating slightly (waiting to eat them was arguably the most difficult part about this recipe). If peanuts aren't your thing, we found that any nut butter would work here. See pages 14–15 for more information about microwaves and softening butter in a pinch.

2 ounces (½ cup) confectioners' sugar

¼ cup creamy or chunky peanut butter

2 tablespoons unsalted butter, cut into 2 pieces and softened

Pinch table salt

3 ounces bittersweet chocolate, chopped fine, divided

1 Using rubber spatula, mash sugar, peanut butter, butter, and salt together in bowl until well combined and lightened in color. Divide into 8 portions, roll into balls, and place on parchment paper–lined plate. Freeze for 15 minutes.

2 Microwave two-thirds of the chocolate in 1-cup liquid measuring cup at 50 percent power, stirring often, until nearly melted, 2 to 3 minutes. Stir in remaining chocolate until melted and smooth. (Return chocolate to microwave if not fully melted, but for no longer than 5 seconds at a time.)

3 Working with one piece at a time, drop peanut butter ball in melted chocolate and, using 2 forks, gently flip to coat all over. Lift ball from chocolate with fork, allowing excess chocolate to drip back into measuring cup, then return chocolate-coated ball to plate. Repeat with remaining peanut butter balls. Refrigerate truffles, uncovered, until chocolate has hardened, about 10 minutes. Serve. (Truffles can be refrigerated for up to 1 week.)

chocolate–peanut butter truffles

total time 45 minutes

makes leftovers

pantry recipe

kitchen improv

use what you've got You can use any type of chocolate (chopped bar or chips) that you have on hand.

level up Sprinkle the truffles with chopped nuts, sprinkles, or coarse sea salt before refrigerating.

edible cookie dough

total time 30 minutes

why this recipe works Who among us hasn't been tempted by the supermarket cookie dough tubes, or sneaking a spoonful from a homemade batch? But health concerns like raw eggs leave many of us feeling queasy at the thought. Whether you're nurturing a bout of childhood nostalgia, or simply don't want to turn on your oven, we developed a safe and delicious recipe that can be easily made from pantry ingredients. The key to making the dough edible was more than just nixing the egg and leaveners, though: Flour is unsafe to eat raw, so we microwaved it to zap any potential bacteria. Because we couldn't achieve caramelization from baking, brown sugar delivered deep, complex flavor. We found that mini chocolate chips were more evenly distributed throughout the dough, but any chips you have on hand would work. Best of all, you can easily double (or triple!) this recipe, freeze the balls, and save them for a rainy day. See pages 14–15 for more information about microwaves and softening butter in a pinch.

2 tablespoons all-purpose flour

1 tablespoon unsalted butter, softened

1 tablespoon packed brown sugar

1 tablespoon mini chocolate chips

1 teaspoon milk

⅛ teaspoon vanilla extract

Pinch table or sea salt

kitchen improv

use what you've got You can use any type of chocolate (chopped bar or chips) that you have on hand. Or, substitute crushed Oreos, toffee pieces, Reese's Pieces, peanut butter chips, cereal, or any bite-size candy or snack.

make it funfetti Use white mini chocolate chips and add rainbow sprinkles.

make it butter pecan Substitute mini butterscotch chips for the chocolate chips and add chopped toasted pecans (see page 15).

make it rocky road Substitute mini marshmallows for the chocolate chips and add chopped walnuts.

1 Microwave flour in small bowl for 45 seconds; set aside to cool, about 3 minutes.

2 Using rubber spatula, mash butter and sugar together in separate bowl until well combined and lightened in color. Stir in cooled flour, chocolate chips, milk, vanilla, and salt until combined. Refrigerate until firm, about 15 minutes. Roll into 3 balls and serve.

why this recipe works Sometimes you just want to treat yourself to some freshly baked chocolate chip cookies. You might not have the time or patience to make an entire batch, but two cookies? Two is perfect. But drastically scaling down a recipe often results in head-scratching measurements like half of an egg, so we did the heavy lifting for you. We rely solely on brown sugar instead of both brown and granulated for caramelized flavor and just-right texture. There's no need for a mixer or even measuring cups here and, best of all, the cookies can be baked in your toaster oven. These cookies have a crispy edge and soft, chewy interior—truly the best of both ends of the cookie texture spectrum. A pinch is equal to $\frac{1}{16}$ teaspoon. See pages 14–15 for more information about microwaves and softening butter in a pinch. You can use a regular rimmed baking sheet if you don't have a quarter-sheet pan, though you'll have to use your oven.

two chocolate chip cookies

total time 35 minutes

pantry recipe

3 tablespoons all-purpose flour

Pinch baking soda

Pinch table salt

1 tablespoon unsalted butter, softened

2 tablespoons packed brown sugar

1 large egg yolk

$\frac{1}{8}$ teaspoon vanilla extract

2 tablespoons chocolate chips

1 Adjust toaster oven or oven rack to middle position and heat oven to 325 degrees. Line small rimmed baking sheet with parchment paper. Whisk flour, baking soda, and salt together in bowl. Using rubber spatula, mash butter and sugar together in separate bowl until well combined and lightened in color. Add egg yolk and vanilla and mix until combined. Stir in flour mixture until just combined then stir in chocolate chips.

2 Divide dough into 2 portions, then roll into balls. Place on prepared sheet, spaced about 2 inches apart. Bake until edges of cookies are set and beginning to brown but centers are still soft and puffy, 8 to 12 minutes. Let cookies cool on sheet for 10 minutes. Serve.

kitchen improv

use what you've got You can use any type of chocolate (chopped bar or chips) that you have on hand. Or try other sweet stir-ins (M&M's, Reese's Pieces, white chocolate chips, or butterscotch chips) in place of the chocolate.

why this recipe works A flour tortilla (leftover after making a Zucchini Quesadilla, page 198, perhaps?) turns into a cross between a crepe and a pancake in this warm, satisfying dessert that comes together in just a few minutes and is hardly more work than making a PB&J. No "queso" in this quesadilla; instead, we spread peanut butter (dealer's choice—creamy or crunchy) over half of a tortilla, then topped the nut butter with a handful of chocolate chips and folded the tortilla in half. We toasted the quesadilla in a little butter until it was crispy and well browned, the peanut butter was warmed through, and the chocolate chips were melted and creamy. This basic formula lends itself beautifully to improvisation with other fillings and toppings.

1 (10-inch) flour tortilla

2 tablespoons creamy or chunky peanut butter

1 tablespoon chocolate chips

1 tablespoon unsalted butter

1 Lay tortilla on cutting board. Spread peanut butter over half of tortilla, leaving ½-inch border around edge. Sprinkle chocolate chips over peanut butter, then fold other half of tortilla over top.

2 Melt butter in 10- or 12-inch nonstick skillet over medium-low heat. Place filled tortilla in skillet and cook until crispy and well browned, about 2 minutes. Flip tortilla and cook until second side is crispy and well browned, 1 to 2 minutes. Transfer quesadilla to cutting board and let cool slightly. Cut into wedges and serve.

peanut butter–chocolate quesadilla

total time 15 minutes

pantry recipe

kitchen improv

use what you've got Use any nut butter in place of the peanut butter and any type of chocolate (chopped bar or chips) that you have on hand.

make it fruity Add sliced banana, apple, or strawberries to the filling.

make it cannoli-inspired Skip the peanut butter and chocolate and fill the tortilla with sweetened ricotta or mascarpone. Add dark chocolate, toasted pistachios, and/or some lemon or orange zest. Sprinkle with confectioners' sugar or cocoa powder.

cheesecake parfait

total time 10 minutes

why this recipe works Cheesecake is notoriously fussy, with the cumbersome water bath and temperamental heat regulation—a lot of work for one serving. And a whole cheesecake packs a lot of richness—it's a classic meant more for a crowd. But the flavors are quite simple: sweetened cream cheese, graham crackers, a berry topping. To bring this simplicity to a single-serve parfait cup, we started by macerating some berries to act as a juicy topping. Next we made a light and fluffy sweetened cream cheese mixture, to which we added a touch of lemon zest to cut through the richness. Finally, we crumbled up a graham cracker to give us classic flavor and some necessary crunch. Layer it or simply mix all the components together and enjoy. If you don't want to wait for your cream cheese to soften, microwave it at 50 percent power for 20 to 30 seconds. See page 15 for more information about microwaves.

¼ cup hulled, chopped strawberries

1 teaspoon plus 1 tablespoon sugar, divided

2 ounces cream cheese, cut into 2 pieces and softened

1 tablespoon heavy cream, half-and-half, or milk

¼ teaspoon grated lemon zest

Pinch table salt

1 graham cracker, crushed into coarse crumbs (¼ cup)

kitchen improv

use what you've got You can use any cookie you have on hand in place of the graham cracker; any berry will work in place of the strawberries.

level up Sprinkle chopped crystallized ginger, fresh thyme or basil, and/or chocolate chips on top of the finished parfait.

make it maple Whisk some maple syrup into the cream cheese mixture.

1 Toss strawberries with 1 teaspoon sugar in bowl; let sit for 2 minutes.

2 Whisk cream cheese, cream, lemon zest, salt, and remaining 1 tablespoon sugar together in separate bowl until smooth. Sprinkle graham crumbs into bottom of bowl, then top with cream cheese mixture and macerated strawberries. Serve.

why this recipe works Warm, rich chocolate cake with a molten chocolate center can be yours in a mere 15 minutes. Even better, no need to turn on the oven, get out your baking pans, or even open up a boxed mix. For this single-serving cake, we use cocoa and chocolate to give it a deep chocolate flavor, and we need only a mug, a bowl, and a microwave to make it happen. While some recipes for mug cakes mix everything in the mug, we found that whisking the dry ingredients in a bowl first ensured they were well-mixed (no unpleasant pockets of baking soda). Using 50 percent power kept the cake moist and tender, and tucking a few pieces of chocolate inside partway through gave us that ooey-gooey molten center. We developed this recipe in a full-size 1200-watt microwave. If the wattage of your microwave is less than 1200 watts, you will need to increase the cooking times throughout. See page 15 for more information about microwaves. We prefer Dutch-processed cocoa in this recipe; the cake will be slightly drier if you use natural cocoa powder. We prefer bar chocolate (milk, dark, or bittersweet), as chocolate chips are harder to insert into the cake to form the molten center.

molten chocolate mug cake

total time 15 minutes

2 tablespoons all-purpose flour

2 tablespoons sugar

1 tablespoon Dutch-processed cocoa powder

¼ teaspoon baking powder

⅛ teaspoon table salt

1 ounce milk or dark chocolate, divided

2 tablespoons unsalted butter, cut into 2 pieces

1 large egg

½ teaspoon vanilla extract

1 Whisk flour, sugar, cocoa, baking powder, and salt together in bowl; set aside. Break ½ ounce of the chocolate into rough 1-inch pieces then add to 12-ounce mug with butter. Microwave butter and chocolate pieces at 50 percent power, stirring often, until melted, 1 to 2 minutes. Add flour mixture, egg, and vanilla and mix until smooth and well combined (being sure to scrape corners of mug).

2 Microwave cake batter at 50 percent power until batter has doubled in size, 50 to 70 seconds. Break remaining ½ ounce chocolate into two pieces and press into center of cake with top of chocolate flush with top of cake. Microwave cake at 50 percent power until cake is firm but top is just wet to the touch, 15 to 30 seconds (cake may rise above edge of mug, but will not overflow). Let cake rest for 2 minutes. Serve.

kitchen improv

level up Add instant espresso powder or grated orange zest with the dry ingredients; top with your favorite ice cream or Whipped Cream for One (page 289).

SOMETHING SWEET

s'mores mug cake

total time 20 minutes

pantry recipe

why this recipe works When you crave that summertime treat of chocolate, marshmallows, and graham crackers but there's not a campfire to be found, try our s'mores mug cake. Tucking marshmallows into a rich chocolate batter created a melted marshmallow center as the cake cooked. Making sure they were well-submerged was key to preventing overflow as the marshmallows expand during cooking. A dusting of graham cracker crumbs gave us the crunchy texture and classic s'mores flavor we wanted. We developed this recipe in a full-size 1200-watt microwave. If the wattage of your microwave is less than 1200 watts, you will need to increase the cooking times throughout. See page 15 for more information about microwaves. We prefer Dutch-processed cocoa in this recipe; the cake will be slightly drier if you use natural cocoa powder.

2 tablespoons all-purpose flour

2 tablespoons sugar

1 tablespoon Dutch-processed cocoa powder

¼ teaspoon baking powder

⅛ teaspoon table salt

½ ounce milk or dark chocolate

2 tablespoons unsalted butter

1 large egg

½ teaspoon vanilla extract

2 marshmallows

½ graham cracker, crushed into coarse crumbs

kitchen improv

level up Drizzle with marshmallow crème and/or hot fudge (see page 289).

make it rocky road Substitute chopped walnuts for the graham crackers.

1 Whisk flour, sugar, cocoa, baking powder, and salt together in bowl; set aside. Break chocolate into rough 1-inch pieces, then add to 12-ounce mug with butter. Microwave butter and chocolate pieces at 50 percent power, stirring often, until melted, 1 to 2 minutes. Add flour mixture, egg, and vanilla and mix until smooth and well combined (being sure to scrape corners of mug).

2 Microwave cake batter at 50 percent power until batter has doubled in size, 40 to 60 seconds. Press marshmallows into center of cake so that top marshmallow is about ½ inch below surface of cake. Sprinkle graham cracker crumbs on top, and press lightly to adhere. Microwave cake at 50 percent power until cake is firm but top is just wet to the touch, 20 to 30 seconds (cake may rise above edge of mug, but will not overflow). Let cake rest for 2 minutes. Serve.

why this recipe works Mug cakes aren't just an excuse to eat gooey, decadent chocolate—the technique can apply to even the lightest and fluffiest of cakes. We created a simple cake batter full of lemon zest and juice, with an egg contributing a lovely yellow hue and a few spoonfuls of poppy seeds adding pleasing texture and contrasting color. After less than 2 minutes in the microwave, we had a soft, pillowy, lemon cake, just waiting for a dollop of whipped cream and a handful of berries. We developed this recipe in a full-size 1200-watt microwave. If the wattage of your microwave is less than 1200 watts, you will need to increase the cooking times throughout. See page 15 for more information about microwaves.

lemon poppyseed mug cake

total time 15 minutes

pantry recipe

3 tablespoons all-purpose flour	¼ teaspoon baking powder
2 tablespoons sugar	⅛ teaspoon table salt
2 teaspoons poppy seeds (optional)	2 tablespoons unsalted butter, cut into 2 pieces
1½ teaspoons grated lemon zest plus 2 teaspoons juice	1 large egg
	½ teaspoon vanilla extract

1   Whisk flour, sugar, poppy seeds, if using, lemon zest, baking powder, and salt together in bowl; set aside. Microwave butter in 12-ounce mug at 50 percent power, stirring often, until melted, 1 to 2 minutes. Add flour mixture, egg, vanilla, and lemon juice and mix until smooth and well combined (being sure to scrape corners of mug).

2   Microwave cake batter at 50 percent power until cake has doubled in size and is firm, but top is just wet to the touch, 1 minute 30 seconds to 2 minutes (cake may rise above edge of mug but will not overflow). Let cake rest for 2 minutes. Serve.

kitchen improv

use what you've got Instead of lemon zest and juice, use orange or lime.

level up Top with Whipped Cream for One (page 289), Blueberry Compote (page 289), lemon curd, berries, or your favorite ice cream, gelato, or sorbet.

no-bake apple crisp

total time 15 minutes

why this recipe works You can skip your trip to the orchard: All it takes is one apple and some simple pantry ingredients to achieve a quintessential fall dessert whenever the mood strikes. We found we could "bake" an apple crisp for one entirely in the microwave and achieve a crispy, crunchy topping and tender, juicy fruit. The key was to cook the topping separately and stir it regularly to achieve evenly golden, crunchy crumbles unaffected by the steam of the cooking fruit. We used a Golden Delicious apple for this recipe, but any sweet, crisp apple you have on hand can be used. We developed this recipe in a full-size 1200-watt microwave. If the wattage of your microwave is less than 1200 watts, you will need to increase the cooking times throughout. See page 15 for more information about microwaves. Be careful when handling the bowls for the topping and filling after microwaving, as they will get hot.

filling

- 1 apple, peeled, cored, and cut into ¾-inch pieces
- 2 tablespoons sugar
- 1 teaspoon lemon juice
- ⅛ teaspoon ground cinnamon

topping

- 1 tablespoon all-purpose flour
- 1½ teaspoons sugar
- 1½ teaspoons old-fashioned rolled oats
- Pinch table salt
- ½ tablespoon unsalted butter, cut into 2 pieces

kitchen improv

level up Top with a dollop of Whipped Cream for One (page 289), a drizzle of caramel, or a scoop of your favorite ice cream, gelato, or frozen yogurt.

make it nutty Add chopped nuts (pecans, almonds, walnuts, and/or pistachios) to the topping.

make it fruity Add dried fruit (raisins, dried cranberries or cherries, currants, and/or chopped dried apricots) to the apples before cooking.

1 for the filling Combine apple, sugar, lemon juice, and cinnamon in bowl and microwave until apple has softened and juices have thickened, 3 to 4 minutes, stirring occasionally. Set aside to cool slightly.

2 for the topping Meanwhile, mix flour, sugar, oats, and salt together in separate bowl. Using fingers, rub butter into flour mixture until mixture has texture of coarse crumbs. Microwave until topping is golden, about 2 minutes, stirring every 30 seconds.

3 Sprinkle topping over apple and serve.

no-bake peach-ginger crisp

total time 20 minutes

why this recipe works We loved our microwaved apple crisp (page 314) so much that we wanted to make an even simpler version using frozen fruit, a freezer staple that is always on hand. But this took some finessing—when we tossed frozen peaches with sugar, lemon zest and juice, and ginger and popped them in the microwave, we ended up with peach soup. Draining the fruit halfway through cooking before adding the other ingredients was key to avoiding an overly liquidy filling. The same oat crumble added crunch and, if you like, a sprinkling of nuts was the finishing touch. We developed this recipe in a full-size 1200-watt microwave. If the wattage of your microwave is less than 1200 watts, you will need to increase the cooking times throughout. See page 15 for more information about microwaves. Be careful when handling the bowls for the topping and filling after microwaving, as they will be hot.

filling

- 2 cups frozen peaches, cut into 1-inch pieces
- 2 tablespoons sugar
- ¼ teaspoon grated lemon zest plus 1 teaspoon juice
- ¼ teaspoon grated fresh or ground ginger

topping

- 2 tablespoons all-purpose flour
- 1 tablespoon sugar
- 1 tablespoon old-fashioned rolled oats
- Pinch table salt
- 1 tablespoon unsalted butter, cut into 4 pieces

kitchen improv

level up Top with a dollop of Whipped Cream for One (page 289) or a scoop of your favorite ice cream, gelato, or frozen yogurt.

make it tropical Substitute frozen mango chunks for the frozen peaches and add shredded coconut to the topping.

make it nutty Add chopped nuts (pecans, almonds, walnuts, and/or pistachios) to the topping.

1 for the filling Microwave peaches in bowl until steaming and juices start to bubble, 3 to 4 minutes, stirring occasionally. Remove bowl from microwave and drain liquid. Toss drained peaches with sugar, lemon zest and juice, and ginger. Microwave until peaches have softened and liquid is thick and syrupy, about 4 minutes. Set aside to cool slightly.

2 for the topping Meanwhile, mix flour, sugar, oats, and salt together in separate bowl. Using fingers, rub butter into flour mixture until mixture has texture of coarse crumbs. Microwave until topping is golden, about 2 minutes, stirring every 30 seconds.

3 Sprinkle topping over peaches and serve.

why this recipe works You may associate milkshakes with an ultratall soda fountain glass filled to the brim with a cold creamy concoction, and an accompanying metal shaker with even more that didn't fit in the glass. At home, we wanted a reasonably sized, but still rich and creamy, serving. We used slightly softened vanilla ice cream (ideal for achieving a creamy, not icy, texture) and transformed it into a decadent smoothie-like treat by adding a mix of thawed frozen berries. To get the texture and consistency we wanted—smooth and sippable through a straw—we turned to our food processor. The food processor blade (larger than a blender blade) broke down the fruit evenly and efficiently, which helped puree the berries into a smooth base. Next we added our ice cream, a splash of milk, and just a pinch of salt to bring out the flavors. Using frozen berries ensures peak ripeness all year long while providing maximum berry flavor; you can substitute fresh, ripe berries, though the milkshake won't be quite as thick. If you don't have a food processor you can use a blender; adjust blending time as needed before adding the ice cream.

fruits of the forest milkshake

total time 20 minutes

---

6 ounces (1 cup) vanilla ice cream

4 ounces (1 cup) frozen strawberries, thawed

4 ounces (¾ cup) frozen blueberries, raspberries, or blackberries, thawed

2 tablespoons milk

Pinch salt

Let ice cream soften on counter for 15 minutes. Process strawberries and blueberries in food processor until smooth, about 1 minute, scraping down sides of bowl as needed. Add ice cream, milk, and salt and process until smooth, about 1 minute. Pour into chilled glass and serve.

kitchen improv

level up Garnish with crumbled cookies, Whipped Cream for One (page 289), shredded coconut, and/or shaved chocolate.

make it tropical Substitute frozen, thawed pineapple and/or mango for the strawberries and blueberries.

make it boozy Substitute your favorite spirit (try rum or gin) or liqueur (try orange or elderflower) for the milk.

coconut paletas

total time 5 minutes,
plus 6 hours for freezing

makes leftovers

pantry recipe

why this recipe works Paletas are Mexican frozen treats that usually rely on fresh fruit juice or milk as their base, with chunks of fresh fruit stirred in—a far cry from sickly-sweet store-bought Popsicles. Using richly flavored coconut milk as the base for our version, we added a small amount of honey for sweetness, vanilla extract for rich, buttery undertones, and salt for balance (bonus: it's all dairy-free!). Adding unsweetened flaked coconut amped up the coconut flavor and gave our paletas some pleasant texture. This recipe takes just 5 minutes of hands-on time, with a big payoff—six treats to stash in your freezer for when you're in need of a single-serving dessert. (And note that the recipe can be easily halved.) Do not substitute low-fat coconut milk or the paletas will taste watery and have an icy texture. You will need an ice pop mold for this recipe.

2 cups canned coconut milk

3 tablespoons honey

1 tablespoon vanilla extract

¼ teaspoon table salt

3 tablespoons unsweetened flaked coconut

kitchen improv

make it horchata Add ground cinnamon and ground cloves to coconut milk mixture and substitute toasted sliced almonds for the flaked coconut.

make it cardamom and lime Add ground cardamom and lime zest and juice to coconut mixture.

1 Whisk coconut milk, honey, vanilla, and salt together in large liquid measuring cup to dissolve honey and salt. Stir in flaked coconut.

2 Divide coconut mixture evenly among six 3-ounce molds. Insert Popsicle stick in center of each mold, cover, and freeze until firm, at least 6 hours. To serve, hold mold under warm running water for 30 seconds to thaw. (Paletas can be frozen for up to 1 week.)

why this recipe works When you're cooking for one, making use of overripe bananas in banana bread isn't practical, because then you're left with a whole loaf. Instead, freeze your bananas and blend them into a creamy ice cream that tastes as decadent as digging into a pint. We simply froze whole peeled bananas (even easier if you do this ahead of time) and then sliced and processed them with a little heavy cream for richness. The result was ice cream with a silky-smooth texture that rivaled custard-based ice cream. A teaspoon of lemon juice and a bit of cinnamon gave our ice cream more dimension, while a whole tablespoon of vanilla rounded out the flavors. Be sure to use very ripe, heavily speckled (or even black) bananas in this recipe. You can skip the freezing in step 3 and serve the ice cream immediately, but the texture will be closer to soft-serve or frozen custard.

banana ice cream

total time 30 minutes, plus 10 hours for freezing

makes leftovers

3 very ripe bananas	½ teaspoon lemon juice
¼ cup heavy cream or half-and-half	⅛ teaspoon ground cinnamon
1½ teaspoons vanilla extract	⅛ teaspoon table salt

1 Peel bananas, place in large zipper-lock bag, and press out excess air. Freeze bananas until solid, at least 8 hours.

2 Let bananas sit at room temperature to soften slightly, about 15 minutes. Slice into ½-inch-thick rounds and place in food processor. Add cream, vanilla, lemon juice, cinnamon, and salt and process until smooth, about 5 minutes, scraping down sides of bowl as needed.

3 Transfer mixture to airtight container and freeze until firm, at least 2 hours. Serve. (Ice cream can be frozen for up to 1 week.)

kitchen improv

level up Top with sprinkles, hot fudge (see page 289), and a cherry.

make it vegan Substitute canned coconut milk or plant-based creamer for the cream.

make it nutty Replace half of the cream with peanut butter or Nutella and/or stir in chopped nuts.

make it chocolate Add some unsweetened cocoa powder with bananas in step 2.

SOMETHING SWEET

nutritional information for our recipes

We calculate the nutritional values of our recipes per serving. We entered all the ingredients, using weights for important ingredients such as most vegetables. We also used our preferred brands in these analyses. We did not include additional salt or pepper for food that's "seasoned to taste."

	calories	total fat (g)	sat fat (g)	chol (mg)	sodium (mg)	total carb (g)	dietary fiber (g)	total sugars (g)	protein (g)
introduction									
toasted nuts (per ¼ cup almonds)	210	19	1.5	0	5	7	4	2	8
fried shallots	30	2.5	0	0	0	3	0	1	0
kale chips	110	10	1.5	0	20	4	2	1	2
frico	100	8	5	25	340	0	0	0	7
spicy whipped feta dip	140	13	5	25	260	2	0	1	4
grapefruit-rosemary spritzer	150	0	0	0	25	20	0	9	1
orange-thyme spritzer	150	0	0	0	25	21	0	19	1
celery gimlet	200	0	0	0	35	17	1	15	0
arugula gimlet	190	0	0	0	0	16	0	15	0
mint julep	170	0	0	0	0	11	1	9	0
rye-basil julep	170	0	0	0	0	10	0	9	0
whiskey-ginger smash	170	0	0	0	0	9	0	9	0
simple syrup (per ½ ounce)	35	0	0	0	0	9	0	9	0
herb syrup (per ½ ounce)	35	0	0	0	0	9	0	9	0
the main event									
crispy-skinned chicken	220	5	1	135	370	0	0	0	41
pan-seared boneless chicken breast	250	9	1.5	125	370	0	0	0	38
crispy breaded cutlets	670	30	3.5	215	500	48	0	2	48
roasted chicken wings	660	50	12	300	500	0	0	0	51
juiciest stovetop pork chop	310	21	3	75	370	0	0	0	30
broiled charred kebab	240	9	3	100	390	0	0	0	38
perfect seared steak	410	28	7	115	380	0	0	0	36
sirloin steak tips	420	30	7	115	380	0	0	0	35
glazed meatloaf for one	670	44	15	310	1570	30	1	10	37
weeknight lamb chops	310	18	4.5	105	400	0	0	0	38
crispy-skinned salmon fillet	350	23	5	95	390	0	0	0	35
pan-roasted cod	270	15	1.5	75	380	1	0	1	30
lemony poached fish	170	1	0	75	390	9	1	3	31
golden tilapia	290	17	2	85	380	0	0	0	34
pan-seared shrimp	220	15	1.5	160	1010	1	0	0	17
cauliflower steak	350	17	2	0	560	45	18	17	17

	calories	total fat (g)	sat fat (g)	chol (mg)	sodium (mg)	total carb (g)	dietary fiber (g)	total sugars (g)	protein (g)
the main event (cont.)									
creamy french-style scrambled eggs	140	10	3	370	290	1	0	0	13
easy cheddar omelet	380	29	14	605	680	2	0	1	26
leveling up									
mint sauce (per 2 tablespoons)	200	21	3	0	150	2	0	0	0
chermoula sauce (per 2 tablespoons)	130	14	2	0	0	2	0	0	0
grapefruit-basil relish (per ¼ cup)	80	2.5	0	0	0	17	6	10	1
orange-avocado relish (per ¼ cup)	120	10	1.5	0	35	9	4	4	1
yogurt sauce (per 2 tablespoons)	20	1	0.5	5	15	2	0	2	1
tahini sauce (per 2 tablespoons)	90	8	1	0	40	4	1	0	3
tonkatsu sauce (per 2⅔ tablespoons)	60	0	0	0	870	13	0	10	1
garlic-herb compound butter (per 1 tablespoon)	100	11	7	30	0	0	0	0	0
rosemary-parmesan compound butter (per 1 tablespoon)	120	13	8	35	95	0	0	0	2
blue cheese compound butter (per 1 tablespoon)	130	13	8	35	80	0	0	0	2
mustard-chive compound butter (per 1 tablespoon)	120	11	7	30	230	0	0	0	0
anchovy-garlic compound butter (per 1 tablespoon)	100	11	7	30	40	0	0	0	0
ras el hanout (per 1 tablespoon)	30	1	0	0	0	5	3	0	1
barbecue rub (per 1 tablespoon)	30	0	0	0	90	7	1	1	0
classic steak rub (per 1 tablespoon)	15	0.5	0	0	3	1	0	1	0
fresh herb salt (per 1 tablespoon)	0	0	0	0	1120	0	0	0	0
cumin-sesame salt (per 1 tablespoon)	10	0.5	0	0	370	1	0	0	0
smoked salt (per 1 tablespoon)	0	0	0	0	1120	0	0	0	0
sides to match or eat on their own									
pan-roasted asparagus	140	10	4	15	0	9	4	4	6
beets with hazelnuts and chives	300	19	1.5	0	770	30	8	22	5
sautéed baby bok choy with umami garlic sauce	210	11	1.5	0	720	23	8	12	13
roasted broccoli with garlic	180	11	1.5	0	370	16	6	4	7
broiled broccoli rabe	180	15	1	0	660	7	6	1	7
skillet-roasted brussels sprouts with lemon and pecorino	210	16	3	5	300	11	4	3	7
roasted butternut squash	130	3.5	0.5	0	300	27	5	5	2
skillet-roasted cabbage with mustard and thyme	220	17	11	45	440	14	5	8	3
roasted carrots	160	8	1	0	740	22	6	11	2
skillet-roasted cauliflower with capers and pine nuts	240	21	2.5	0	460	13	5	5	6

	calories	total fat (g)	sat fat (g)	chol (mg)	sodium (mg)	total carb (g)	dietary fiber (g)	total sugars (g)	protein (g)
sides to match or eat on their own *(cont.)*									
cauliflower rice	80	3	0.5	0	430	12	5	5	5
broiled eggplant with honey-lemon vinaigrette	190	14	2	0	510	16	5	11	2
lemony skillet-charred green beans	80	5	0.5	0	150	8	3	4	2
sautéed mushrooms with shallots and thyme	110	8	4	15	10	7	0	4	3
fastest-ever baked potato	90	0	0	0	5	20	1	1	2
creamiest mashed potato for one	360	17	11	50	350	42	0	2	7
roasted feta potatoes	240	10	3	15	290	31	0	1	6
sugar snap peas with pine nuts and tarragon	150	11	1	0	590	11	3	5	5
roasted sweet potato wedges	240	7	1	0	410	40	7	12	4
sautéed radishes with crispy bacon	80	6	2	10	430	5	2	3	3
simple ratatouille	220	19	1.5	0	380	11	4	6	2
easiest-ever white rice	220	0	0	0	530	49	0	1	6
easiest-ever quinoa	130	2	0	0	430	21	2	1	5
couscous with cumin and pine nuts	330	11	1	0	440	46	3	1	9
creamy orzo with parmesan	220	10	6	25	610	22	0	2	10
no-fuss parmesan polenta	200	10	6	25	590	20	2	0	8
easy cuban black beans	200	8	0.5	0	530	31	1	3	9
garlicky braised chickpeas	270	17	2.5	0	400	24	7	2	8
curried lentils	250	9	0.5	0	580	33	9	3	12
making a side the main event									
savory seed brittle *(per 2 tablespoons)*	80	5	1	0	135	6	1	2	3
cheesy toasted panko	80	4.5	1	5	80	8	0	0	3
take a crack at it									
poached egg	70	5	1.5	185	220	0	0	0	6
fried egg	110	9	2	185	220	0	0	0	6
hard-cooked eggs	70	5	1.5	185	70	0	0	0	6
soft-cooked eggs	70	5	1.5	185	70	0	0	0	6
simple soups and stews									
gingery carrot soup	140	9	2	5	770	14	3	8	3
creamy curried cauliflower soup	190	10	4	0	900	19	6	8	9
creamy butternut squash soup	230	9	2	5	530	37	5	15	7
weeknight miso soup with tofu	150	8	1	0	1060	9	1	4	14
5-ingredient black bean soup	210	2.5	1.5	5	1080	43	1	3	13
5-ingredient sun-dried tomato and white bean soup	230	3.5	0.5	5	1230	37	10	2	14
5-ingredient creamy chickpea and roasted garlic soup	210	4.5	0	0	950	32	10	1	12

	calories	total fat (g)	sat fat (g)	chol (mg)	sodium (mg)	total carb (g)	dietary fiber (g)	total sugars (g)	protein (g)
simple soups and stews *(cont.)*									
sausage and tortellini florentine soup	370	18	4.5	35	1760	40	3	11	13
pantry garlicky chicken and rice soup	290	9	1.5	80	1200	30	2	5	22
beef and barley soup	520	17	4	80	2320	58	11	11	35
almost-instant ginger beef ramen	540	17	4.5	75	2140	60	1	4	35
beef pho	530	8	2	60	1300	79	1	8	34
thai-style hot-and-sour soup	250	2.5	0	105	1700	38	2	9	18
easy beef chili	510	22	6	60	1380	51	16	11	30
thai-style coconut chicken curry	430	17	12	105	1250	38	2	11	30
chicken tagine	540	12	1.5	85	1840	71	11	41	39
shrimp and sausage gumbo	450	23	7	215	1420	22	2	6	39
spanish-style fish stew	580	30	9	125	1840	20	6	9	47
clam and cannellini bean stew with sausage	490	26	13	85	2040	42	1	4	20
mexican street-corn chowder	420	23	4.5	25	930	46	7	14	20
quinoa and vegetable stew	300	10	1	0	530	44	6	6	11
sandwiches and salads									
avocado toast	340	23	3	0	330	31	7	4	5
breakfast sandwich	660	50	20	270	1020	29	0	1	24
sweet potato–bacon wrap	630	35	11	35	1660	65	7	8	16
packable pita sandwich	390	15	3.5	370	1090	42	1	2	24
lamb pita sandwiches with tzatziki	700	43	20	130	1110	41	1	4	41
zucchini quesadilla	470	28	10	40	1230	40	1	4	17
simplest ground beef tacos	420	26	9	75	570	23	3	2	24
chipotle shrimp tacos	400	10	3.5	305	960	42	2	6	37
asian barbecue chicken lettuce cups	190	7	1.5	80	470	12	1	7	18
creamy deli salads									
classic egg salad	200	17	4	285	260	2	0	1	10
curried egg salad	200	18	4	285	260	3	2	1	10
egg salad with capers and anchovies	210	17	4	285	440	2	0	1	10
chickpea salad	310	23	3.5	10	960	21	7	1	7
curried chickpea salad	380	23	3.5	10	890	37	8	15	8
classic tuna salad	260	11	1.5	60	840	3	1	1	34
curried tuna salad	280	11	1.5	60	840	10	1	7	34
tuna salad with apples, walnuts, and tarragon	360	20	2.5	60	840	11	3	6	36
tuna salad with cornichons and whole-grain mustard	260	11	1.5	60	1060	3	1	1	34

	calories	total fat (g)	sat fat (g)	chol (mg)	sodium (mg)	total carb (g)	dietary fiber (g)	total sugars (g)	protein (g)
sandwiches and salads *(cont.)*									
chopped chicken salad with fennel and apple	320	13	3.5	70	750	28	7	17	25
moroccan chicken salad	490	30	4	60	660	32	6	14	26
green goodness salad	300	17	3	65	390	12	6	3	26
sriracha-lime tofu bowl	280	14	1	0	540	23	5	14	14
harvest salad	400	24	7	25	790	40	6	20	7
mexican street-corn salad	360	23	6	35	720	34	4	10	13
arugula and steak tip salad	500	32	8	125	500	12	2	7	39
seared scallop salad with snap peas and radishes	370	22	3	40	1000	15	3	5	23
tuscan tuna salad bowl	390	25	3.5	30	900	18	5	3	22
italian pasta salad	960	49	17	105	1860	90	1	4	40
warm spiced couscous salad	640	28	7	35	1230	73	7	18	24
quinoa salad with red bell pepper and cilantro	360	18	2.5	0	230	41	5	3	9
chilled soba noodle salad	350	10	1	0	380	56	1	10	9
one-pan dinners									
skillet-roasted chicken and potatoes	540	21	3.5	145	1050	47	1	3	37
weeknight chicken cacciatore	610	38	9	190	1460	22	5	11	38
chicken sausage hash	500	28	6	280	1460	34	2	5	30
spice-rubbed flank steak with celery root and lime yogurt sauce	610	30	9	155	810	31	8	6	57
beef and broccoli stir-fry	550	36	9	115	1690	17	3	3	41
garam masala pork chop with couscous and spinach	680	26	6	125	770	48	4	0	58
crispy sesame pork chops with wilted napa cabbage salad	1040	71	7	205	540	43	6	5	53
sheet pan sausages with sweet potatoes, broccoli rabe, and mustard-chive butter	700	51	21	110	1660	30	7	7	33
pomegranate-glazed salmon with black-eyed peas and walnuts	850	49	9	95	1210	57	8	25	47
spiced crispy-skinned salmon with tomato-mango salad	680	42	8	95	690	39	3	12	39
couscous with shrimp, cilantro, and garlic chips	610	30	2.5	215	890	52	4	1	32
risotto primavera	400	20	6	25	870	45	3	4	14
stovetop spinach macaroni and cheese	830	36	22	110	1260	79	1	10	43
lemony spaghetti with garlic and pine nuts	770	46	7	10	1390	69	1	5	22
fastest-ever carbonara	700	35	12	235	1610	64	0	4	31

	calories	total fat (g)	sat fat (g)	chol (mg)	sodium (mg)	total carb (g)	dietary fiber (g)	total sugars (g)	protein (g)
one-pan dinners (cont.)									
weeknight pasta with meat sauce	810	30	13	95	1160	90	6	17	38
vegetarian fideos	450	13	1.5	0	1210	71	8	7	15
peppery sesame noodles with bok choy	670	32	4.5	5	1310	75	5	10	20
spicy peanut rice-noodle bowl	660	29	4.5	0	910	84	3	9	18
lemon-herb zoodles with artichokes, feta, and walnuts	320	26	4.5	10	600	17	3	7	7
dal with tofu and spinach	330	14	4	15	580	36	9	6	15
skillet flatbread with goat cheese, sun-dried tomatoes, and prosciutto	640	36	13	50	1770	52	1	4	28
tex-mex cheese enchiladas	800	55	21	100	1440	57	4	8	32
asparagus and goat cheese frittata	350	24	10	575	790	6	2	3	28
something sweet									
solo sundae									
strawberry-balsamic topping with pepper	15	0	0	0	0	4	0	4	0
honey-ginger fig topping	30	0	0	0	0	8	1	7	0
classic hot fudge sauce (per 2 tablespoons)	130	6	3.5	10	40	19	1	16	1
whipped cream for one	220	22	14	70	15	4	0	4	2
blueberry compote	20	1.5	1	5	20	2	0	2	0
dipping hot chocolate	170	12	8	35	10	15	0	13	2
chocolate haystacks	220	13	5	0	190	20	1	8	5
cinnamon-sugar pita chips	420	23	14	60	470	48	1	13	6
paper bag popcorn	170	7	3.5	15	580	23	4	7	3
chocolate–peanut butter truffles	630	44	20	30	220	57	5	31	10
edible cookie dough	270	15	9	30	150	34	0	21	2
two chocolate chip cookies	440	22	12	215	120	57	1	38	6
peanut butter–chocolate quesadilla	550	35	14	30	780	49	3	11	13
cheesecake parfait	340	24	15	85	380	27	1	22	5
molten chocolate mug cake	590	39	23	245	470	53	2	26	11
s'mores mug cake	570	34	20	245	490	59	1	34	10
lemon poppyseed mug cake	480	29	16	245	470	44	1	26	10
no-bake apple crisp	300	6	3.5	15	150	62	4	49	2
no-bake peach-ginger crisp	450	11	7	30	150	87	6	68	5
fruits of the forest milkshake	460	20	12	80	300	66	5	52	8
coconut paletas	600	52	46	0	320	34	1	25	5
banana ice cream	280	11	7	35	150	45	5	24	2

conversions and equivalents

Some say cooking is a science and an art. We would say that geography has a hand in it, too. Flours and sugars manufactured in the United Kingdom and elsewhere will feel and taste different from those manufactured in the United States. So we cannot promise that the loaf of bread you bake in Canada or England will taste the same as a loaf baked in the States, but we can offer guidelines for converting weights and measures. We also recommend that you rely on your instincts when making our recipes. Refer to the visual cues provided. If the dough hasn't "come together in a ball" as described, you may need to add more flour—even if the recipe doesn't tell you to. You be the judge.

The recipes in this book were developed using standard U.S. measures following U.S. government guidelines. The charts below offer equivalents for U.S. and metric measures. All conversions are approximate and have been rounded up or down to the nearest whole number.

example

1 teaspoon	=	4.9292 milliliters, rounded up to 5 milliliters
1 ounce	=	28.3495 grams, rounded down to 28 grams

volume conversions

u.s.	metric
1 teaspoon	5 milliliters
2 teaspoons	10 milliliters
1 tablespoon	15 milliliters
2 tablespoons	30 milliliters
¼ cup	59 milliliters
⅓ cup	79 milliliters
½ cup	118 milliliters
¾ cup	177 milliliters
1 cup	237 milliliters
1¼ cups	296 milliliters
1½ cups	355 milliliters
2 cups (1 pint)	473 milliliters
2½ cups	591 milliliters
3 cups	710 milliliters
4 cups (1 quart)	0.946 liter
1.06 quarts	1 liter
4 quarts (1 gallon)	3.8 liters

weight conversions

ounces	grams
½	14
¾	21
1	28
1½	43
2	57
2½	71
3	85
3½	99
4	113
4½	128
5	142
6	170
7	198
8	227
9	255
10	283
12	340
16 (1 pound)	454

conversions for common baking ingredients

Baking is an exacting science. Because measuring by weight is far more accurate than measuring by volume, and thus more likely to produce reliable results, in our recipes we provide ounce measures in addition to cup measures for many ingredients. Refer to the chart below to convert these measures into grams.

ingredient	ounces	grams
flour		
1 cup all-purpose flour*	5	142
1 cup cake flour	4	113
1 cup whole-wheat flour	5½	156
sugar		
1 cup granulated (white) sugar	7	198
1 cup packed brown sugar (light or dark)	7	198
1 cup confectioners' sugar	4	113
cocoa powder		
1 cup cocoa powder	3	85
butter†		
4 tablespoons (½ stick or ¼ cup)	2	57
8 tablespoons (1 stick or ½ cup)	4	113
16 tablespoons (2 sticks or 1 cup)	8	227

* U.S. all-purpose flour, the most frequently used flour in this book, does not contain leaveners, as some European flours do. These leavened flours are called self-rising or self-raising. If you are using self-rising flour, take this into consideration before adding leaveners to a recipe.

† In the United States, butter is sold both salted and unsalted. We generally recommend unsalted butter. If you are using salted butter, take this into consideration before adding salt to a recipe.

oven temperatures

fahrenheit	celsius	gas mark
225	105	¼
250	120	½
275	135	1
300	150	2
325	165	3
350	180	4
375	190	5
400	200	6
425	220	7
450	230	8
475	245	9

converting temperatures from an instant-read thermometer

We include doneness temperatures in many of the recipes in this book. We recommend an instant-read thermometer for the job. Refer to the table above to convert Fahrenheit degrees to Celsius. Or, for temperatures not represented in the chart, use this simple formula:

Subtract 32 degrees from the Fahrenheit reading, then divide the result by 1.8 to find the Celsius reading.

example

"Roast chicken until thighs register 175 degrees."

To convert:
175°F − 32 = 143°
143° ÷ 1.8 = 79.44°C, rounded down to 79°C

index

Note: Page references in *italics* indicate photographs.

c

Cabbage
Napa, Salad, Wilted, Crispy Sesame Pork Chops with, 248, *249*
Skillet-Roasted, with Mustard and Thyme, 90, *91*
Spicy Peanut Rice-Noodle Bowl, *272,* 273
Sriracha-Lime Tofu Bowl, 214, *215*

Cakes. See Mug Cakes

Canned or jarred items, 11, 20

Capers
and Anchovies, Egg Salad with, 206
and Pine Nuts, Skillet-Roasted Cauliflower with, 94, *95*

Cardamom
Ras el Hanout, 72, *72*

Carrot(s)
Beef and Barley Soup, 160, *161*
Pantry Garlicky Chicken and Rice Soup, 158, *159*
Roasted, *92,* 93
Soup, Gingery, *142,* 143
Sriracha-Lime Tofu Bowl, 214, *215*
Warm Spiced Couscous Salad, 228, *229*

Cauliflower
Rice, 96, *97*
Skillet-Roasted, with Capers and Pine Nuts, 94, *95*
Soup, Creamy Curried, 144, *145*
Steak, *62,* 63

Celery Gimlet, 28

Celery Root and Lime Yogurt Sauce, Spice-Rubbed Flank Steak with, 242, *243*

Cheddar
Breakfast Sandwich, *190,* 191
Omelet, Easy, 66, *67*
Simplest Ground Beef Tacos, 200, *201*
Stovetop Spinach Macaroni and Cheese, *260,* 261
Tex-Mex Cheese Enchiladas, 280, *281*
Zucchini Quesadilla, 198, *199*

Cheese
Blue, Compound Butter, 70, *71*
Breakfast Sandwich, *190,* 191
buying from cheesemonger, 17
Cheesecake Parfait, 306, *307*
Cheesy Toasted Panko, 137
Chopped Chicken Salad with Fennel and Apple, 208, *209*
Creamy Orzo with Parmesan, *126,* 127
Easy Cheddar Omelet, 66, *67*
Enchiladas, Tex-Mex, 280, *281*
Fastest-Ever Carbonara, *264,* 265
freezing, 20
frico made with, 27

Cheese (cont.)
Goat, and Asparagus Frittata, 282, *283*
Goat, Prosciutto, and Sun-Dried Tomatoes, Skillet Flatbread with, *278,* 279
Harvest Salad, 216, *217*
Italian Pasta Salad, 226, *227*
Lemon-Herb Zoodles with Artichokes, Feta, and Walnuts, 274, *275*
Mexican Street-Corn Salad, 218, *219*
No-Fuss Parmesan Polenta, *128,* 129
Quinoa Salad with Red Bell Pepper and Cilantro, *230,* 231
rinds, uses for, 21
Roasted Feta Potatoes, 108, *109*
Rosemary-Parmesan Compound Butter, 70, *71*
Simplest Ground Beef Tacos, 200, *201*
Skillet-Roasted Brussels Sprouts with Lemon and Pecorino, 86, *87*
spicy whipped feta dip, preparing, 27
storing, 20
Stovetop Spinach Macaroni and, *260,* 261
Zucchini Quesadilla, 198, *199*

Cheesecake Parfait, 306, *307*

Chermoula Sauce, 68

Chicken
Asian Barbecue, Lettuce Cups, 204, *205*
Breast, Pan-Seared Boneless, 34, *35*
buying from butcher, 17
Cacciatore, Weeknight, 238, *239*
Coconut Curry, Thai-Style, *170,* 171
Crispy Breaded Cutlets, 36, *37*
Crispy-Skinned, 32, *33*
Green Goodness Salad, 212, *213*
and Potatoes, Skillet-Roasted, 236, *237*
and Rice Soup, Garlicky Pantry, 158, *159*
Salad, Chopped, with Fennel and Apple, 208, *209*
Salad, Moroccan, 210, *211*
Tagine, 172, *173*
Wings, Roasted, *38,* 39

Chicken Sausage Hash, *240,* 241

Chickpea(s)
Chicken Tagine, 172, *173*
Garlicky Braised, *132,* 133
Moroccan Chicken Salad, 210, *211*
and Roasted Garlic Soup, 5-Ingredient Creamy, *154,* 155
Salad, 206
Salad, Curried, 206
Vegetarian Fideos, 268, *269*
Warm Spiced Couscous Salad, 228, *229*

Chiles
chipotle, in adobo, freezing, 20
5-Ingredient Black Bean Soup, 150, *151*
Mexican Street-Corn Chowder, 180, *181*

Chili, Easy Beef, *168,* 169

Chili powder
Barbecue Rub, 72, *72*

Chilled Soba Noodle Salad, 232, *233*

Chipotle
chiles in adobo, freezing, 20
5-Ingredient Black Bean Soup, 150, *151*
Shrimp Tacos, 202, *203*

Chive(s)
and Hazelnuts, Beets with, 78, *79*
-Mustard Compound Butter, 70, *71*
storing, 21

Chocolate
Chip Cookies, Two, 302, *303*
Classic Hot Fudge Sauce, 289
Dipping Hot, *290,* 291
Haystacks, *292,* 293
Molten, Mug Cake, 308, *309*
-Peanut Butter Quesadilla, 304, *305*
-Peanut Butter Truffles, 298, *299*
S'mores Mug Cake, 310, *311*

Chopped Chicken Salad with Fennel and Apple, 208, *209*

Chowder, Mexican Street-Corn, 180, *181*

Cilantro
Chermoula Sauce, 68
Mexican Street-Corn Salad, 218, 219
and Red Bell Pepper, Quinoa Salad with, *230,* 231
Shrimp, and Garlic Chips, Couscous with, 256, *257*

Cinnamon-Sugar Pita Chips, 294, *295*

Citrus
stocking up on, 10
zest, dehydrating in microwave, 14
see also specific citrus fruits

Clam and Cannellini Bean Stew with Sausage, 178, *179*

Classic Egg Salad, 206

Classic Hot Fudge Sauce, 289

Classic Steak Rub, 72, *72*

Classic Tuna Salad, 207

Clean-Out-Your-Fridge Soup, 184–85

Coconut
Chicken Curry, Thai-Style, *170,* 171
milk, storing, 20
Paletas, 320, *321*

Cod
Lemony Poached Fish, 56, *57*
Pan-Roasted, 54, *55*
Spanish-Style Fish Stew, *176,* 177

Compound Butters
Anchovy-Garlic, 71
Blue Cheese, 70, *71*
Garlic-Herb, 70
Mustard-Chive, *70,* 71
Rosemary-Parmesan, 70, *71*

Condiments, buying, 10, 11

i

Ice Cream
   Banana, *322, 323*
   Fruits of the Forest Milkshake, *318,* 319
   Solo Sundae, *288,* 288–89
Ingredients
   basic, for pantry, 10
   common, easy swaps for, 5
   flavor-boosting, 11
   small amounts, using up, 22–23
   substitution guidelines, 5
Italian Pasta Salad, 226, *227*

j

Juiciest Stovetop Pork Chop, 40, *41*

k

Kale
   Chips, 15
   Harvest Salad, *216, 217*
   Vegetarian Fideos, 268, *269*
Kitchen Improv suggestions, 6–7

l

Lamb
   Chops, Weeknight, *50,* 51
   Pita Sandwiches with Tzatziki, 196, *197*
Leeks, storing, 21
Leftovers
   using up leftover ingredients, 20–21
   see also Makes leftovers
Lemon
   -Herb Zoodles with Artichokes, Feta, and Walnuts, *274,* 275
   -Honey Vinaigrette, Broiled Eggplant with, *98,* 99
   Lemony Poached Fish, 56, *57*
   Lemony Skillet-Charred Green Beans, *100,* 101
   Lemony Spaghetti with Garlic and Pine Nuts, 262, *263*
   Poppyseed Mug Cake, *312,* 313
Lentils
   Curried, 134, *135*
   Dal with Tofu and Spinach, 276, *277*
   stocking up on, 10
Lettuce
   Chopped Chicken Salad with Fennel and Apple, 208, *209*

Lettuce *(cont.)*
   Cups, Asian Barbecue Chicken, 204, *205*
   Lamb Pita Sandwiches with Tzatziki, 196, *197*
   Mexican Street-Corn Salad, *218,* 219
   Moroccan Chicken Salad, 210, *211*
   Tuscan Tuna Salad Bowl, *224, 225*

m

Main dishes (one-pan)
   Asparagus and Goat Cheese Frittata, 282, *283*
   Beef and Broccoli Stir-Fry, 244, *245*
   Chicken Sausage Hash, *240,* 241
   Couscous with Shrimp, Cilantro, and Garlic Chips, 256, *257*
   Crispy Sesame Pork Chops with Wilted Napa Cabbage Salad, 248, *249*
   Dal with Tofu and Spinach, 276, *277*
   Fastest-Ever Carbonara, *264,* 265
   Garam Masala Pork Chop with Couscous and Spinach, *246,* 247
   Lemon-Herb Zoodles with Artichokes, Feta, and Walnuts, *274,* 275
   Lemony Spaghetti with Garlic and Pine Nuts, 262, *263*
   Peppery Sesame Noodles with Bok Choy, *270,* 271
   Pomegranate-Glazed Salmon with Black-Eyed Peas and Walnuts, 252, *253*
   Risotto Primavera, 258, *259*
   Sheet Pan Sausages with Sweet Potatoes, Broccoli Rabe, and Mustard-Chive Butter, *250,* 251
   Skillet Flatbread with Goat Cheese, Sun-Dried Tomatoes, and Prosciutto, *278,* 279
   Skillet-Roasted Chicken and Potatoes, *236,* 237
   Spiced Crispy-Skinned Salmon with Tomato-Mango Salad, *254,* 255
   Spice-Rubbed Flank Steak with Celery Root and Lime Yogurt Sauce, 242, *243*
   Spicy Peanut Rice-Noodle Bowl, *272,* 273
   Stovetop Spinach Macaroni and Cheese, *260,* 261
   Tex-Mex Cheese Enchiladas, 280, *281*
   Vegetarian Fideos, 268, *269*
   Weeknight Chicken Cacciatore, 238, *239*
   Weeknight Pasta, *266,* 267
Main dishes (simple)
   Broiled Charred Kebab, 42, *43*
   Cauliflower Steak, *62,* 63

Main dishes (simple) *(cont.)*
   Creamy French-Style Scrambled Eggs, *64,* 65
   Crispy Breaded Cutlets, 36, *37*
   Crispy-Skinned Chicken, 32, *33*
   Crispy-Skin Salmon Fillet, *52,* 53
   Easy Cheddar Omelet, 66, *67*
   Glazed Meatloaf for One, 48, *49*
   Golden Tilapia, 58, *59*
   Juiciest Stovetop Pork Chop, 40, *41*
   Lemony Poached Fish, 56, *57*
   Pan-Roasted Cod, 54, *55*
   Pan-Seared Boneless Chicken Breast, 34, *35*
   Pan-Seared Shrimp, *60,* 61
   Perfect Seared Steak, *44,* 45
   Roasted Chicken Wings, *38,* 39
   Sirloin Steak Tips, *46,* 47
   Weeknight Lamb Chops, *50,* 51
Makes leftovers
   about the recipes, 3
   see also meal types below
Makes leftovers (desserts)
   Banana Ice Cream, *322,* 323
   Chocolate Haystacks, *292,* 293
   Chocolate–Peanut Butter Truffles, *298,* 299
   Coconut Paletas, 320, *321*
Makes leftovers (one-pan meals)
   Asparagus and Goat Cheese Frittata, 282, *283*
   Beef and Broccoli Stir-Fry, 244, *245*
   Dal with Tofu and Spinach, 276, *277*
   making brown bag lunches with, 284–85
   Risotto Primavera, 258, *259*
   Skillet-Roasted Chicken and Potatoes, *236,* 237
   Spice-Rubbed Flank Steak with Celery Root and Lime Yogurt Sauce, 242, *243*
   Tex-Mex Cheese Enchiladas, 280, *281*
   Weeknight Chicken Cacciatore, 238, *239*
Makes leftovers (sandwiches and salads)
   Asian Barbecue Chicken Lettuce Cups, 204, *205*
   Chopped Chicken Salad with Fennel and Apple, 208, *209*
   Green Goodness Salad, *212,* 213
   Harvest Salad, *216,* 217
   Italian Pasta Salad, 226, *227*
   Lamb Pita Sandwiches with Tzatziki, 196, *197*
   Mexican Street-Corn Salad, *218,* 219
   Moroccan Chicken Salad, 210, *211*
   Quinoa Salad with Red Bell Pepper and Cilantro, *230,* 231
   Simplest Ground Beef Tacos, *200, 201*
   Sriracha-Lime Tofu Bowl, 214, *215*
   Warm Spiced Couscous Salad, 228, *229*